IS IT ADHD?

Common signs of ADHD include:

- Failure to pay attention to details or making careless mistakes

- Difficulty maintaining attention during work or play

- "Zoning out" while others speak

- Difficulty organizing tasks and activities

- Avoidance of tasks that require long-term mental effort, such as homework

- Easy distractibility

- Frequent forgetfulness

- Extreme hyperactivity that may include fidgeting, squirming, leaving one's seat in class, inappropriate running or climbing, or excessive talking

- Impulsive behavior, including blurting out answers in class, inability to wait one's turn, and intruding on others

Avon Books are available at special quantity discounts for bulk purchases for sales promotions, premiums, fund raising or educational use. Special books, or book excerpts, can also be created to fit specific needs.

For details write or telephone the office of the Director of Special Markets, Avon Books, Dept. FP, 1350 Avenue of the Americas, New York, New York 10019, 1-800-238-0658.

Do We Really Need RITALIN?

A Family Guide to Attention Deficit Hyperactivity Disorder (ADHD)

Josephine Wright, M.D.

The ideas, procedures, and suggestions in this book are intended to supplement, not replace, the medical advice of a trained medical professional. All matters regarding your health require medical supervision. Consult your physician before adopting the suggestions in this book, as well as any condition that may require diagnosis or medical attention. The author and publisher disclaim any liability arising directly or indirectly from the use of this book.

AVON BOOKS
A division of
The Hearst Corporation
1350 Avenue of the Americas
New York, New York 10019

Copyright © 1997 by CMD Publishing, a division of Current Medical Directions, Inc.
Published by arrangement with CMD Publishing, a division of Current Medical Directions, Inc.
Visit our website at **http://www.AvonBooks.com**
Library of Congress Catalog Card Number: 97-93746
ISBN: 0-380-79356-3

All rights reserved, which includes the right to reproduce this book or portions thereof in any form whatsoever except as provided by the U.S. Copyright Law. For information address CMD Publishing, 114 East 32nd Street, New York, New York 10016.

First Avon Books Printing: December 1997

AVON TRADEMARK REG. U.S. PAT. OFF. AND IN OTHER COUNTRIES, MARCA REGISTRADA, HECHO EN U.S.A.

Printed in the U.S.A.

WCD 10 9 8 7 6 5 4 3 2 1

If you purchased this book without a cover, you should be aware that this book is stolen property. It was reported as "unsold and destroyed" to the publisher, and neither the author nor the publisher has received any payment for this "stripped book."

Contents

Introduction — 1

Part One

Chapter 1: Is It Really ADHD? — 11

Chapter 2: ADHD in Children and Adolescents — 31

Chapter 3: ADHD and Adults — 57

Part Two
What to Do About It

Chapter 4: Everything You Need to Know About Ritalin — 79

Chapter 5: Other Treatments for ADHD — 103

Chapter 6: Psychotherapy and Its Place in a Multimodal Treatment Plan — 129

Chapter 7: The Family's Role — 159

Chapter 8: The School's Role — 187

Chapter 9: Your Choice — 211

Chapter 10: Resources for the ADHD Family 239

References 251

Index 257

Introduction

Perhaps you have been told that you or someone in your family has attention deficit hyperactivity disorder (ADHD). You may already have been told that Ritalin is the answer. Now you are looking for accurate information that will help you make wise choices about how and where to proceed from here.

This is precisely what this book is about. It is different from other books about Ritalin and ADHD. It is not simply trying to stir up controversy. It is not advocating one miracle treatment. It is not joining the bandwagon by trashing stimulant medications. It is not offering a simple cure.

This book aims to give you all the information you need to understand ADHD and to be an effective advocate for yourself or a family member who suffers from this disorder. Much has changed in this field in just the last few years. This book brings, to you, the family, new information about research, about the basic underlying disorder, and about its comprehensive treatment.

This book describes in great depth the signs and symptoms of ADHD, how they affect and interact with a child's development from the earliest days of life and in what manner these symptoms persist into adolescence and adulthood. Then this book looks, with critical scrutiny, at the various treatment methods used and shows how a comprehensive individualized approach can be developed. This almost always means using several different modalities of treatment simultaneously, such as medication, therapy, and tutoring. Hence, this approach is called the multimodal treatment of ADHD.

Undoubtedly, many questions have already occurred to you about this disorder. Just what is ADHD? What causes it? How can you be certain that your child has it? Will he grow out of it, or will he always have it? How will it affect his future success in school, in relationships, in life? What is the best form of treatment for him? Should he take Ritalin? Is this drug really safe? How long will he have to take it? What can you do at home, as his parents, to help him overcome the difficulties caused by ADHD?

ADHD has become a very well-known diagnosis. You have probably heard it discussed on television or radio talk shows, read about it in magazines and newspapers, or seen it listed as the topic of discussion at your local school PTA meeting. You may have heard that Ritalin, a stimulant medication used to treat ADHD for the past twenty years, is one of the most widely prescribed medications in the United States today.

Unfortunately, there is also much misinformation about ADHD. Frequently families come to me burdened unnecessarily with misinformation and fears and with no knowledge of where to begin to find answers to their questions.

This is precisely why I wanted to provide families with a readable and accessible source of accurate and up-to-date information about ADHD and its treatments. In my practice, the first step after an ADHD diagnosis is to educate the sufferer and his family. In order for you to become an effective advocate for your child or for yourself, it is essential that you too be armed with as much accurate information as possible.

Just what is ADHD and how common is it? The media has suggested that as many as 20 percent of school-age children may have ADHD. What do scientific studies say about this? The answer to this begins to point to the complexity of the whole situation. For in order to find the incidence of a condition, investigators have to agree on how to define what it is that they are counting. But ADHD is not a clearly defined disease, like pneumonia. It is a syndrome, a collection of symptoms that tend to cluster together in the same individual and remain constant over time and in different situations. And this collection of symptoms is shared by a significant number of individuals. Calling this collection of symptoms a syndrome and giving it a name, however, does not imply that it is a disease, with the same etiology (i.e., cause) in all individuals or even with only one etiology in one individual.

Even the name can be a problem. When this group of symptoms was first put together to describe a common syndrome in the 1940s, the name minimal brain damage was given. This was a diagnosis that stated an assumption about causality, that is, that there was evidence of brain damage to account for the symptoms. Over the years, as understanding of the condition changed, the name also changed several times, to minimal brain dysfunction, hyperkinetic impulse disorder, hyperkinesis, and, finally, attention deficit hyperactivity disorder as research began to suggest that the underlying disturbed function was in focusing attention. This historical development and the research into the causes of ADHD are discussed more fully in Chapter 1.

Today, it is our best understanding that the syndrome we call ADHD is very common and probably affects about 5 to 10 percent of the school population. About three times as many boys as girls are diagnosed with it.

Knowing how the diagnosis has come about, how can we now define ADHD? Just what are doctors talking about when they use this term? ADHD is a syndrome that can affect children, adolescents, and adults and is characterized by inattention, distractibility, hyperactivity, and impulsivity.

By the time an individual has come to professional attention, these problems have already been compounded due to the ways in which they have interfered with his or her development right from the beginning of life. So these children may now have low self-esteem, poor academic records, and repeated experiences of failure, leading to a sense of hopelessness and often depression and anxiety. By adolescence, they may be unmotivated, bored, angry, and have disturbed interpersonal relationships. They may be defiant, extending to trouble with the law or even car accidents. Or they may have turned to drugs or alcohol to appease their sense of failure and frustration. As adults, they may not have met their academic potential and therefore have less job satisfaction and socioeconomic success than their peers. They may have disturbed relationships or suffer from some psychiatric condition.

These problems may be present to different degrees. Some may be absent. And they will have different characteristic appearances at different ages. Chapters 1, 2, and 3 will describe these characteristic appearances in much more depth. Of course, it may occur to you immediately that any of these symptoms could be present in an individual for many different reasons, and it is certainly true that they are not specific to ADHD.

In order to make a firm diagnosis of ADHD, other possible causes must be ruled out, such as a specific learning disability or other psychiatric or medical conditions. A thorough history and examination should be performed by an ADHD specialist (usually a child psychiatrist). I will discuss the diagnostic process more fully in Chapter 1, but you should understand that a fifteen-minute visit to your family doctor will *not* allow for sufficient information-gathering to make a firm diagnosis. Ideally, *many* sources of information need to be considered by the evaluator, including parents' descriptions of the child at home; teachers' reports and observations; academic reports; any psychological, neurological, or academic testing that has been done; descriptions of the child by the significant adults in his life; and direct observation of the child on at least two occasions. Sometimes a home visit or school visit may be indicated to observe the child directly in the setting where he is most symptomatic.

Much of the symptoms present when ADHD is first diagnosed are a result of the complex interactions of the underlying disturbed operations with the developmental, familial, and social environment. While much research is currently underway into the etiology of ADHD (see Chapter 1), it is generally accepted that no one etiology will be found. In fact, it appears the symptom cluster of ADHD is the final common pathway by which complex interacting neurobiological, genetic, and environmental variables are expressed.

In Chapters 2 and 3, I will discuss in more detail the possible underlying operational dysfunctions that may be the neurobiological component to this disorder. I will also show how these underlying dysfunctions interact with the developmental tasks and emotional environment at each particular developmental level to bring about the evolving picture and ongoing difficulties of ADHD. This approach may make you wonder about the long-term outcome of ADHD. Is it inevitable that ADHD is a lifelong condition, or can one grow out of it? Will treatment make any difference to the long-term outcome? What can be done now to diminish the secondary effects of ADHD in the future?

In the section on adolescents in Chapter 2, and on adults in Chapter 3, I will discuss some of the outcome studies that have been published. There are now many long-term prospective studies underway, and these results will not be available for many years. Many of the older studies look at more poorly defined populations and treatments limited to medication, and many of these studies have methodological problems.

In spite of these shortcomings, the studies available so far show over and over again that most people do not outgrow ADHD. The symptoms, though often modified, persist into adulthood. In addition, the secondary effects reverberate throughout life, resulting in lower levels of education achieved, less satisfying occupations in life, less socioeconomic success, trouble with relationships, more likelihood of a significantly disturbed personality, and a greater risk of anxiety and depression. An alarming finding has been the significantly increased risk of antisocial personality disorder found in the adult subjects who had ADHD as children.

This alarming and relatively new information from the followup studies raises several important questions.

- Is there something about the cognitive, psychological, or neurological difficulties of ADHD that may interfere with normal emotional and psychological development, not just with academic and intellectual development?
- Do these difficulties make a child more susceptible to significant psychological distress in his life?
- Is there anything you, as a parent, can do now to try to affect that outcome?
- Have traditional treatments like Ritalin been enough?

The high incidence of ADHD in the adulthood of children previously diagnosed with the syndrome (30 to 60 percent) suggests that, on the whole, traditional treatments have not affected the outcome. Is it the correct treatment? Are we trying to treat the right symptom? Do current treatment methods aim at the underlying disorders or only at the most visible symptoms?

Perhaps Ritalin, the most popular and widespread treatment for ADHD, has been used a bit like a stretch sock, i.e., "one size fits all." But feet are all different sizes, and soon that stretch sock gets very misshapen, or that foot begins to feel abused by a too tight or a too loose, poorly fitting sock. And so it is with ADHD, an extremely varied disorder. No two individuals are the same, and neither should any two treatment plans be the same. The diagnosis must fully examine all areas of functioning, assess where intervention is needed, and determine what combination of interventions and treatment strategies will be most effective for that individual.

Such a combination may well include Ritalin or one of the other medications discussed in Chapter 4. However, treating the symptoms of hyperactivity and inattentiveness with medication alone is really only applying a Band-Aid. And perhaps this is a Band-Aid that can never be discarded because it does not heal the underlying problem. Is a more comprehensive approach to the underlying disorder possible, an approach that perhaps has more long-lasting effects on the underlying problems? I certainly think this is the case.

I will give some examples of how, in my practice, I evaluate a person referred with possible ADHD and how I set up a multimodal treatment plan for that child or adult and his or her family. The treatment plan is often far-reaching, in that it may involve school, tutors, extended family, medication, sometimes group or family counseling, and almost always individual psychotherapy.

Psychotherapy does, in fact, offer the possibility of true change, not just symptomatic support. The aims of psychotherapy are to deal with and even change some of the psychological consequences of ADHD, as well as to actually approach the underlying difficulties themselves in a way that can stimulate corrective development. The therapy can be used to set in motion a learning process in which the individual develops new skills, strengths, and strategies that may compensate for his difficulties and may even change them. I will discuss the latter in much more detail in Chapter 6.

I also work very closely with the family. I try to guide parents in helping their children develop the best work habits and in assessing and providing any necessary academic support. I try to help parents approach their child flexibly, knowing that what works best for him may be very different from their expectations. Parents need the courage to ask themselves what is really going on with their child, with their relationship to this child and with the whole family. How have the difficulties posed by their child's disorder already affected their relationships, marriage, and family in ways that may not be helpful to the child or to them? If parents can look at and understand the whole complex situation as it affects their child, they are much better equipped to become their child's helper and advocate.

It is both appropriate and vital that you should have many questions after being told that your child has ADHD and needs Ritalin. You should be asking just what will help your child maximize his chance of success in the future. Stimulant medications, like Ritalin, may well play a role in helping him pay attention in school and be less of a behavior problem. But will Ritalin also help him do better academically? Will it help him succeed in interpersonal relations and in learning the skills for social intercourse that are so essential to a successful life? Will Ritalin help him deal with his affective states, his inner conflicting feelings? Will it give him the inner tools to sort out his emotions and communicate effectively and to soothe himself and learn emotional strategies to deal with life's stresses? Will Ritalin help him learn how to be loving and intimate in a way that can ensure his ability to develop satisfying emotional relationships outside of his family? Is it realistic to hope that any one form of treatment can help with all these things?

Of course it is not. And this is why it is so essential that you and the professionals you consult create a treatment plan that includes many approaches. Your child psychiatrist can act as the coordinator of this treatment plan, as well as be an advocate for you and your child in dealing with all the other systems and professional people involved.

But it is most important that you, the family, feel empowered to become your child's advocate. You must become a superbly educated consumer who can take charge of your child's treatment, education, and all the other support systems that are going to be necessary. This book is the first step to acquiring that education and information. The various professionals in your child's life may focus on the need to modify the child to better fit in with his or her environment, and medication may be the mainstay of this approach. But it is essential for you to have the courage to focus on the need to modify the environment to better suit your child. This will not just mean at home; you will have to become a gutsy advocate at your child's school, in the medical system, with your health insurance company, and elsewhere. This book gives you tips and helps you to become that powerful advocate.

While I have most often referred to the ADHD sufferer as "he," this does not reflect a dominance of males in my own practice. It is purely an arbitrary choice to save the necessity of the cumbersome double pronoun.

I have described several people with whom I have worked over the years in order to illustrate discussions of diagnosis, symptoms, and treatment. Their identities have, of course, been carefully disguised. I wish to express my gratitude to the many individuals and families who have shared with me the stories of their struggles with ADHD, and I hope you can learn from their stories as I have. I am also grateful to Sarah Butterworth at Current Medical Directions for her guidance and editorial input into this project and to Don Vaughan for his skillful help and research. Thanks also to my husband, Richard, for his scholarly input and his interest and to my sons, David and Nicholas, for their patience and support.

Further updated information on ADHD can be obtained from my Web page at http://www.geocities.com/HotSprings/Spa/4218/.

PART ONE

ONE

Is It Really ADHD?

Ryan's day begins at 7 a.m. His mother wakes him, tells him to get dressed, then comes back five minutes later and tells him again. It takes the freckle-faced eight-year-old fifteen more minutes to complete the task. In the kitchen, Ryan races around, unable to sit still for more than thirty seconds.

At school, the other children are frightened of Ryan's explosive temper and tendency to strike out. He talks out of turn, races around the classroom, and can't seem to stay at his desk. He finds it impossible to concentrate on a simple spelling test, despite the fact that he knew all the words perfectly the night before. When time is called, Ryan's page is full of doodles and scrawls.

Later, on the playground, Ryan gets into a fight when a classmate accidentally brushes by him while playing kickball. Ryan flies into a rage, and, screaming, he knocks the boy down.

Back home, Ryan's mother orders him to clean his room. Instead, Ryan dashes into the living room and turns on the television. His mother grabs him by the arm and drags him, kicking and screaming, into his bedroom.

Getting Ryan to do his homework proves equally difficult. It takes sixty minutes and several angry reprimands from his mother and father before he is able to write down fifteen simple spelling words. When his mother checks his work, ten of the words are impossible to read.

A fight ensues when his parents try to put him to bed at nine-thirty. After that, they can hear Ryan in his bedroom, talking to himself and playing with one toy after another. By the time he finally falls asleep, it's 11 p.m.

Despite his best efforts, Ryan simply can't control his behavior. He has attention deficit hyperactivity disorder (ADHD), a mental disorder believed to affect between 3 and 5 percent of all children—possibly as many as two million youngsters in the United States alone.

Once known as *minimal brain dysfunction* or *hyperkinesis*, ADHD is now considered by most experts to be an umbrella *syndrome* characterized by the presence of several distinct symptoms, most commonly hyperactivity, impulsivity, and inattention. It affects three times as many boys as girls and frequently continues into adolescence and adulthood.

There is no cure for attention deficit hyperactivity disorder, but in most cases it can be effectively managed with medication (most commonly Ritalin), psychotherapy, behavior modification, and other approaches. Left untreated, children and adults with ADHD typically find it difficult to do well in school or at work, maintain friendships or interpersonal relationships, and generally enjoy life. It's an often maddening existence that leaves the victim feeling powerless, confused, and angry.

But there is hope. Every day, researchers worldwide are discovering more and more about the biological workings and potential causes of ADHD, as well as new treatments for the syndrome and perhaps, one day, even a cure. In the meantime, victims must learn to manage one day at a time, constantly aware that the most disruptive symptoms of ADHD always lie just below the surface, ready to wreak havoc.

Following are some of the most commonly asked questions regarding ADHD, its presentation, suspected causes, and prognoses.

Q: Could you give us a more detailed definition of ADHD? What are the most common symptoms of this disease?

Is It Really ADHD?

A: First of all, it must be stressed that ADHD is *not* a disease in the traditional sense, like measles or chicken pox. It's known medically as a syndrome and is characterized by a wide range of common symptoms that must be present for at least six months and impact in a detrimental way on the victim's life.

These potential signs are discussed in detail in *Diagnostic and Statistical Manual IV (DSM IV)*, a book published by the American Psychiatric Association to help professionals diagnose specific mental disorders. The most common signs of ADHD include the following.

- Failure to pay attention to details or making careless mistakes in schoolwork or other activities.
- Difficulty maintaining attention during work or play.
- Apparent lack of attention when spoken to by another, commonly known as "zoning out."
- Difficulty organizing tasks and activities.
- Avoidance of tasks that require long-term mental effort, such as homework.
- Easy distractibility.
- Frequent forgetfulness.
- Extreme hyperactivity that may include constant fidgeting or squirming, leaving one's seat in class without permission, inappropriate running or climbing and excessive talking.
- Impulsivity that may include blurting out answers before instructed to do so, an inability to wait one's turn, and intruding on others.

Secondary characteristics that also may be present include social clumsiness (an inability to make friends due to social inappropriateness), insatiability (such as an inability to calm down after becoming overexcited during play), inflexibility (seeing everything as black or white), physical clumsiness, short-term memory problems, low self-esteem, anxiety and depression, low frustration tolerance, and sleep problems.

The American Psychiatric Association states that in order to be classified as ADHD, the primary symptoms must be numerous, apparent before age seven, cause impairment in two or more settings (such as school and home), and not be attributable to other mental disorders.

Most specialists tend to divide ADHD into three specific subtypes when making a diagnosis, based on whether hyperactivity or inattention has been the predominant symptom for the previous six months. These subtypes are as follows.

1. Attention Deficit Hyperactivity Disorder, Combined Type. This is used if six or more symptoms of inattention and six or more symptoms of hyperactivity/impulsivity were persistent for the previous six months. The majority of children with ADHD fall into this subtype.
2. Attention Deficit Hyperactivity Disorder, Predominantly Inattentive Type. This subtype is used if six or more symptoms of inattention but fewer than six symptoms of hyperactivity/impulsivity have been predominant for the previous six months.
3. Attention Deficit Hyperactivity Disorder, Predominantly Hyperactive-Impulsive Type. This subtype is used if six or more symptoms of hyperactivity/impulsivity but fewer than six symptoms of inattention have been predominant for the previous six months.

Let me explain the concepts of inattention, impulsivity, and hyperactivity in more detail. People who are inattentive find it extremely difficult to focus on any one task for an extended period and thus are very easily bored. It's not uncommon for them to pay automatic attention to things they like, such as television or video games, but most inattentive people find it nearly impossible to focus for more than a few minutes on completing a given task or learning something new. In youngsters, inattention usually manifests itself in an inability to learn a new classroom lesson, complete homework assignments, or clean up their rooms. Their minds wander when they should be concentrating on the task at hand.

Is It Really ADHD?

People who are extremely hyperactive always seem to be on the move, and not in a good way. Hyperactive youngsters find it nearly impossible to stay in their seats or sit still without fidgeting or bouncing around. Their need for constant motion makes it difficult for their parents to take them out in public, such as to a restaurant or the movies, because their hyperactivity bothers everyone else. Trying to keep up exhausts most parents.

Impulsivity can be equally annoying both in public and private. A small amount of impulsivity can make a person endearing and interesting to be around, but extreme impulsivity—as seen in youngsters and adults with ADHD—can be extremely difficult to tolerate. Overly impulsive people usually act before they think, blurting out answers inappropriately, talking out of turn, and making a general nuisance of themselves. Impulsivity can also be dangerous: youngsters may run into a busy street without thinking or perform an equally hazardous act without considering the consequences.

Of course, everyone experiences bouts of inattention, hyperactivity, and impulsivity now and then. Zoning out when a boring person is talking to you or blurting out an answer when it isn't your turn are all part of being human. But when these characteristics are ceaseless and have a negative impact on family and school, it's time to get help.

Q: Can other problems accompany ADHD?
A: Unfortunately, other problems often accompany ADHD. For example, many youngsters with ADHD also have a certain type of learning disability that makes it difficult for them to master language or learn certain academic skills, such as math or reading. ADHD is not in itself a learning disorder, notes the National Institute of Mental Health, but because it impedes concentration and attention, it can exacerbate those learning disorders that accompany it.

Nearly half of all children with ADHD—especially boys—develop a condition known as oppositional defiant disorder (ODD), characterized by stubbornness, outbursts of temper, aggression, and a general defiance of those around them. Youngsters with ODD run a much greater risk of getting into trouble in school and later, with the law. Other emotional problems that can go hand-in-hand with ADHD include extreme anxiety, depression, sadness, worry, and fearfulness. While these problems may occur independent of ADHD, they are often secondary effects of the syndrome's impact on the young person's development.

In addition, a small percentage of people with ADHD have a rare disorder known as Tourette's syndrome, which is characterized by uncontrollable tics, twitches, and other facial movements, as well as grimaces, shrugs, hand-clapping, and the barking out of words, often obscenities. Thankfully, Tourette's syndrome and related disorders can be successfully managed with medication.

Q: Is ADHD found only in one race or group of people?
A: No. Although researchers have found that ADHD afflicts more boys than girls, more whites than other races and, in all likelihood, more Americans than other nationalities, it is not exclusive to any of these groups. Anyone of any age in any country may show symptoms of this syndrome.

Q: Is ADHD a newly discovered problem, or have doctors known about it for a long time?
A: The history of ADHD's "evolution" is both fascinating and lengthy. It's not a new ailment, but it's taken doctors and researchers quite a long time to understand what it is and how to effectively treat it.

The first description of ADHD in the medical literature was made in 1902 by an English doctor named George Still, who described a group of young patients stricken with extreme hyperactivity, inattention, and impulsivity. Not surprisingly, the group consisted of three boys for every girl, and in each case the problems manifested themselves before age eight. From his report, it's apparent that Still was dealing with almost textbook examples of ADHD. Based on the fact that most of the children in his study came from good, loving homes, Still theorized that their condition was biological rather than environmental and might even have a genetic component.

It's interesting to note that during that period, disruptive children were generally viewed as simply poorly disciplined, and much of the responsibility for their behavior was placed on their parents' shoulders. Parenting books and even many medical texts advocated spanking and other forms of corporal punishment as the answer to hyperactivity and inattention. Now, of course, we know that corporal punishment does nothing to eliminate the symptoms of ADHD, and can, in fact, make them worse.

A 1917 encephalitis outbreak in the United States stimulated still more interest in attention deficit syndromes because many children stricken with the disease developed problems strikingly similar to ADHD, including hyperactivity and attention deficit. Doctors reasoned that the virus responsible for encephalitis damaged the same parts of the brain suspected to be immature in ADHD children. By the 1940s, the term *minimal brain damage* was used to describe this disorder. However, once it was determined that these children often had no evidence of brain damage, the term was changed to *minimal brain dysfunction*.

Hyperactivity became the focus of study in the 1950s, when doctors started referring to the condition as "hyperkinetic impulse disorder." It was during this period that Ritalin and other stimulants became the treatment of choice for children with ADHD, though the number of prescriptions then was dramatically lower than what we're seeing today.

During the latter part of the 1960s, doctors and researchers began to realize with greater certainty that the symptoms that make up ADHD are biological and possibly genetic in origin—not the result of poor parenting, environment, or children just being "bad." The use of stimulants, particularly Ritalin, became increasingly common as parents looked desperately for an effective treatment.

The 1970s saw greater research into both the causes and effects of ADHD, with strong emphasis on impulsivity and distractibility. Scientists became increasingly convinced of a biological and probably genetic cause, although they couldn't prove it. As studies attempted to understand the underlying deficient cognitive operations that result in the syndrome, the name given to the disorder changed. Thus the term *attention deficit disorder* reflected the conviction, largely following the work of Virginia Douglas in the 1970s and 1980s, that a deficit in attention was the primary underlying disorder. In *DSM IV*, hyperactivity was added to the nomenclature, so that now the syndrome is referred to as attention deficit hyperactivity disorder.

Q: It's frequently stated that up to 5 percent of all kids have ADHD. This seems like a pretty high number. Is it really that many?

A: No one really knows just how prevalent the disorder is among children and adults. The National Institute of Mental Health (NIMH), in a special report on ADHD, confirms the 3 to 5 percent figure. The *Washington Post* says the number of ADHD cases has skyrocketed from slightly more than 900,000 in 1990 to more than 2 million in 1995. However, there is ongoing debate within the medical community as to whether it's really that high—or even whether ADHD really exists.

Recent media coverage suggests that many cases of so-called ADHD are just normally active, enthusiastic, and energetic children and that the dramatic increase in Ritalin use is merely a panacea for parents and teachers who don't know how or don't have the time to manage these children.

As a child psychiatrist, I believe that ADHD is a useful medical diagnosis to describe a group of symptoms that co-exist in and cause a great deal of trouble for a significant number of children. There's no question that some children diagnosed with ADHD probably don't have the disorder and really don't need to be on Ritalin. But this shouldn't detract from the hundreds of thousands of youngsters and adults who *do* have ADHD and *do* benefit from the use of Ritalin and other therapies. It is clear that an ADHD diagnosis should not be made lightly and that other conditions that may explain the symptoms should be ruled out first.

Q: This may be a silly question, but are there any advantages to having ADHD?

A: That's not a silly question at all. Hallowell and Ratey, in their book *Answers to Distraction* (Bantam), note that people with ADHD tend to have a high energy level, are extremely creative and resourceful, have a strong intuitive sense, and are tenacious, hardworking, warmhearted, and forgiving. They also tend to have a strong sense of loyalty and a great sense of humor.

Q: Someone told me recently that ADHD has become a cottage industry. What does this mean?
A: Over the past few years, as more and more young people and adults have been diagnosed with ADHD, there has been a tremendous grassroots market in goods and services designed to help them. They range from special camps and boarding schools to testing services, videotapes, interactive newsletters, and other items. A listing of national ADHD organizations, help groups, and other services can be found at the end of this book.

Q: How does ADHD typically present itself? Do symptoms differ with age?
A: Yes, they do. The presentation of ADHD in a six-year-old is much different than in an adolescent or adult. The symptoms are very similar, but their *manifestation* changes with age.

A small child may present ADHD through behavior such as extreme hyperactivity, inattentiveness, and impulsivity. All small children exhibit these characteristics now and then—they're part of growing up—but a child with ADHD will be like that every waking moment.

An adolescent with ADHD will present the syndrome in a much different way. He may do very poorly in school despite obvious intelligence, have a tendency to "zone out" during class or while his parents are talking to him, be moody or irritable and exhibit serious behavior problems that result in few friends. Again, a great many teenagers are moody, irritable, and difficult to be around—but not all the time. Nor do most normal adolescents present such a neat package of telltale symptoms.

ADHD is a bit trickier to see in an adult, though the symptoms are similar. He may have trouble focusing on and finishing projects at work, experience difficulty relating to bosses and co-workers, be irritable and moody at home, and have problems with interpersonal relationships because of his temper and inability to focus.

The presentation of ADHD symptoms will be addressed in greater detail in the next two chapters.

Q: How does ADHD first come to the attention of a health care professional? Who is the first person to notice that something's wrong with a child?

A: Parents and teachers are usually the first to notice that something is "different" in an ADHD child. Very often, indicators are detected in infancy—ADHD children tend to be more colicky, have more sleep problems, cry more, and show earlier signs of high intelligence.

Sally B., for example, detected differences between her second son, Jacob, and his older brother, Nathan, immediately. Whereas Nathan had slept soundly as an infant, Jacob was up at all hours, fussy and difficult to get to sleep. He cried frequently. "It was hard to believe that the boys were related," Sally says now. Jacob also started walking and talking at an earlier age than Nathan and gave every indication of being gifted.

But, as Jacob grew older, his "antsy" behavior never settled down. In fact, he stayed in constant motion from the moment he woke up to the moment he grudgingly went to sleep. And despite his obvious intelligence, Jacob did poorly in school, and developed a reputation as a discipline problem and a bully. "I knew there was something wrong with Jacob. I just didn't know what it was," Sally says. "I knew in my heart he was a good boy and I loved him, but because of his behavior, there were times when I didn't like him very much."

Help came in the form of Jacob's second-grade teacher, who suspected that Jacob had ADHD. She suggested he be seen by a child psychiatrist specializing in the syndrome, and after an extensive battery of tests, the diagnosis was confirmed.

Teachers are also often the first to suspect ADHD in older children. Whereas parents may just assume their teenager's aggravating behavior is merely a phase, teachers usually know better. They're around teenagers all the time, know their moods and behaviors and have greater knowledge of the symptoms that identify ADHD.

An ADHD diagnosis in adults, of course, is a completely

Is It Really ADHD?

different story. A professional workup and diagnosis usually only follows ADHD-related problems at work or home (such as disciplinary action for not completing a project or the threat of a divorce because of violence or irrational behavior). Very often, adults with ADHD suspect for quite a long time that there's something wrong with them, but they have lived with the disorder for so long that they can't quite put a finger on it. Like someone with an alcohol or drug problem, they must often "reach bottom" before seeking help.

Q: Do doctors know yet what causes ADHD?
A: Doctors know a lot about ADHD, but they are not completely certain what causes it. The current view is that the syndrome has underlying biological-neurological origins (possibly with a genetic, or inherited, component) that interact with the individual's environment to result in the manifestation of ADHD.

Previous hypotheses regarding the causes, or etiologies, of ADHD have focused on brain damage caused during pregnancy or birth; other causes of brain damage early in life, such as trauma or infections; troubled family environments; inadequate parenting; food additives; sugar in the diet; and malnutrition. It is now clear that no one of these etiologies is universally present. The question of food additives and sugar has been carefully examined in controlled studies and has been convincingly ruled out as an etiology. While some people with ADHD have undergone prenatal fetal distress or birth trauma, and while some, upon examination, show signs suggestive of brain dysfunction, others may have no such history and may have a completely normal physical examination.

One of the problems with researching the possible biological causes of ADHD is the difficulty in defining just what brain functions are disturbed. Researchers have attempted to break down the function of attention into its components, which can then be studied and even localized to specific parts of the brain. For example, Dr. Alan Mirsky of the NIMH has divided attention into the following three components:

1. the capacity to select a part of the environment to focus on,

2. the ability to sustain that focus over time, and
3. the ability to change or shift focus, i.e., to stop focusing on one part of the environment and start focusing on another part of the environment.

With the advent of positron emission tomography (PET), researchers are now trying to localize brain function while it is occurring. For example, in one study adult subjects were asked to learn a list of words while a PET scanner analyzed how much glucose different parts of their brain used while they worked. In people with ADHD, the brain areas involved in attention used less glucose than in normal control subjects.

Another area of research involves the dramatic results achieved in improving some ADHD symptoms through the use of the stimulants methylphenidate (Ritalin) and dextroamphetamine (Dexedrine). Studies have shown that these stimulants increase the amount of dopaminergic neurotransmitters, the chemicals that carry electrical messages from one nerve cell to the next, available in the central nervous system. Stimulants may also increase the amount of another transmitter, norepinephrine, in the parts of the brain related to activation and arousal. However, the impact of these stimulants is very complex, and it does not follow that ADHD is caused by a simple deficiency in the quantity of these transmitters. What is very likely is that the underlying biological disorders somehow cause a disturbance in neurotransmitter functions. Research in this area will hopefully continue to enhance our knowledge of both the etiology and management of ADHD.

From the moment of conception, the environment has an impact on the fetus. Obviously poor nutrition, absence of adequate prenatal care, metabolic and toxic factors (such as alcohol, cigarette, or drug use by the pregnant mother), infections, stress, birth trauma, premature delivery, and low birth weight can all affect the health of the newborn infant. In fact, studies have shown a correlation between these factors and later ADHD.

Environmental influences become ever more complex as an individual proceeds through development after birth. While there are no firm correlations between ADHD and family and parenting variables, it is clear that from the beginning of life, the environment of these youngsters interacts in complex ways to bring about the complicated symptom picture that we call ADHD. This interplay between biology and environment will be enlarged upon in the next chapter's discussion of ADHD at different developmental stages.

For now it is clear that many different variables, including genetic, biological, and psychosocial factors, combine and interact to form the syndrome known as ADHD.

Q: How long does ADHD last? Does it always progress into adulthood?

A: There are few absolutes when discussing attention deficit hyperactivity disorder, including its duration. Some young people do seem to outgrow the symptoms of the disorder and go on to lead relatively normal adult lives; however, studies suggest that in the vast majority of cases the disorder continues, at least to some degree, into adulthood.

ADHD expert Gabrielle Weiss and her colleagues reported in the *Journal of the American Academy of Child Psychiatry* that 66 percent of patients who had ADHD as children have at least one or more "mild to severely disabling" symptoms as adults. That's why it's so important that ADHD children be placed on a management program as early as possible. Studies show that almost 80 percent of ADHD victims who needed medication as children also need it as teenagers, and 50 percent need it as adults. Early and aggressive intervention is the best way to ensure that these children will grow up to live productive and fulfilling lives.

Q: How is ADHD diagnosed? Can my child's pediatrician make the diagnosis, or should I see someone else?

A: Attention deficit hyperactivity disorder isn't an easy problem to accurately diagnose. As mentioned earlier, it's not a disease like the flu or measles, but a collection of common symptoms, not all of which are present in all patients and some of which may also be caused by other disorders. Most children are brought in for evaluation because they exhibit several of the telltale signs of ADHD, such as extreme hyperactivity and inattention, and these problems are causing an adverse effect on their lives at home and at school.

Parents and teachers are usually the first to suspect ADHD, and pediatricians are typically the first line of diagnosis. However, not all pediatricians are well versed in the disorder, and they may suggest the child be examined by someone with greater expertise, such as a child psychiatrist who specializes in behavior disorders.

It must be stressed that an accurate diagnosis of ADHD cannot be made following a simple fifteen-minute meeting with the child and his parents. If your doctor diagnoses ADHD following such a brief interview and recommends no further testing, you should consider seeking a second opinion, preferably by an ADHD specialist.

In most cases, the child must first undergo a thorough and extensive physical examination to ensure that his problems are not the result of other ailments, such as mental or emotional illness, hearing problems, undetected seizures (known as petite mal), food allergies, poor nutrition, or other medical conditions. The initial diagnostic interview should also include taking a full history of the child's birth, infancy, and subsequent development, as well as the health history of all related family members.

Once the child receives a clean bill of health, the next step is to gather as much information about the child and his environment as possible. This usually includes an examination of all report cards, tests, classwork, and academic and psychological testing, as well as extensive interviews with the child's parents, siblings, pediatrician, teachers, and others who work closely with him. They may be asked to describe the child's behavior in a variety of situations and fill out a rating scale to indicate how severe and frequent his behaviors seem to be. The ADHD specialist may visit the child's school or home to further observe him in his own setting.

In addition, the child may undergo a battery of psychological, behavioral, and observational tests to determine the degree of his symptoms and rule out common learning disorders. How extensive is his hyperactivity? What makes him "zone out," and how often does he do it? On which tasks does he find it most difficult to concentrate? Is he prone to bursts of anger or aggression? The answers to these and many other questions help doctors rule out other possible causes and confirm an accurate diagnosis of ADHD based on the criteria listed in the *DSM IV*.

Q: How early in a child's development can ADHD be diagnosed?

A: That's a good question. As mentioned earlier, parents often notice signs that their child is "different" during early infancy, but it's difficult to establish a diagnosis of ADHD in children younger than four or five because their personality and behavior patterns are still developing and often are similar to symptoms of ADHD. Typically, ADHD is not suspected, or confirmed, until a child is in nursery or elementary school, where his problematic behavior conflicts with environmental expectations.

In infants, signs that might suggest ADHD include extreme and prolonged irritability (being "colicky"), erratic sleep patterns, and somewhat faster motor development. As mentioned earlier, ADHD children sometimes show early signs of being gifted, which is what makes their poor grades in school such a mystery to parents and teachers.

In toddlers, possible signs of ADHD include extreme hyperactivity (constant movement even during quiet periods), a need to touch everything, a need to be the constant focus of attention, inattention when others are speaking, and an inability to concentrate for extended periods (such as when being read a book). Some of these children also seem unresponsive to normal reward or punishment incentives.

In elementary-school–age children, symptoms might include greater hyperactivity, talking back to adults in authority, an inability to concentrate on schoolwork, an explosive temper, and a frightening disregard for personal safety (e.g., running into the street without consideration for oncoming traffic or jumping from a tree that's too high).

In adolescents, possible symptoms of ADHD include extreme and prolonged moodiness, poor grades despite obvious intelligence, an inability to make or keep friends, rebelliousness, outbursts of anger or aggression, and frequent zoning out in class or during conversation.

Q: You mentioned earlier that certain disorders and conditions can mimic symptoms of ADHD. Could you please clarify this?

A: ADHD is a syndrome characterized by a collection of common symptoms, any one of which can be mimicked by numerous other problems. This is why making a careful diagnosis is so essential. The ADHD specialist, as part of this diagnosis, will consider all other possible causes of the clinical picture and will take a history, do an examination, and sometimes give tests to rule out these other causes. The most common include the following.

- **Mental retardation**.
- **Borderline low intelligence**. When these children are placed in academic settings beyond their intellectual ability, they frequently show symptoms of inattention and hyperactivity.
- **Intellectually gifted children**. If these children are placed in an academically understimulating environment, they may be bored, fidgety, and inattentive and may even exhibit behavior problems.
- **Learning disabilities**. There are several different kinds of learning disabilities that may occur in children of normal and superior intelligence and that can be diagnosed by neuropsychological testing. If not treated, these can result in academic underachievement, frustration, and low self-esteem and secondary inattention and behavior problems. It is essential that learning disabilities be ruled out as a cause of academic and behavioral difficulties in a hyperactive youngster. They may take several forms, including disorders of reading, mathematics, written expression, motor skills, or language.
- **Vision or hearing impairment**. If the pediatrician has any suspicion that one of these is present, the child should be examined by a specialist.
- **Pervasive developmental disorder**. This disorder includes what used to be called autism. It should be con-

sidered when a child with the features of ADHD also has severe language impairment, seems unable to relate to people and has strange, stereotypically autistic behaviors.

- **Family problems**. Situations such as divorce, a death in the family, or the loss of a parent's job can greatly affect the emotional well-being of young children and adolescents, resulting in disruptive behavior, anger, aggression, and low self-esteem. In most cases, the child's behavior returns to normal once the problem issue has been resolved or the child comes to terms with it. Excessively permissive or extremely punitive parenting, inadequate and chaotic home environments, and parental neglect may result in a clinical picture similar to that of ADHD.
- **Oppositional defiant disorder (ODD)**. While some children with ADHD may develop ODD, it is possible for this condition to exist on its own. Signs of ODD include impulsive aggressivity, defiance of adults, deliberately annoying or hurting people, blaming others for behavior, and refusing or avoiding academic tasks.
- **Conduct disorder**. This diagnosis implies a persistent pattern of aggression toward people and animals, destruction of property, deceitfulness, theft, and serious violations of rules. In children this may include running away from home, drug use, and school truancy.
- **Manic episode**. The manic phase of a bipolar illness can resemble ADHD with its agitation, mood lability, restlessness, distractibility, and impulsivity. Usually, a careful history and exam will reveal differences.
- **Depression**. Similarly, a severe depression could look like ADHD, just as a person with ADHD may be secondarily quite depressed. It is important for the specialist to try to determine which is the primary condition.
- **Adjustment disorder**. An acutely traumatic situation or event can lead to an ADHD-like reaction. However, in this case, symptoms would not have the long history

present in attention deficit hyperactivity disorder.
- **Child or adolescent antisocial behavior**.
- **Antisocial personality disorder**. This diagnosis is reserved for adults with a clinical picture similar to the conduct disorder described above. While antisocial personality disorder should be considered as an alternative diagnosis to adult ADHD, it is, unfortunately, often a coexisting condition.
- **Food allergies**. This is much less common than generally believed, but if a child is proven to be allergic to certain foods, then the symptoms of hyperactivity should abate when the food is omitted from the diet.
- **Drug use**. It is an unfortunate fact that children as young as elementary school age are already experimenting with marijuana, alcohol, speed, hallucinogens and other illicit drugs, and certain symptoms of ADHD, such as zoning out, irritability, poor attention, and hyperactivity may be the results of such use. No parent wants to believe that his or her child is involved in drugs, but it's an issue that needs to be addressed if your child's condition is to be diagnosed and managed.
- **Viral diseases**. Following the 1917 encephalitis outbreak, many children had a persistent post-encephalitis syndrome that closely mimicked ADHD. A rare cause like this should certainly be ruled out during the preliminary, thorough medical history and examination.
- **Other medical conditions**. Poor medical care, chronic infections, hormonal disorders, anemia, malnutrition, and sleep deprivation can all produce symptoms reminiscent of ADHD, and need to be ruled out during the preliminary health checkup.
- **Temperament**. Some children are just naturally energetic and rambunctious. Temperament is determined by a great many factors, including genetics, parenting, and environment, and can change dramatically from one developmental stage to another. A child who is colicky in infancy, for example, may grow up to be

quiet and peaceful, while another who is calm in infancy may grow up to be hyperactive and difficult to manage. With this in mind, it's important to remember that a child's temperament is not always a predictor of ADHD. Other factors must also be taken into consideration.

- **Hunger**. It's frightening to think that there are children in this country who go to bed hungry every night, but it does occur and in far greater numbers than many people realize. Sadly, many of these children may be exhibiting symptoms of ADHD. Poor nutrition can have a tremendous impact on a child's ability to think, learn, and behave. Fatigue can have a similar impact.
- **School difficulties**. A poor student-teacher relationship, problems with friends or classmates, and other related classroom difficulties external to the child may cause otherwise healthy and normal youngsters to behave in ways that mimic ADHD. In the majority of cases, when these problems are properly addressed and students are placed in a class that's on their level, behavior returns to normal.

TWO

ADHD in Children and Adolescents

Attention deficit hyperactivity disorder is not something that develops at a specific age, like acne. Research suggests that ADHD children are probably born with the syndrome, and many strong indicators may be present from the very first day of life.

It's usually during the many developmental stages of infancy and childhood that ADHD begins to show itself in its myriad forms. The underlying symptoms of the disorder are strikingly similar throughout life, but manifest themselves differently according to a child's age and developmental level. For example, in infancy an ADHD child may be "colicky" and have crying fits. At age seven, his impulsivity and hyperactivity may exhibit themselves in temper tantrums and an inability to remain still. The symptom is the same, but it manifests itself quite differently according to age.

In determining whether a child has ADHD, doctors and specialists perform what's known as a "differential diagnosis." In brief, this means that all the patient's symptoms are analyzed and all possible causes are eliminated one by one until only the true cause remains.

A differential diagnosis is especially important when working with children because the potential causes of their disruptive behavior can be numerous, depending on their age and developmental stage. Some of the most common include conduct disorder, separation anxiety or overanxious disorder, bipolar affective disorder (mania or depression), schizophrenia, mental retardation, learning disabilities, lead poisoning, and medical problems such as hyperthyroidism or migraine headaches. See Chapter 1 for a more in-depth look at disorders that can mimic symptoms of ADHD.

In this chapter, we will answer common questions regarding the symptoms of ADHD at each developmental period and how they can impact on the different developmental tasks appropriate to infancy, school age, and adolescence. Chapter 3 will discuss ADHD in adults.

Q: If the symptoms of ADHD are relatively similar throughout life, why is it necessary that they be analyzed according to age and developmental level?
A: It's important to break it down this way because children look very different at various ages, their developmental tasks are different, and the environment in which they are behaving and living is different. Consequently, the underlying disorders of ADHD will manifest themselves uniquely at those ages and have a distinct effect on the most crucial aspects of development.

When ADHD presents itself in an older school-age child, an adolescent, or even an adult, so much has gone into developing that person's character that to say ADHD is the only force at work is extremely simplistic. We must go back to the beginning and look at how the syndrome first appeared, as well as how the difficulties related to it interacted with the child's environment to distort his development right from the start.

It often helps to think of attention deficit hyperactivity disorder as an onion, made up of layers, each having a dramatic impact on the next. Parents need to have a strong understanding of this multilayered aspect of ADHD in order to design the treatment approach that will be most helpful for their child.

Q: Could you please explain how ADHD can influence the developmental stages of infancy? I don't understand how a disorder like this can

have such a dramatic impact on a child so young.

A: Infancy is the period in which the least amount of research has been accomplished, and thus it's where we have the least amount of clinical information. Nonetheless, researchers are learning more and more every day about how ADHD affects the earliest months of life, and how it can impact on development in later years.

Research in infants is difficult for many reasons. For example it is not possible to subject infants to some of the exciting new ways to study brain functioning, such as positron emission tomography, because of the radiation involved, the need to use isotopes, and so on. On the other hand, infants cannot participate in studies that rely on verbal instruction or carefully structured tasks. However, researchers have found many innovative ways to study infant attention, arousal, and learning. For example, infants are presented with a visual image that becomes familiar to them. That image is then presented among other distracting images, and the researcher can observe whether the infant remembers the first learned image according to whether the infant's gaze is preferentially focused on it.

Many studies are now focusing on states of arousal in infants, on what allows for focused attention, what interferes with it, how infants learn, what states they need to be in to best learn new information, and so on. There is some convincing evidence to suggest that children who have the hallmark signs of ADHD already had disrupted attentional systems and abnormal arousal states.

Arousal is the state of neurophysiological activation and the nature of its organization. In ADHD infants, there may be abnormally high levels of arousal, which do not respond normally to organizing input. Let us look at the normal baby first.

Consider the normal baby who cries and thrashes about due to hunger or feeling cold and wet. This baby becomes highly aroused in response to a specific stimulus and will usually calm down rapidly when certain soothing activities are performed by the caretaker. These may be tactile activities such as holding or rocking the baby or putting a nipple in the baby's mouth. Or they may be auditory experiences, such as when the caretaker croons to the baby. Or they may just be removal of the offending stimulus. There is apparently some feedback between these sensory experiences and the state of arousal.

What we see is that the baby responds by quieting and by *organization*; that is, by focusing his or her attention. The baby may simply look at the soothing person, or perhaps exhibit sucking behavior if a bottle or nipple is offered. Or the quieting and focus may result in sleep. When all this is working ideally, the caregiver is also learning and focusing, learning just how to match the baby's degree of arousal with the intensity of soothing activity, and learning just which specific soothing activities will work for this particular child in each particular situation.

Something goes awry with this complex interactive loop in the ADHD child and the problems may be multiple. First, these children may respond to stimuli with far greater levels of arousal. Second, their neurophysiological system does not respond as well or as quickly to the organizing sensory input which we call soothing activities. For reasons as yet unknown, the feedback loops in the brain that inhibit arousal are less responsive. This may have to do with neurotransmitter function in parts of the brain used to focus attention. Similarly, the neurological function of enhancing certain options over others, and hence focusing conscious attention on the enhanced pathways, seems disrupted.

This means several things for the ADHD baby. First, she may suffer longer and more intense states of disorganizing arousal. She may have significantly less time in an organized, calm, alert state. This state is essential for her to focus on her environment, including her interactions with her caregiver, and it is during these times that all her important learning and experimenting can take place. In addition, she may need much more stimulation to override the state of high arousal, reach the attentional system, and focus attention. And of course it means a loss for the caregiver too, who may experience repeated failure in attempts to soothe her baby. For both the baby and the caretaker, this means a loss of the important mirroring, sharing, and intimacy.

In fact, it is this baby-caretaker interaction that is most important in the first two years of life to so much of the infant's development. Through this relationship, the baby will develop a sense of self, the ability to trust and relate to other human beings, and the ability to love and empathize. This all begins within the context of a baby and mother or significant parent figure. However, if this earliest bond is disrupted by something biological within the infant, it can cause a ripple effect that may have consequences years, even decades later.

Children start learning from the day they're born. But we usually don't know how well or how effectively until they're in school and we see they're not learning as well as they should in the school setting. In ADHD children, the internal learning process has probably been interfered with since birth.

The impact of these early problems on the development of ADHD sufferers extends to their emotional development, the development of language, and the ability to sustain satisfying, loving relationships. Chapter 6 will discuss how psychotherapy can play a very specific role in healing some of these effects.

Q: What are the most common signs of ADHD in infants?

A: There are many—but it's important to stress that these signs don't always mean a child will develop ADHD in later years. Sometimes a fussy child is just fussy; it's part of his personality. When he grows up, he may be a normal, active child with no symptoms of ADHD at all.

As described above these infants may often be fussy and distressed, with frequent bouts of crying at a greater intensity and for longer periods than other babies. It's not uncommon for newborns to suffer from occasional colic, but studies have shown that hyperactive youngsters tend to cry excessively at an earlier age and for longer periods. Of particular note is the fact that such children are almost impossible to soothe. Mothers report that no matter what they did—rocking, walking, gentle talking—they could not get their children to settle down.

Researchers believe that the mothers' desperate efforts, as well as the crying bouts themselves, can be problematic in that they result in higher periods of arousal and less frequent periods of quiet, mother-child interaction—an important part of a child's emotional development.

Excessive bouts of crying can also influence a child's cognitive development, studies suggest, because a child who is in constant turmoil is less able to explore and learn from his external environment. These children may also be much more difficult to soothe.

The parents of ADHD children often recall that their children had sleep disturbances as infants. Some were very sleepy and unresponsive during the first months of life, while others had trouble falling asleep and were noticeably overactive. Mothers of infants with poor sleep patterns also often note that once asleep, their children were restless and frequently awoke with a start, which led to long bouts of crying that were difficult to soothe.

Many of these sleep difficulties in infancy are no doubt due, at least in part, to an inability to "turn off" external stimuli. It's a problem also seen in ADHD children and adults. It is not yet known if there is an actual physiological difference in the way ADHD infants sleep. However, further research in this area may yield interesting results, since there is some overlap in the parts of the brain involved in sleep and in attention.

Another potential sign of ADHD in infancy is feeding difficulties, such as poor sucking, crying during feeding or, in later months, an irritating finickiness. Some mothers also report a strange irregularity in their child's desire for food. Most babies feed on a regular schedule, but some hyperactive infants appear to be on their own unique timetable.

These problems may have numerous causes, including an overexcited physiological state. But it might also be that the earliest sense of trust and comfort with the parenting figure has been interfered with. In order for a baby to feed well, he must feel comfortable with the person who is holding and feeding him. If he doesn't, he's likely to be fussy at feeding time.

Some mothers worry that their baby's feeding problems may lead to poor nutrition, but studies show that this is rarely the case. Of greater consequence is how the feeding problems affect the mother-child relationship.

Other potential signs of ADHD in infancy include the following.

- **Uncharacteristic inattention**. Granted, infants and toddlers aren't known for their long attention spans, but most two- or three-year-olds will sit quietly with mom or dad while reading a book or playing a game. Toddlers with symptomatic ADHD may become antsy and bored after just a couple of minutes.
- **Poor vocalization**. Most healthy infants begin babbling during their first year of life, a phenomenon known as vocalization that's a precursor to learning to talk. Studies and parent interviews show that many hyperactive infants do not begin to vocalize until well after their first birthday, and are often equally delayed in speaking their first words.

    Illustrating the importance of this issue, a study published in the journal *Pediatrics* found neurological and behavioral difficulties in a seven-year followup study on youngsters who failed a speech screening examination at age three.
- **Lack of cuddling response**. Parents of hyperactive infants often report, in retrospective studies, that their babies were not cuddly. That is, they squirmed and fretted and showed a great dislike at being held. Not surprisingly, this problem can lead to increased difficulties in the mother-child relationship because cuddling is usually an activity enjoyed equally by mother and infant.

Q: How can symptoms of ADHD in infancy affect development in later years? I don't understand the connection.

A: It must be understood that the developmental stages of life are interconnected, and that the many stages of infancy have a dramatic impact on school-age development, adolescence, and adulthood. If development is disturbed today, then tomorrow's development will also be disturbed.

When an ADHD child arrives at the next developmental

milestone, he does not have the full range of necessary skills that he should have acquired during previous stages. His developmental skills have been interfered with, and often remain immature. That's why ADHD becomes so complex as the child grows older.

Q: Can the symptoms of ADHD in infancy have an adverse effect on personality development later in life?

A: Yes, they can. One of the things researchers have found repeatedly is that older adolescents and adults with this condition show a higher incidence of antisocial personality disorder and related problems.

It makes sense when you think about it. The origins of antisocial personality disorder seem to be connected to a child's earliest relationships—his ability to trust and to empathize, as opposed to dehumanizing others and then committing antisocial acts against them. If that trust doesn't develop and mature with age, dangerous antisocial behavior may result.

Q: Could you elaborate on how the early signs of ADHD can affect a mother's ability to parent? It must make this already difficult job much harder.

A: It certainly can. Parents must work much harder than usual to provide the emotional support that ADHD children need.

A new mother may feel like a failure if she can't soothe her child, or believe that she's a bad parent or simply doesn't know what she's doing. But research has shown that if a parent can rise to the challenge and see her child as having special needs, she can help that child enormously.

Several important studies have found that parenting problems are most severe when a hyperactive baby is a woman's first child. She may find it difficult to be with the child, may express anger over his difficult behavior, and may show him less love and affection.

But if a woman's first child shows normal growth and development, she will be more confident in her parenting skills and realize that her new baby's behavior problems are not her fault. As a result, she will continue to do all she can to be a good mother and not give up.

Unfortunately, few pediatricians are really attuned to the early signs of ADHD, and that can be a problem for new mothers. Even though we know quite a bit about ADHD in older childhood, little is known about the kinds of support that parents need in order to be the right kind of parent for a very young child with these special demands. I think that this is where parents need the most support. They need to know that this is about their child, not about them failing as new parents. They can't say, "Oh, I just have a difficult kid" and that's that. It means they're going to have to rally around and work extra hard to provide what's needed so that these problems don't interfere with their child's development later on.

Q: Is preschool too early to contact a specialist regarding a child's hyperactivity or other behavior problems?
A: No, but you should realize that at this age few children are perfect angels, and that misbehavior and hyperactivity are relatively common and usually no cause for alarm. However, while most children are not brought for diagnosis until they are of school age, earlier diagnosis may offer help that might prevent later problems from developing.

A doctor should be consulted if the child's behavior is causing serious problems at home, in school, or in other social situations. If you feel your baby does have severe difficulties in calming down, or if your toddler seems especially hyperactive, inattentive, or very difficult to soothe, you should consult with your pediatrician, and perhaps ask for a referral to a child psychiatrist. Similarly if your child has not begun babbling during the first year, or is not speaking words during the second year, or if your child seems to not relate to you, it would be advisable to seek a consultation.

I will illustrate the picture of ADHD in a preschooler, by describing Peter, who already exhibited severe symptoms of ADHD by the age of four.

Peter, a four-year-old preschooler

Peter was first brought to see me when he was four years old, a few months after beginning pre-kindergarten. His teachers had told his parents that he never communicated with them or other children, did not play with his peers, and never joined in group activities. He either kept to himself in a corner with books, or he careened around the room in an unrelated, hyperactive state. He could only tolerate an hour or two a day before becoming disruptive and demanding to go home. At times he became babyish, for example, crawling around the classroom and mouthing toys.

His parents said these were also long-standing problems at home. While Peter had a large vocabulary and fund of knowledge, he rarely spoke to them directly about his needs or feelings and they felt he did not listen to them. He seemed to tune them out when they tried to speak to him, particularly when they asked him to do something. He spoke incessantly, but rarely about any real events or interactions. His speech was irrelevant and filled with fantasy. He reacted with increased hyperactivity and uncontrollable behavior whenever a change of situation was required, such as when leaving the house or having to end an activity or go to bed.

Peter was his parents' first child, a second having arrived when he was three. His mother's pregnancy with Peter was normal but the labor lasted three days, and monitoring of the baby's heartbeat in the birth canal showed there was some fetal distress during the end stages. However, he seemed healthy at birth and went home with his mother on schedule. She remembered that he was colicky and very difficult to soothe, often requiring prolonged carrying. Now, at age four, he still became uncontrollably distressed when upset or overstimulated, had tantrums and banged his head on the wall. He still seemed unresponsive to his parents' attempts to soothe him or to control or punish him.

A further troubling symptom was that he had never achieved full bowel training. He would retain his feces, and then have repeated accidents in his clothing (encopresis). Sometimes he would actually disrobe and defecate on the floor, but he very rarely defecated in the toilet. He preferred to wear diapers and, though not wearing them to preschool, was continuing to wear them at night. His pediatrician found no physical abnormality to account for this encopresis and, in fact, found him in excellent health except for his recurrent ear infections. These infections may well have interfered with his hearing at various times during his infancy. His speech development had been delayed, and he did not start speaking in full sentences until after three years of age.

When I first met Peter, he came bursting into my office enthusiastically, his mother at his side. I invited her to stay in the room, and he proceeded to explore hectically, talking continually with an immature articulation at times difficult to understand. Sometimes he spoke about the toys and asked me about broken things and missing pieces, but often his streams of speech seemed irrelevant to the situation at hand, and were just another medium of motor discharge. Suddenly, after about ten minutes, his activity stopped, and he went and stood by his mother and stared at me, as though he had only just realized I was a stranger and he needed to take stock of the situation.

I easily engaged him again, and found I had to keep my own energy level very high to keep up with him, following him around the room, talking, answering his questions. He was not rough with the toys, however, and worked with great perseverance to carefully free a stuck car from a garage elevator. When I suggested that his mother could wait in the waiting room while he and I continued, he said that she would have nothing to do there. When she went anyway, saying she had lots to do, he seemed not to respond, and went on playing.

In her absence, Peter's activity level increased even further. He went to the cold woodstove and started to rub his hands in the ashes. He wanted to open my drawers, in addition to other activities that I had to prohibit. He clearly was now reacting to his mother's absence with some anxiety. He couldn't express it or acknowledge it; rather, he just became more disorganized, distracted, and hyperactive. I felt that he wasn't listening or couldn't really focus on what I said. When I asked him to draw, however, it became clear he had heard me because he immediately said he was no good at drawing. He began to gather paper and tape it together into a long strip because he wanted me to draw a six-foot-high picture of a volcano. It was to be Mount Vesuvius, and as he became more excited and paced around, he spoke rapidly, loudly, and in great detail about the volcano, its massive eruption, the burying of Pompeii, and his voluminous instructions for my drawing.

Q: What are the effects of ADHD during the normal developmental stages of school-age children?

A: Obviously, the developmental tasks facing a child in the first grade through early adolescence differ considerably from those met during infancy. The telltale symptoms of ADHD, such as hyperactivity and inattention, are also far more pronounced. As a result, this is the period during which most ADHD children are first brought to their doctors for testing and a diagnosis is made.

One of the most important developments in a child this age is a move outside the family into a school setting where there are many more requirements. Some families have been extremely flexible up to this point and haven't really challenged the ADHD child's disruptive behavior; the child's impulsivity and hyperactivity have been absorbed into the family setting, and the child may not seem different. Other times, a child is viewed as being "just like his father" because of his rambunctious behavior and thus considered typical (in cases like this, the father may have undiagnosed ADHD, too). But once in the school setting, with its requirements for standardized behavior, the child's difficulties come under sharper scrutiny.

This can happen right at the beginning or further along in the child's education; it all depends on the school environment, the teachers, and the severity of the child's condition. If a school has a laid-back, unstructured setting with relaxed teachers and small groups of children, the child's behavior may not seem unacceptable. And if the child is bright enough, he may develop sufficient academic skills to hide his condition for years.

It's imperative that a child at this age learn to deal with the classroom situation. This may mean controlling his activity level, focusing his attention on the tasks required of him, listening to the teacher, being able to wait and delay action, making appropriate responses to a stimulus, and tuning out stimuli so that he can focus on the task at hand. It also means learning tasks that require attention, sitting still, and a certain level of cognitive skill. At this age we may begin to see that the child hasn't developed balanced judgment and this may be a problem.

Q: What are the most common symptoms of ADHD in school-age children?
A: Children ages six to twelve with clinically diagnosed ADHD typically display most (but seldom all) of the following.

- **Inappropriate activity**, either too much or unrelated to the task. The child may be fidgety, getting up out of his seat, knocking things off his desk, or playing with books or pencils, doodling, making paper airplanes, and so on.
- **Impulsive behavior**, making quick and perhaps aggressive responses to other children, reacting impulsively to stimuli in the classroom or talking incessantly and out of turn, unable to restrain himself. He may also be impulsive in his work, rushing to answer a question or finish a task without focusing on what is needed, thus often making impulsive errors, ignoring instructions, and handing in inadequate and too little work.
- **Poor attention-focusing**. This may lead him to daydream in class, to not be able to concentrate on the task at hand, and to make impulsive or hyperactive responses to try to compensate.
- **Extreme distractibility**. He may respond to every possible distraction and be unable to sustain attention for more than a few minutes.
- **Falling behind academically**, even when his intelligence may seem more than adequate.
- **Poor organizational skills**, losing work and books, not doing homework, a chaotic desk and backpack.
- **Behavioral problems**, which may result from some of the above problems, but which may also be the main area that affects the teacher and classmates. Some of

these children may turn to others in their distractibility and impulsivity, trying to get them to talk or play with them, or they may act impulsively and aggressively in response to feeling humiliated or rejected. In an attempt to enhance their social standing, such children may try to act as the class clown or may openly defy the teacher in the hope of being admired by peers. Or, feeling frustrated and a failure, they may react angrily and lose all motivation to try to please or comply.

- **Low self-esteem**, related to the child's sense of failure, conclusion that he is dumb, and his experiences of peer rejection.
- **Difficulty in adapting to change**. Parents may notice that their child's behavior worsens when a change of activity is needed, such as getting ready to leave the house for school in the morning, or preparing for bed at night. There may be an element of perseveration in this, i.e., once having started an activity, it is very difficult to stop it and to shift attention onto something else. This may have a neurophysiological basis. But also it is possible that anxiety about a change, about the unfamiliar, or about leaving the safety of home can act as a disorganizing stimulus. Whatever the cause these children are often extremely inflexible and this can be very disruptive to a family's life.

By the time Peter (described above) reached first grade, his symptom picture was a rather typical example of how ADHD can impact on a child's school experience. He attended a fairly traditional school that required him to sit at a desk, face the teacher, and listen carefully to instructions. His day was punctuated by changes in activities, including leaving the classroom for music, gym, library, and science periods. His teacher soon found that these requirements were all very hard for Peter.

He could not stay in his seat, but would get up and wander around the room, often only finally settling down in the reading corner, where he would curl up on a pillow on the floor and read a book while rocking himself. He rarely could follow instructions given to the whole class, though once the teacher or her assistant came over to him, perhaps gently laid a hand on his shoulder and then went over with him what was required, he could often begin the task. However, as soon as the teacher walked away, he would become distracted by other activity in the room and seem to forget about his task. When the class had to end an activity and line up to move to another part of the school for another activity, he would become hyperactive and anxious and at times openly defiant, leading to punishments and time-outs which did not seem to help him contain himself.

As I will discuss in the chapter on the school's role, it became essential for his teachers to understand his difficulties and to plan special approaches to him, which, fortunately, they were willing to do. But it meant that often his needs had to be given special consideration, just as, at home, his disruptive behavior and special needs meant that the family life often had to center around him. This a frequent complaint made by parents of school-age children with ADHD: "He needs so much attention. We have to structure the whole family's life and schedule around him. It is just not fair to the other children!" This is an unfortunate fact of life for a family living with ADHD. However, it is possible to make that extra input and focus much more effective and worthwhile.

Q: Can you describe how a girl of this age with ADHD might differ in presentation from a boy?
A: That is a good question, for although girls may have the same symptoms as boys, the symptoms may often look quite different. I will illustrate by telling you about Stephanie, who was first brought to see me when she was eight.

Stephanie, an eight-year-old third-grader

Stephanie's mother was not aware of any possibility of ADHD, but had been persuaded by her daughter's school to bring her in for assessment because of her tendency to daydream, fabricate stories, and not complete academic tasks. Her mother was concerned about her daughter's emotional welfare, as she was a single parent and felt her daughter worried too much about her, frequently talking about the possibility of either her mother's or her own death.

Upon meeting Stephanie, I was struck by several things: She was very fidgety and restless and seemed unaware of herself in space, frequently bumping into furniture, knocking over a chair, or bumping into me. Neither her mother nor the school had been concerned about this, but upon careful questioning, I found that indeed, she was very physically active, always climbing on furniture, up trees, and "even walls," her mother proudly asserted. In fact, both school and home environments were exceedingly supportive and flexible, so her activity level had never posed a problem.

The next thing that struck me was Stephanie's use of language. Like Peter, she spoke constantly. Her speech was clear, and she used an astonishing vocabulary. At times she used phrases and expressions that made her seem uncannily grown up. In many ways she came across as a small adult, very poised, articulate, and proper except for her physical activity level. Finally I was struck by a strange inauthenticity, a feeling that the true Stephanie was somehow hidden. Not only did she tell me stories about her life which I knew to be quite untrue, but her entire demeanor and affect seemed to be an act. She was charming, obviously very intelligent, and incredibly watchful. She remembered every detail of our play and sessions and would refer to them the next time I saw her. If she noticed any changes in me or my office she would speak of them or ask about them. She often tried to direct our conversations by asking me detailed questions about my life.

You may wonder why I speak of Stephanie as an illustration of ADHD when she seems so vastly different from Peter, who demonstrated such an obvious and extreme case. While I do not think that ADHD describes the whole problem (in fact, it almost never does), as I began to work with Stephanie in therapy, it became clearer to me that some of her difficulties could well be the result of some of the deficits of ADHD and their impact on her early development. As the academic demands increased at school, she began to have more difficulty, fell behind in math and couldn't focus on homework, and her impulsivity sometimes caused her social troubles. Neuropsychological testing was able to pinpoint definite attention deficits and distractibility as well as some specific visual-spatial problems that were affecting her math abilities.

I soon saw that Stephanie's superior verbal skills were masking her inability to use language to gain a clear and firm picture of herself and her emotional states. She seemed unable to use language internally to understand and process interactions with other people. The false stories and feelings she created (sometimes borrowed whole from others or from books or television) acted as a substitute for a real sense of her self and her own story. She used this "as if" world to try to impose some order on her scary and confusing mental life, with its overwhelming states of loneliness, feelings of inadequacy, and fears of abandonment and rage. Her own states frightened her, for she had no secure sense that they could be managed or understood. Her mother had suffered some significant periods of depression and traumas in her own life. Stephanie had been a challenging baby who cried a lot. Her mother had often felt overwhelmed by her and at a loss as to how to calm her. While she tried to protect Stephanie from her own despair, she feared that it must be involved in Stephanie's sense that emotions were dangerous and had to be replaced by fiction. Stephanie experienced her emotions as overwhelming states of confusing, intense distress that could not be understood or tolerated. Instead, they had to be hidden and denied by erecting her false world. In addition, she feared that her mother was vulnerable and would be hurt or perhaps even destroyed by these emotions. I do believe these factors have been active from the beginning of Stephanie's life and have been much compounded by the kind of problems posed by the deficits of ADHD.

Q: How can ADHD affect a child's ability to make and keep friends during this period in life?
A: ADHD can play a very detrimental role in a child's ability to make and keep friends. And as ADHD children grow older, the situation becomes even more complicated.

All very young children are impulsive and active, so in nursery school there is less reflection regarding others who behave differently. But in elementary school, children begin to observe and compare each other. The normal child is better able to delay gratification, to delay impulse, to sit and listen, and to model his behavior according to group norms. But in a child with ADHD, those abilities are impaired on many different levels. They may be more hyperactive than the other children and unable to delay their response to stimuli. This may mean talking too much, not completing classroom assignments, and running around rather than sitting still.

In addition, ADHD children of school age are not as well equipped to make interpersonal judgments. They don't understand what's transpiring emotionally in others or how to read the expressions in other people's faces. Consequently, they have to work much harder than normal youngsters to evaluate what's going on socially and to find their own place in it. This can be a serious struggle because they already have so many other problems. They can't concentrate, they're easily distracted, and nothing they do seems right. It's a tremendous uphill battle for many of these children.

By the first grade, children start to observe and make comments about each other. They notice right away that an ADHD child's behavior is different, and they react to him. They may not want to play with him, for example, or they may call him names, which only compounds the situation by lowering his self-esteem even further.

We know that ADHD children have a great amount of trouble tolerating uncomfortable internal emotions because, as infants, they didn't have the learning experiences that teach them how to cope. They don't know how to find significant people within the environment to help them cope either. Consequently, the only thing they can do is react in the same way as the screaming infant does. They may throw screaming tantrums, be overtly aggressive, pick fights, and even lose control of their urine or bowels.

This was a problem of Peter's. His severe encopresis recurred at times of stress even as he grew older and advanced through grade school, causing him enormous humiliation among his peers. This was an older child's version of the uncontrolled bodily outbursts he had as an infant.

Once school-age children develop the most telling symptoms of ADHD, they may become social pariahs. Classmates refuse to play with them and often tease them unmercifully because of their strange behavior. Not surprisingly, this can severely hamper any possibility of academic success, which is already difficult for the ADHD child.

Q: Are the developmental problems of adolescents with ADHD much different from those experienced by school-age children?

A: There are a lot of similarities, but the differences can be significant.

The preteen, or early adolescent, may look somewhat like the school-age child. She may have some of the hyperactivity and impulsivity as well as the academic difficulties. She may also still experience behavior problems in the classroom. However, at this age it may look more like oppositional and defiant behavior or perhaps like anxiety and depression.

By now, ADHD children are often very angry and frustrated. They have no confidence in their abilities to deal with difficult situations, and their opinion of themselves is probably that they're stupid even if they're quite intelligent; they have not experienced satisfaction and success from their own activities. Some of these children, if their families have been incredibly supportive, may find areas in which they are somewhat successful, such as sports or a particular academic or artistic area. But for many of these youngsters, there is an overriding sense of failure by this age.

Making matters worse is what's going on within their bodies and minds. They are beginning to think of themselves as young adults and may find themselves interested in the opposite sex, which makes the social situation much more complicated. Their bodies are changing; the peer pressure surrounding attractiveness and body changes is getting stronger. And there are internal changes. They are becoming increasingly stimulated by the hormone changes that come with the onset of puberty, and that can result in many different feelings about themselves and others.

For a child who already has a fragile sense of himself and a pessimistic view of being able to control inner states, these changes can be frightening and overpowering. Boys may experience nocturnal emissions or have sudden erections or unexpected feelings of attraction to a girl. This can be very unnerving because they don't have a secure sense of their bodily functions or mental functions. A young woman with ADHD reported to me that she was made so confused and anxious by her breast development at age thirteen that she cut up and hid the first bra her mother bought her.

Around this time, age eleven or twelve, the ADHD child is often seen as immature by his peers. He is not ready to get involved in what the other children are doing socially, and he may continue certain problem patterns of behavior in an attempt to make friends, get attention, or become popular with his fellow students. But his behavior seems more and more inappropriate in the social setting because the others are moving on; they are feeling more mature, and suddenly they're interested in the opposite sex. The hyperactive ADHD preteen is still trying to be a child, to get attention in ways that are not respected by his classmates.

Very often the dramatic physical and mental changes that occur with the onset of puberty can lead to serious problems. I had one patient, a twelve-year-old boy named Allan, who was diagnosed as having ADHD and had used Ritalin. He was a very intelligent boy who did not do well in school and had no friends. He had extremely low self-esteem and was seen by his teachers as very immature. In a preadolescent surge of excitement, he had one day engaged in some inappropriate sexual play with a younger child. It was as a result of this I was asked to assess him and found that his ADHD was being inadequately treated. Psychotherapy and tutoring were added to the medication.

My understanding was that his impulsive action was in response to pressures he was unfamiliar with and didn't know how to handle. He didn't have the social outlet of being "one of the gang" and, thus, was unable to share these normal sexual feelings with his peers and learn how to deal with them. Because he had no socially defined way of handling these experiences, Allan acted impulsively when he felt aroused.

Another patient of mine, an eleven-year-old girl named Andrea, is very much caught up in her need to develop friendships. But because of her ADHD, her behavior makes her different, and her peers want nothing to do with her. As a result, Andrea feels lonely, has low self-esteem, and is angry at her peer group because she feels rejected by them, so she reaches out even more inappropriately. She tries to talk with them over and over again about the same things, giggling and laughing. She tries practical jokes and pranks, and the other girls see her behavior as more and more deviant.

Andrea has no way of understanding the other girls' changing interests, such as boys, clothes, and makeup. She's developmentally stuck and behaves more like an immature nine-year-old than an eleven-year-old on the verge of teenage maturity. Her peers want nothing to do with her, so she suffers from increased anxiety, deeper depression, and academic problems—enhanced by the impact of this developmental period on her social relations.

With older adolescents, the situation changes a bit. Frequently, by this age, ADHD children have learned to control their hyperactivity or social inappropriateness somewhat. They may be able to behave the way they're expected to in a social or classroom situation, at least for short periods. However, their long-standing academic difficulties typically become more evident. The weak base they've had through elementary school seriously impairs their ability to handle high school.

One of the ways this inability frequently presents itself is through a lack of motivation. By this time these young people have not had successful intellectual experiences. They don't treasure curiosity and learning and are unable to motivate themselves to complete a project or pursue a topic of interest. All they know is that it's required of them, and they fear failure.

Often, when an undiagnosed ADHD teen is brought to my office for the first time, it's because his parents can no longer tolerate his inexplicable lack of motivation. They have yet to realize the child's long history and the many biological problems that are playing a role in it. All they see is the psychological outcome: depression, low self-esteem, impaired academic performance, and other symptoms.

Older adolescents with ADHD often try to ease their mental anguish by looking for satisfaction elsewhere, such as experimenting with alcohol, drugs, sex, or defiant behavior.

Rebecca, a sixteen-year-old high-school student

The picture of lack of motivation was very much what brought Rebecca to treatment. She was referred by her school guidance counselor, who was concerned that she was underachieving academically. For years her teachers had felt she was a student with promise and talents, but who seemed to be unmotivated. She seemed to give up quickly, to be easily distracted and "dreamy," and to perform well below her capabilities. Her parents focused on her lack of following through, her poor motivation, and her disorganization. They wondered if she cared at all about her schoolwork and were very frustrated with her.

Neuropsychological testing had also been sought to rule out any learning disability or attentional problems. The testing revealed that Rebecca was of superior intelligence, but that while she had enormous strengths in the verbal sphere her ability to mentally manipulate math problems was very poor, as was her skill on visual organizing and visual memory tasks. Other tests showed she was very distractible and had great difficulty focusing attention, especially when the task was difficult for her, such as those tests requiring visual processing.

When I met Rebecca, she struck me as a sad-looking, pretty teenager, wearing old, dark-colored clothes, and somewhat inadequately dressed for the cold. Her eyes were heavily and colorfully made up, as though to undo her otherwise unhappy and drab appearance, and to be more acceptable to her peers. It was hard for her to talk about herself, due to a combination of shyness and of an inability to put into words what she was really feeling. She spoke of not knowing what the matter was, of just knowing she felt bored and uninterested in things. Maybe school just wasn't for her. It just didn't seem relevant to anything. She felt her parents, both professionals with advanced degrees, and her school just expected too much from her. Neither she nor her parents understood the layers of effects of her ADHD that had occurred over the years and had certainly affected her learning and her experience in school from the very beginning.

All of these issues have affected Rebecca's peer relations.

ADHD in Children and Adolescents

She is at risk of becoming promiscuous, which is common among ADHD girls who feel unsuccessful and unwanted. They desire very much to be accepted and loved, and one answer is to be sexually valued. However, because of difficulties establishing trust and intimacy, these relationships tend to be loveless and temporary.

The situation with older adolescent boys is a little different. They're more likely to become involved with alcohol or drugs and with behavior that gets them in trouble with the law. In fact, many followup studies have shown that by late adolescence, more of these youngsters have had some brush with the police than children who don't have ADHD. They tend to channel their impulsivity, as well as their chronic sense of failure and lack of motivation, into areas where they may get satisfaction, though it's usually short-lived.

A variety of odd clinical problems may also be seen in adolescents with ADHD, especially those with extreme impulsivity. These include a fascination with fire, bed-wetting, excessive lying, and even food hoarding. The correlation between these acts and impulsivity remains a mystery, but a thorough history should include questions about them to find out if they are present.

Older adolescents with ADHD are also more likely to be susceptible to group pressure out of their need for acceptance and value in the social scene. If they can't feel valued as a student or athlete, another way is through daring, dangerous, and often socially unacceptable behavior.

Boredom can be the gasoline tossed onto this very dangerous fire. Unmotivated and lacking in any satisfying academic achievement, many adolescents with ADHD find themselves suffering from a stifling sense of boredom that can only be cured through impulsive, often perilous acts. Studies have shown that young people with ADHD have far more automobile accidents than young people without ADHD, as well as a greater incidence of defiant behavior.

Colin, a seventeen-year-old high-school student

Colin attended a boarding high school. He came from another country, where he had witnessed a fair amount of political unrest and street violence during his childhood. His parents had arranged for boarding school both as a wonderful academic possibility for him, as well as a way to remove him from a very noxious cultural environment. What they had not told the school, but became subsequently clear, was that Colin had already been expelled from school at home due to some drug use and sexual acting out and had a chronically poor academic record. His uncle had been murdered just a few weeks into Colin's second year at this school, and his behavior and grades began to slip noticeably. This brought him to the attention of the school authorities, who referred him to me for evaluation.

Colin was an expensively dressed boy, small for his age, who deliberately wore his clothes too large, slicked back his hair in an exaggerated '50s look, and sashayed into my office with a nonchalant air. He seemed uninterested in the reasons his school had sent him to my office, but tried, in a practiced way, to charm me with observations about my office, about his drive in the taxi, and about other apparently irrelevant topics. He was not at a loss for words and spoke English fluently, even though it was his second language. When I asked about his family and why he was at boarding school, he spoke in a grandiose way about his talents, about his family's wealth and social standing, and about his own control over the choices that had been made for him. He would jump up and down from the chair to make a point or to show me a dance move, and sometimes clicked his fingers or drummed on his knees.

I knew from the school that he was disruptive in class, always talking and joking with other students and trying to one-up the teachers. He frequently lied to students and teachers. He was often fidgety in study hall and sometimes skipped it, despite the penalties imposed. Some of the girls in the school had complained that he was too forward, pressuring them to date him and even to have sex with him. All his teachers were concerned that his academic progress seemed well below what he was capable of.

I arranged for neuropsychological testing to be done and interviewed Colin's parents on the telephone. It soon became clear that he was suffering from very severe distractibility, inattention, and hyperactivity, as well as showing evidence of some specific learning disabilities. Much of his behavioral problem could be seen as both an expression of these symptoms as well as of his low self-esteem. His poor expectations of any success from academic work had diminished his motivation and convinced him that he was "dumb." In turn, he had turned to his peers to look for the support and esteem-building that he craved. Unfortunately, in his impulsive and nonempathic way he sought to fulfill his own emotional needs, often at the expense of others.

Q: I've heard that many stimulant medications like Ritalin lose their effectiveness when a child reaches puberty. Is this true?

A: No, that's a very common myth. It's very well documented that postpubertal adolescents, as well as adults with ADHD, continue to benefit from stimulant therapy, as well as other forms of treatment.

The discontinuation of stimulants and other medications at puberty can have dire consequences, including a flare-up of symptomatic behavior, hyperactivity, and uncontrolled impulsiveness.

Q: My fourteen-year-old has mild ADHD and claims that he can study better while listening to heavy metal music. This makes no sense to me. Isn't the music just another distraction?

A: It may seem on the surface that loud music would be a major distraction to anyone trying to study, but many youngsters with ADHD report that they can study more effectively with music playing in the background.

One possible explanation for this phenomenon is that the music masks all other background noise, such as family conversations and television—real distractions that can interfere with a child's ability to concentrate. After a while, the music becomes mere background noise, and the child is better able to focus on the task at hand.

My advice is this: Monitor your son's homework, and if music really does allow him to study more effectively, let him play it. Just don't allow him to crank up the volume to the point where it disturbs others.

Q: Can a daily dose of Ritalin help an ADHD child overcome the social problems caused by his disorder?

A: There's no question that Ritalin is a beneficial drug that has worked wonders for a great many young people and adults with ADHD. But Ritalin isn't a panacea, and seldom does it help with peer and social relations. Those problems are best handled through a multimodal treatment plan with a strong emphasis on therapy, perhaps including group therapy.

Q: Is there a big difference in treatment between school-age children and older adolescents?

A: Approaches to treatment for these age groups may be similar, but the small differences can be dramatic. Foremost, it must be stressed that these two groups have decidedly different developmental tasks. Medication and therapy may work well for both, but ultimately, treatment must be tailored to the age and development of the child. You wouldn't treat a seven-year-old the same way you'd treat a twelve-year-old, and you wouldn't treat a twelve-year-old the same way you'd treat an eighteen-year-old. The differences are more striking than the similarities, and must be addressed as treatment is decided. This issue will be discussed in greater detail in later chapters.

THREE

ADHD and Adults

Until very recently, it was believed that children with ADHD eventually outgrew the condition and that it was relatively unknown among the adult population. However, numerous long-term followup studies have found this to be untrue, and experts now believe that between 1 and 2 percent of adult men and women—possibly as many as five million in the United States alone—are affected to some degree with attention problems, impulsivity, and hyperactivity.

Unlike childhood, in which boys with ADHD outnumber girls three to one, men and women seem prone to the syndrome in equal numbers. One possible explanation is that young boys develop more visible and disturbing symptoms and thus are more quickly diagnosed than girls, who tend to be more subtle in their presentation. Another answer could be that attention deficit, impulsivity, and other problems develop later in females than males.

Between 30 and 70 percent of youngsters with ADHD show some symptoms in adulthood, researchers report, though the presentation tends to change with age. In a high percentage of cases, the syndrome has an adverse effect on the patient's personal and professional well-being.

Adults with ADHD are usually self-sufficient, but often have a lower academic performance, are less successful at work, and have a lower socioeconomic status than their siblings. Studies also show that adults with ADHD get divorced more frequently and have more job changes, more car accidents, greater personal distress and more interpersonal problems.

In this chapter, we will answer common questions regarding attention deficit hyperactivity disorder in adults, its presentation, effects, and treatment.

Q: My husband was recently diagnosed with what his doctor called "residual ADHD." Is this different from traditional attention deficit hyperactivity disorder?

A: No. Residual ADHD is a phrase used by some doctors and psychiatric specialists when discussing the persistence of ADHD symptoms from adolescence into adulthood.

The majority of youngsters with ADHD see a reduction in symptoms around late adolescence. Sometimes this improvement is so dramatic that the child is considered cured of the syndrome. However, in most cases, some residual effects continue to appear through late adolescence and into adulthood. Approximately 60 percent will have mild ADHD, and 20 percent will have a more severe presentation.

Most adults with mild ADHD are able to live a normal life with a minimum of difficulty. They are able to function well at work and at home with only slight behavior modification, and few need medication. However, adults with severe ADHD may have great difficulty coping with work and family and may require intensive treatment.

Many adults with residual ADHD also suffer from secondary problems related to their ADHD in childhood, such as poor academic skills, low self-esteem, and clinical depression and personality problems. These must be addressed along with the primary symptoms.

Q: Why have researchers had such a difficult time determining the prevalence and effects of ADHD among adults who had it in childhood?

A: It's only in the last decade or so that doctors have come to accept that ADHD is not just a childhood problem. In fact, until recently, most studies and most physicians did not follow

ADHD sufferers beyond adolescence. As a result, there have been very few long-term followup studies. And as with any scientific investigation, the studies that have been done have shown similar but not identical results.

Most studies currently available are what are termed retrospective ("looking back") studies. In one method, researchers check old clinic records and find a population of children previously diagnosed with ADHD perhaps ten to twenty years before. After attempting to contact these subjects, the researchers study those they succeed in finding who agree to participate. Various methods (such as questionnaires, rating scales, interviews, and checking medical, academic, and police records) are used to evaluate current symptoms of ADHD and life achievements, as well as the psychiatric, social, and emotional variables of these grown-up subjects.

Another method of retrospective study is to find a group of adults diagnosed with adult ADHD and to try, through history taking and looking through old school and medical records, to trace the history of their condition and to determine the presence or absence of various symptoms at earlier stages.

For example, a controlled twenty- to twenty-five-year retrospective study conducted by B. L. Borland and H. K. Heckman analyzed twenty of thirty-seven men who had been diagnosed as hyperactive in childhood. Nineteen brothers were used as a control group. The researchers found that the majority of the men who had earlier been diagnosed as hyperactive were living normal and productive lives, though more than half continued to show symptoms of hyperactivity and a noticeable number demonstrated clear antisocial behavior. They also found that the hyperactive subjects had not done quite as well as their brothers socially or economically.

A similar followup study conducted in Rhode Island analyzed eighty-one adults, averaging twenty-one years of age, who had been diagnosed with ADHD in childhood. Thirty-two older brothers were used as a control group. The researchers found results similar to those of Borland and Heckman, but with a lower percentage of antisocial problems among the ADHD subjects.

Several other studies have strived to analyze the impact and occurrence of ADHD in adults of varying ages and socioeconomic status, with interesting results. Most importantly, nearly all follow-back studies have concluded that symptoms of ADHD continue into adulthood and can predispose individuals to alcoholism and certain psychiatric problems, most notably character disorders.

There are obviously many problems with trying to reconstruct a clinical picture that may be from twenty years before. A more accurate form of study is the prospective study. The researchers begin with a group of children who have been diagnosed as having ADHD and match them with a group of control subjects, i.e., children matched in age, socioeconomic variables, and intelligence, but with no evidence of ADHD or behavioral problems. These two groups are then followed extensively over many years, with intermittent interviews of the child and family, testing, and so on. These studies necessarily take a long time to complete, and since it is only recently that ADHD in adulthood was recognized, there are not yet many groups of studied children with ADHD who have reached adulthood.

Drs. Gabrielle Weiss and Lily Hechtman of the Montreal Children's Hospital have published the fifteen-year followup data of an ongoing study of, originally, 104 hyperactive children. They have studied many aspects of these young adults' lives, including the persistence of ADHD symptoms; psychiatric status; personality pathology, including antisocial behavior; educational and vocational status; socioeconomic status; beliefs and values; as well as general life course and achievements.

They have found that hyperactives had greater difficulties as young adults in several areas when compared with a group of normal controls. Among these are the following.

- The hyperactive young adults had more impulsive personality traits.
- They were more likely to have been involved in traffic and other accidents.
- They were likely to have some persistence of hyperactivity, distractibility, and attentional problems.
- They also had a significantly lower level of education

and were more prone to leaving school because of poor grades and expulsion.
- They were more likely to have a diagnosable psychiatric condition; in particular, a significant number fulfilled the criterion for antisocial personality disorder.
- They had much lower self-esteem.
- They had less successful social and emotional relationships.

Many questions remain unanswered in the study of adult ADHD, and obviously much more research is needed in this area. The most obvious questions include: Why does ADHD afflict some adults who had it as children, but not others? And to what degree does ADHD in childhood predict personality and psychiatric disorders in adulthood? Which treatment measures can most improve the long-term outcome?

These questions and others are now being addressed. Over 600 children have been enrolled in a six-site NIMH study undertaken with the U.S. Department of Education. This study will compare medication, behavior therapies, psychotherapy, and other clinical treatments available in the child's community. The first data from that study will be available in fall 1997. But the NIMH intends to continue the study over a long period, providing a look at the long-term course of ADHD and the influence of various treatments on its course and outcome.

Q: Are adults with ADHD always first diagnosed in childhood?

A: No. In fact, a sizable percentage of adult ADHD patients manage to get through elementary school, high school, and even college without having their condition diagnosed by a physician or specialist.

Many times, a diagnosis of ADHD is made only after an adult sees a doctor for a seemingly unrelated medical or psychological reason, such as mood swings or insomnia. Others are diagnosed after bringing their child to a specialist because of disruptive behavior; in my practice I've often heard a mother say, "His father has the same problem!" And, sadly, many ADHD sufferers don't receive the help they need until their condition has caused them to hit rock bottom socially or professionally.

One of the biggest problems in diagnosing ADHD in adults is that few physicians are aware of its existence outside of childhood. They don't consider ADHD to be an adult disorder and thus often overlook the obvious when making a diagnosis. That's why people who suspect they or a loved one may have ADHD should see a psychiatrist.

Q: How is ADHD diagnosed in adults? Is it similar to making a diagnosis in a child?

A: Yes, it's very similar. A physician who suspects that a patient has ADHD should do a differential diagnosis, noting the various telltale symptoms of ADHD and gradually eliminating all other possible causes, such as depression, mania, obsessive-compulsive disorder, severe personality disorder, or an organic medical condition.

As with childhood ADHD, the dominant signs in adulthood are hyperactivity, inattention, and impulsivity. A doctor should examine the pervasiveness of these and other symptoms and note how dramatically, if at all, they affect the patient's life. The most common sources of information are the patient himself, his spouse and family, childhood and adolescent history, and school and work history.

Often a doctor will find that the patient received medication for hyperactivity as a child and that the medication was discontinued in adolescence with the assumption that the problem had been corrected. Alternatively, an adult patient may never have been accurately diagnosed, though his symptoms can be traced back to childhood, where they may have contributed to an unhappy, unsuccessful school experience. By the time he reaches adulthood, the patient may be convinced that he is not a good student or worker and is not intelligent. He may have chronic low self-esteem, experience shame and guilt, and lack motivation.

Q: Just what does ADHD look like in an adult?

A: The primary symptoms of ADHD—inattention, hyperactivity, impulsivity, etc.—don't really change in adults, but their presentation does. They're often less pronounced, but seldom do they disappear completely.

It's important to remember that our adult lives resemble childhood and adolescence in many ways. Instead of going to school, we go to work. But we must still interact with our peers, pay attention to our superiors, and complete our assignments as instructed and on time. In social situations, we interact with others, read their faces and emotions, and react appropriately. The same goes for our interaction with members of the opposite sex. These tasks are often difficult for children with ADHD and equally so for adults with the syndrome.

In adulthood, common signs of ADHD include the following.

- An inability to concentrate for any length of time.
- An inability to finish assigned projects on deadline.
- Poor organizational skills.
- Procrastination, especially where work is concerned.
- Difficulty in sustaining interest and focus over a length of time or through to completion of a project.
- Few interests and hobbies; a tendency toward boredom.
- Difficulty interacting with superiors and co-workers (and often family and friends).
- Difficulty coping with the small "waits" in life, such as traffic lights, supermarket checkout lines, and business meetings.
- Poor memory. Many ADHD sufferers overcome this problem by writing down everything they need to remember throughout the day or placing reminders in visible locations.
- Extreme distractibility and restlessness.
- Impulsivity, such as blurting out an answer before being asked, interrupting another speaker, or saying something before considering the consequences. This may also manifest in impulsive actions, like frequently changing jobs, impulsively shopping or spending

money, impulsive eating, and rapidly changing one's mind.
- An overwhelming need to be in motion. Adults with ADHD usually don't run around the room like they did when they were children, but it's not uncommon for them to constantly jiggle a leg, tap their fingers, or suddenly stand up in a meeting and walk out of the room.
- An addictive personality.
- Poor self-esteem, based on years of perceived failure.
- A hair-trigger temper.
- A tendency toward physical aggression.

Obviously, not all adults demonstrate every one of these symptoms. And as with any condition, the presentation of symptoms may be very obvious or very subtle. It all depends on the individual. I will illustrate this picture by describing Leslie, who first came to my attention when she was twenty-eight years old.

Leslie, a twenty-eight-year-old woman

Leslie, an attractive, slender brunette, came to see me in a state of great distress and anguish. She informed me that she had moved to a large country town near my northern Connecticut practice determined to start a new life. She hated the southern city she had recently moved from, but now feared the country wasn't the place for her, either. She felt her life was slipping through her fingers and that she would never have the husband and children she longed for. She hated all the jobs she'd had, did not know what to do with herself, and hoped that by talking to me a few times, she could make the right decision regarding where to move.

Her mother had died during her sophomore year in college, and since then Leslie had roamed around lost and mainly unattached. She changed colleges several times, took time off in between and took many years to finally graduate. Her older brother had been out of contact for years, and her father, devastated by his wife's death, had been emotionally unavailable and now was remarried. She did not connect grief regarding her mother's death to her ten years of wandering. In fact, she asserted, she never even cried and certainly did not miss her mother. She felt she had always been depressed and anxious, "since she was born," and now it seemed obvious to her why anyone would be so depressed in her situation. She was sure she was getting old, losing her looks, had no talents or intelligence, and feared no man would ever love her because there were so many younger and more attractive women to be had.

As we began to meet frequently and I got to know Leslie better, certain features stood out. One was her emotional storminess. Frequently our sessions were filled with deluges of crying, angry yelling, panicky anxiety, and states of enormous anguish and pain. She would speak continually, moving from one incomplete sentence to another, constantly changing her mind as to what she wanted to say and rarely even attempting to explain any connections between her emotions and an immediate event. It seemed as though she experienced her life as a globally painful experience, with no meaning or reasons, and that all she needed to do in therapy was to show me the pain. She described regularly waking up at night in terror, convinced that it was too late, that she was already growing old and ugly and would never be loved by a man. And she seemed unable to find any way to calm herself down or to soothe herself, other than to put herself into a sleepy state, when she would nap on and off during the day, or to exercise excessively, often running ten miles a day.

Leslie's difficulty in speaking about herself, either in terms of her feelings or in terms of her life history, was another feature. She did not seem able or willing to use language as a way of describing or of investigating pain. She even seemed unable to describe to me, or narrate, her daily experience. However, at times she showed that she had quite an unusually rich vocabulary. And her fund of knowledge indicated an intelligence well above average. She did not have the disordered thoughts characteristic of a psychotic person. In fact, her difficulty in communicating clearly and, I suspected, in thinking clearly mainly centered around her own life story and her emotional states.

Another striking feature was her lack of interests. There seemed to be nothing that she cared about or felt passionately about. She went from one activity to another, taking courses that she dropped after one class, starting jobs that she left within the first week, and meeting people that she lost interest in on the first encounter. For her, any choice about where to live, what to do, or what kind of work to engage in was totally arbitrary, as she had never been interested in anything.

Leslie claimed that she could not understand things, was confused, and had an impaired memory. She said school had always been difficult for her, even though at times she had done well. It was terribly hard for her to remember anything she read, and although she tried to read novels, she couldn't describe what one was about after she finished it. She claimed that reading anything else was just too much of a struggle and that this was why she could never go to graduate school. She remembered having enormous difficulties organizing her thoughts to write papers. College was a constant nightmare for her.

Other features that were evident were an overriding sense of guilt, poor self-esteem, an enormous amount of anger, poor frustration tolerance, a tendency to impulsive action, and an inability to feel empathy toward or understanding of others. In Chapter 6 I will describe how the treatment proceeded and how I gradually became convinced that a major part of the picture for Leslie was due to previously undiagnosed, rather severe ADHD that had interfered with her emotional, academic, and social development since her earliest childhood.

Q: Does ADHD differ greatly in men and women?
A: The differences aren't great, but they are distinct. For example, men and women share the same symptoms of ADHD (especially inattention and impulsivity), but women tend to be less hyperactive and problematic in childhood and thus are often diagnosed later in life.

In general, women with ADHD experience more depression and guilt than men, and the dominant cause of these problems is often failed interpersonal relationships. Women typically try to be the stable ballast in a relationship, and when it goes sour, they tend to blame themselves. ADHD can exacerbate these feelings of failure, plunging a woman into an ever-deepening abyss of sadness and shame.

Of course, many of the telltale symptoms of ADHD contribute greatly to this situation. A woman may drive away potential mates with her inattention or impulsivity, or her perpetual disorganization and forgetfulness may cause conflict with family and suitors. Many women with ADHD strive to be the perfect wife and mother, but their condition makes this an impossibility.

Q: How often do adults with ADHD have serious emotional problems?

A: Unfortunately all studies that have looked at the adult outcome have found an increased incidence of diagnosable psychiatric conditions, as well as less emotional well-being as rated by the adults themselves, compared to control groups. Findings do vary from study to study. However, most agree that there is not a significant increase in the rates of psychotic illness, such as schizophrenia, or in the serious affective disorder known as manic depressive (bipolar) disorder. By contrast, there is a significant increase in conditions such as neuroses; personality disorders, especially antisocial personality disorder; addictions; anxiety and depression; and suicide attempts.

Since the Weiss and Hechtman study referred to earlier in this chapter is the major prospective study available thus far, I will refer to the rates of psychiatric and emotional disturbance that they found in their adult subjects who had been diagnosed with ADHD in childhood.

- 66 percent had disabling symptoms of the original ADHD syndrome.
- 23 percent had antisocial personality disorder. (This rate is smaller than many of the other studies; the difference is discussed further below.)
- 20 percent had sexual problems.
- Nearly 50 percent had some significant difficulties in interpersonal relations.
- Overall, there were increased diagnoses of phobic anx-

iety and somatic disorders related to emotional problems.
- Over 40 percent seemed to have significant self-esteem problems.
- Twenty-four subjects out of sixty-one reported suicidal thoughts in the last three years.
- 20 percent had problems with physical aggression.

Q: What is antisocial personality disorder, and why is it so frequently found in ADHD children as adults?

A: The essential feature of this condition is a pattern of disregarding the rights of others. This may begin in childhood, and is certainly manifested by adolescence, when it is diagnosed as conduct disorder. In adults it has variously been called psychopathy, sociopathy, or dissocial personality disorder. Individuals with antisocial personality disorder fail to compy with social norms and laws. They disregard the wishes, feelings, and rights of others and may engage in lawless behavior, such as aggression toward people and property and stealing. They are frequently manipulative or deceitful in order to gain pleasure or personal profit. They also exhibit a pattern of impulsivity and a tendency not to plan ahead and hence may live fairly disrupted lives. They tend to be irritable and impulsively aggressive and hence may perpetrate domestic violence against spouses or children. They tend not to show remorse or guilt and cannot empathize with their victims. They are often highly verbal, charming, and glib, with an arrogant self-appraisal.

The followup studies did not just rely on interviews with the subjects themselves. Family members were also interviewed and criminal and school records checked to determine the rates of this disorder. Several studies suggest that adults who were diagnosed with ADHD as children have a higher incidence of potentially dangerous antisocial behavior and often demonstrated such behavior in childhood. Most studies found that the disorder was more likely to occur in the adults who still had significant ADHD symptoms, rather than in the ones whose ADHD had improved or lessened. Some of the most telling studies include the following.

- A retrospective analysis of eighty-three children diagnosed as hyperactive, reported in the *Journal of Nervous and Mental Disease*. Researchers interviewed the children's mothers and found that nearly 22 percent of the youngsters had extensive histories of antisocial behavior, including lying, fighting, stealing, setting fires, carrying weapons, and general destructiveness. Fifty-nine percent of the children had had contact with police because of their behavior, and 23 percent had been taken to the police station on one or more occasions.
- A comprehensive, five-year, controlled followup study of ninety-one ADHD subjects, ages ten to eighteen, reported in the *Archives of General Psychiatry*. Researchers found that nearly 25 percent of the youngsters had a history of antisocial behavior. Ten had been in court as a result, and two had been sent to reform school.
- An examination of the arrest records of 110 boys who were diagnosed with ADHD in childhood, reported in the *American Journal of Psychiatry*. Researchers compared the group to eighty-eight normal control subjects and found that those diagnosed with ADHD had a dramatically higher number of arrests for robbery, car theft, assault with a deadly weapon, and other serious offenses.

Another series of studies analyzed the biological parents of children diagnosed with hyperactivity and other symptoms of ADHD and found a high prevalence of alcoholism, hysteria, and sociopathy. These problems were not found in the adoptive parents of youngsters with hyperactivity.

And then, as mentioned above, in the Weiss and Hechtman prospective study 23 percent were diagnosed with antisocial personality disorder in the 15-year followup.

The reason for this terrible incidence in adults with ADHD is not yet known. However, as discussed in Chapter 2, the underlying biological components of ADHD can have a profound impact on early development. This effect may be the most devastating on the earliest relationship between the ADHD infant and his or her significant parenting figures. ADHD interferes with the development of trust, empathy, and a stable internal image of the self and the other, as well as the development of language both as a tool to organize inner experiences and a tool of communication. The profoundly distorting effect this may have on a child's ability to relate to others, to empathize, and to love and be loved may well predispose this child to the later development of antisocial personality disorder.

Q: Can the presence of ADHD worsen the effects of premenstrual syndrome? My sister has ADHD and is a monster immediately before her monthly period.

A: There has been very little clinical research in this area, but anecdotal evidence suggests that women with ADHD suffer more severe symptoms of PMS (including mood swings, depression, and rage) than those who don't have the disorder.

One possible answer could be the hormone shifts responsible for menstruation. Prolactin and estrogen are known to influence the brain's serotonin neurotransmitter system, which controls certain functions, including mood. Women with ADHD already have problems with the brain's neurochemical system, so it's safe to assume that the onset of menstruation only makes matters worse.

Treatment with serotonin-active drugs, such as Paxil and Zoloft, often helps keep the painful symptoms of PMS (and thus ADHD) under control. Your sister should consult with her gynecologist to determine which treatment regimen would work best for her.

Q: Has anyone ever established a correlation between ADHD and eating disorders, such as anorexia nervosa or bulimia?

A: Psychiatrist Hans Huessy reported such a connection nearly twenty years ago, and several clinical and anecdotal studies appear to confirm his findings.

Many women with ADHD note that they suffered from anorexia or bulimia while in high school or college. How the connection works remains a mystery, but women commonly report that their eating disorder actually seemed to reduce the impact of their ADHD. Anxiety and depression eased, and their ability to concentrate improved.

Some experts speculate that a lack of food and energy affects the brain's neurochemical system in such a way that it reduces ADHD symptoms. However, the detrimental physical effects of starvation are far worse than any possible advantages. A dramatic reduction in food intake should never be considered a treatment for ADHD.

Q: How can ADHD adversely affect the life of an adult who has it?

A: Not surprisingly, the manifestation of symptoms can have many dire consequences professionally, socially, and personally.

At work, an adult with ADHD may receive reprimands and poor work evaluations from superiors because of his inability to complete assignments as directed or remain focused on the task at hand. He may also have a poor relationship with coworkers and superiors because of concentration difficulties, mood swings, or a fiery temper. All of this, of course, can lead to depression and poor self-esteem, which only exacerbate his problems at work.

Socially, adults with ADHD often have a hard time making and keeping friends because of their impulsivity and inattention. They may misread common social cues and speak or behave in ways that make others dislike them. And their often unintentionally abusive behavior can put a tremendous strain on interpersonal relationships. ADHD has destroyed countless marriages because it takes an exceptionally strong, understanding, and compassionate mate to live with someone so unpredictable and difficult to be around.

On the personal front, unmanaged ADHD can, in extreme circumstances, result in a destroyed life and even suicide. As in childhood, adults with ADHD often feel that they're stupid, untalented, and undeserving of whatever success they've managed to achieve. Their often addictive personality puts them at risk of alcoholism, drug addiction, gambling addiction, and other problems. And when inebriated or under the influence of drugs, they may get into fights that they can't win or behave in a dangerous and reckless manner that puts them and others in jeopardy.

Q: Are there any positive effects at all to having ADHD as an adult?

A: Some characteristics of ADHD can be useful under certain circumstances. For example, some adults in extremely active and mobile jobs have turned their hyperactivity into an asset. They enjoy being on the go and find that they get much more work done in a day than their co-workers. Others report that their condition has turned them into excellent problem-solvers. And because of their drive for excitement and stimulation, a great many people with ADHD find tremendous success in sports, business, and entertainment.

As mentioned earlier, people with ADHD are often very friendly, forgiving, innovative, and creative individuals—characteristics that can serve them well both professionally and personally. Some ADHD adults have even refused treatment because they feel it would adversely affect their careers. That's their right, and I support it, but only if their symptoms aren't causing difficulties at home or in the office.

Q: What are the best jobs for adults with ADHD?

A: It all depends on the degree to which the syndrome's symptoms manifest themselves. If a person's symptoms can be well managed with medication and other therapies, then theoretically he should be able to hold any job he wants. But if his symptoms are severe and only moderately managed with treatment, he should be careful about what profession he pursues and hope for a boss that is flexible.

An office job requiring a lot of concentration and management of details, for example, would almost certainly be a nightmare for a person with severe ADHD. Such a person would probably be happier in a position that would allow him to stay on the move and interact with people.

Self-employment, preferably in a job that requires a certain amount of creativity, is another good option for people with

ADHD, especially those who are independent and have trouble working for others. The only problem with self-employment might be motivation.

Ultimately, the best advice I can give regarding careers is to follow your dream. Almost everyone finds pleasure in a job that challenges them and gives them deep personal satisfaction. ADHD can be an obstacle, but it doesn't have to be insurmountable. Do what you really want to do, and fulfillment is sure to follow.

Q: I have ADHD and work as a clerk in a large law office. I'm able to manage the symptoms of my disorder fairly well with the help of Ritalin, but I still find it hard to make and keep friends. Two of my co-workers have told me to my face that they find me very difficult to be around. What can I do to make myself more likable?

A: The fact that you recognize you have a problem is the first step toward getting better. As you probably know, ADHD can result in a wide variety of personality quirks that seem normal to the patient, but are almost intolerable to others. It's very likely that your condition has resulted in several problematic personality nuances, such as a hot temper or abrupt manner, that make people feel uncomfortable in your presence.

One answer is to ask someone you trust to give you regular feedback regarding your behavior and attitude at work. Ask this person to be brutally honest in describing what it is about you that turns people off. Then do what you must to eliminate these characteristics. Most people in your situation don't realize what they're doing until problems result. Being alert to troublesome personality quirks is the best way of making sure they don't recur. Practice at home with family and friends until it becomes second nature to you.

It might also be helpful to gather your coworkers together for a meeting so you can explain your condition and how it affects you. It's possible that they aren't aware you have ADHD and thus don't realize your actions are often out of your control. It is also wise to keep in mind that it is precisely these interpersonal problems that psychotherapy can be effective in helping. I will discuss this in more detail in Chapter 6.

If your problems with co-workers and friends seem to form a repetitive pattern, you might want to consider some psychotherapy.

Q: Is a person ever too old to be diagnosed with ADHD?

A: No. A person with symptoms at age thirty is just as likely to manifest those same symptoms at age sixty or older—and to benefit just as much from treatment.

Q: Does the treatment of adult ADHD differ greatly from treatment in childhood and adolescence?

A: There's almost no difference at all. A multimodal approach involving medication (typically stimulants such as Ritalin or dextroamphetamine), counseling, and education can help most adults with ADHD manage their condition and lead a normal and happy life.

It should be noted that the use of stimulants and antidepressants has not been approved by the Food and Drug Administration for the treatment of adult ADHD, but these compounds are well known for their effectiveness in correcting the cognitive symptoms of the syndrome. Controlled studies have found that the three most commonly used stimulants—methylphenidate (Ritalin), dextroamphetamine (Dexedrine), and pemoline (Cylert)—work very well in about two-thirds of the cases. Methylphenidate is the stimulant of choice because of its quick action and minimal side-effects, but patients who fail to respond to it almost always do well with one of the alternative medications.

With most patients, issues of drug dosage, timing, and the management of potential side-effects are handled as they would be in children and adolescents, with regular monitoring and adjustments as needed.

Interestingly, the height, weight, or age of the patient has little to do with the size of the drug dose he may need. Often an effective dose is smaller in adulthood than it would be in adolescence.

Group and individual therapy are also beneficial because they can help the patient better understand himself, his emotions, and the numerous effects his condition can have on his professional and personal life. In addition, family therapy can be useful in helping family members understand and cope with the patient's unpredictability, inattention, mood swings, and other problems. In Chapter 6, we'll discuss the use of psychotherapy for adults with ADHD, and offer an example to more effectively illustrate its usefulness.

The treatment of secondary problems resulting from a lifetime of ADHD must also be addressed. Often these problems are in the academic arena and have been present since school age or earlier. Sometimes the answer is remarkably simple—using a tape recorder instead of taking notes during a lecture, using a computer or typewriter instead of writing longhand, and using a spell-checker to ensure proper spelling. Those who enjoy literature but find reading difficult should consider books on tape. And adults facing exams should ask for a little more time to complete the assignment (after explaining their condition to their instructor). The key is not to be embarrassed by your limitations or suffer in silence. Most people are very understanding once they know the facts and will do whatever is needed to help you deal with these issues.

It is often necessary for an adult to sit down and try to systematically analyze his or her organizational and work difficulties. It is thereby possible to find specific weaknesses that can be addressed with specific remedial strategies. Sometimes it is helpful to undergo a battery of neuropsychological tests to better focus on these cognitive weaknesses and to devise these strategies. Often, however, the ADHD specialist and the adult can together isolate the most difficult areas and devise a plan of attack without the aid of tests. Sometimes a spouse can be helpful in planning better ways to get things done, for example, a different division of tasks or a system of paperwork organization. It may involve learning a rhythm of work periods and breaks that cuts down on the chance of fatigue and distractibility interfering; or strategies of dividing work into smaller, manageable portions, with a more limited focus. Often the ADHD specialist can help with this kind of practical, behavioral planning.

Q: How actively are researchers looking for new drugs to treat adult ADHD?

A: Very actively indeed. One of the most promising is venlafaxine, a new compound designed to combat depression. In a recent Case Western Reserve University study reported in the *Journal of Clinical Psychiatry*, ten adults diagnosed with attention deficit hyperactivity disorder were placed on the compound for eight weeks; nine completed the study. Of that number, seven reported a significant reduction in symptoms, with minimal side-effects.

Q: Is ADHD covered under the Americans With Disabilities Act?

A: Yes, it is. The Americans With Disabilities Act (ADA) protects individuals from discrimination based on physical, learning, or mental disability. This means a person with ADHD can't be penalized by an employer because of problems directly attributable to his condition.

The ADA also prevents discrimination in places of public accommodation, such as movie theaters, restaurants, and nightclubs; state, county, and municipal services; public and private transportation systems, and public telecommunications services.

If you feel you've been discriminated against because you have ADHD, contact the Equal Employment Opportunity Commission and ask for ADA information.

PART TWO

What to Do About It

Once a diagnosis of ADHD has been established, the next obvious concern is what to do about it. Since the early '70s, the main approach has been stimulant medication, namely drugs such as Ritalin, Dexedrine, and Cylert. However, a recurring finding of long-term followup studies has begun to alarm those involved with ADHD, both the professionals and the sufferers themselves: In spite of years of treatment with stimulants, many children with ADHD enter adolescence and adulthood still suffering from significant symptoms. And many of the long-term effects of ADHD on their development, personality, self-esteem, and academic achievement continue to interfere with their personal and professional success as adults.

Other methods of treatment can help with different aspects of ADHD. These include psychotherapy, behavioral modification techniques, behavioral cognitive techniques, remedial education as well as tutoring to strengthen academic and organizational skills, and special classroom techniques to minimize distractibility. For some individuals, other medications have proven to be more helpful than stimulants. These include antidepressants such as Prozac and Wellbutrin.

New followup studies are now examining how a combination of these approaches can affect the long-term well-being of the ADHD sufferer. In the preceding chapters, I have described how ADHD is a syndrome brought about by a complex combination of factors, including an underlying biological problem and the increasingly complex way that underlying problem interacts with an individual's experience of his surroundings. Just as there are many causes and effects of ADHD, so must the treatment approach be multiple, combining several different modes of treatment according to an individual's needs. This approach is called a multimodal treatment plan. In the chapters that follow, I will discuss the many different types of treatment that might be used and how they can be coordinated into a multimodal treatment plan for a given individual.

FOUR

Everything You Need to Know About Ritalin

At the turn of the century, the most common management technique for youngsters with ADHD was a sound thrashing when they misbehaved. Today, spanking has been replaced by an array of stimulant drugs. These drugs can often significantly curb the disruptive behaviors of ADHD and help patients lead a more normal life. However, stimulants are so widely prescribed in the United States today that some people wonder if they have become a method, like the spanking of yesteryear, that is indiscriminately and overly used.

Stimulants were first prescribed for symptoms of hyperactivity and distraction in youngsters following an outbreak of encephalitis in 1937. Doctors were amazed at the drugs' paradoxical effectiveness on children who exhibited hyperactivity as a result of the viral infection, and stimulants have been used to curb all kinds of hyperactive behaviors ever since.

Researchers estimate that in 1970 about 150,000 children nationwide were taking prescribed stimulant medication. A decade later, that figure had escalated to between 270,000 and 541,000. By 1988, the number of school-age youngsters receiving stimulants was estimated at between 750,000 and 1.6 million, a figure that didn't include the 25 percent of children in special education classes who received stimulants to improve academic performance. Today, the number of youngsters in the United States receiving various forms of stimulant medication is well over two million and climbing.

Benzedrine was the drug of choice in the 1940s and 1950s. Today it is methylphenidate (Ritalin), which is quite similar structurally to amphetamine. Doctors prefer Ritalin because it is fast-acting, clears the system well, and has a minimum of side-effects. Also effective are dextroamphetamine (Dexedrine) and pemoline (Cylert).

In this chapter we will discuss at length Ritalin and other drugs commonly used to treat ADHD, the way they work, and their benefits and disadvantages.

Q: The use of stimulants in treating ADHD makes no sense to me. How can a stimulant help someone who is already hyperactive?

A: The use of stimulants to calm someone who is already stimulated is somewhat of a medical paradox. But more than fifty years of clinical trials and patient use have found stimulants amazingly effective in reducing hyperactivity and inhibiting disruptive behaviors in individuals with ADHD.

If a normal, healthy person were to take a stimulant such as methylphenidate or dextroamphetamine, it may make him feel jittery. But stimulants have the opposite effect on someone with ADHD, possibly because of a malfunction or deficiency in the brain's neurotransmitter system. One theory suggests that stimulants work by temporarily boosting levels of certain essential brain chemicals, such as dopamine or norepinephrine, resulting in more normal behavior.

Q: Are the benefits of stimulant drugs used in the management of ADHD really as remarkable as doctors would have us believe? Do the efficacy studies confirm these benefits?

A: The benefits of stimulants are many and often amazing. My patients tell me that their medication helps them control distractibility, improves their motor control (such as handwriting), and allows them to better organize their thoughts, to pay attention, and to concentrate more clearly. However, it should be mentioned that stimulants appear to have no effect on any learning disabilities that might be present along with ADHD. Similarly, stimulants do not alter a patient's ability to communicate or develop empathy and social understanding and often seem not to affect impulsivity. In addition, it is important to note that the improvement seen with Ritalin only occurs as long as the stimulant is present in the body. It is not a permanent or structural change, but is a direct chemical effect.

As for efficacy studies, there are many. In fact, more than 900 scientific papers on the use of stimulants for ADHD appeared between 1983 and 1992, and many more have been published since then.

One of the first studies to prove the effectiveness of Ritalin in ADHD children involved a group of ten adolescents ages thirteen to seventeen and was reported in the *New York State Journal of Medicine*. The children received doses ranging from 20 to 60 milligrams daily, and all demonstrated a marked improvement in school performance after receiving the drug.

Another important study, reported in the *Journal of the American Academy of Child Psychiatry*, demonstrated the effectiveness of Ritalin in sixteen of twenty-two adolescents with attention deficit hyperactivity disorder. The children were divided into two groups, with some receiving active medication and the others receiving a placebo (an inert or nonactive pill, often made of sugar, which is designed to look like the active medication). None of the youngsters, their parents, or teachers knew who was receiving the active drug and who was receiving a placebo. The researchers concluded that both low- and high-dose levels of Ritalin were much more effective than a placebo in calming disruptive behaviors and improving academic skills. They also noted that there was no apparent decrease in effectiveness once a child reached puberty. Many other clinical studies have analyzed the effects of stimulant medications with equally positive findings.

Q: Are stimulants as effective in adults with ADHD as they are in children and adolescents who have the syndrome?

A: There haven't been as many studies on ADHD adults as there have been on young people, but the limited studies we do have, as well as anecdotal reports, suggest that stimulants are an effective therapy for ADHD patients of all ages.

One of the first series of controlled studies involving adults with ADHD was conducted at the University of Utah in Salt Lake City. Researchers there selected fifteen adults—nine of them women—who showed strong symptoms of ADHD, including inattention, impulsivity, and irritability, but no signs of any other mental disorder or condition.

Eleven of the fifteen subjects participated in a double-blind study comparing Ritalin and a placebo. Double-blind means that neither the subjects nor the interviewers knew which pill the subject had been given, thus removing the influence of suggestion from the results. Eight subjects showed good response to the active drug; in particular, patients given Ritalin reported that they felt less irritable, were able to concentrate better, and had better control of their tempers.

Later, all fifteen participants were given an open trial of pemoline (Cylert) or the tricyclic antidepressants amitriptyline or imipramine. Four responded well to pemoline, and two who had failed to respond to stimulants improved with the antidepressants. Followup studies also found that two of the women stopped abusing their children, two achieved orgasm for the first time (an occasional side-effect of Ritalin use), and five reported some improvement in their marriages.

A subsequent replication of this study involving sixty adults with characteristic signs of ADHD used pemoline (Cylert) instead of methylphenidate (Ritalin) because the researchers felt it had less euphoriant properties and thus was less likely to be abused. Pemoline was found to be much more effective than a placebo in reducing hyperactivity, attention deficit, impulsivity, and other symptoms of ADHD, particularly in those subjects who had evidence of severe childhood ADHD.

Q: How does a doctor determine which stimulant is best for a particular patient?
A: Predicting which drug will be most effective is difficult because every patient is unique. Some will react poorly to one stimulant, but remarkably well to another. Most doctors begin with Ritalin, which is the stimulant most commonly used in the treatment of ADHD. It is safe, has few side-effects, and is

short-acting (i.e., it starts to work within an hour and its effects last for four hours). Because it acts rapidly and clears the body quickly, it is possible for the child psychiatrist to closely monitor the drug's effect and to tailor the dose schedule to the person's needs during the day. In other words, the medication will be at its most active exactly when the ADHD patient most needs it. If a patient doesn't respond after a week or so, the doctor may increase the Ritalin dosage and wait another week or two. If it becomes evident that Ritalin just isn't working, the doctor may then switch the patient to Dexedrine or Cylert.

Sometimes pemoline (Cylert) is the first choice of stimulant as it does not have the potentially euphoriant properties of Ritalin and therefore minimizes the risk of being abused as an addictive drug. This is important if the subject is an adolescent or adult who has a tendency to use drugs or is surrounded by drug-using peers. Sometimes Cylert is also preferred because of its longer-lasting effects. It can be taken in the morning and remains active throughout the school day. This can be a benefit to older schoolchildren or teenagers who do not want to take time out to go to a nurse's office for medication, or who do not want to be seen taking their medication.

Q: What is the typical daily dose, for a child and an adult, of the three most commonly prescribed stimulants?

A: The strange thing about the use of stimulants in managing ADHD is that the size and age of the patient have only partial bearing on how much of a particular compound he should receive. A child with severe symptoms, for example, may receive a daily dose considerably larger than that received by an adult with only mild symptoms. Blood monitoring is one way of establishing dosage, but doctors and parents should also keep a close eye on therapeutic effects.

The typical dose of Ritalin is 15 to 30 milligrams per day, usually in divided doses, between 0.5 and 1.0 milligram per kilogram of weight. However, some patients may require as much as 60 milligrams per day or more. In high-dose cases, close monitoring for efficacy and side-effects is essential.

The typical dose of Dexedrine is 15 milligrams per day,

with an upper dose of 40 milligrams or more with close monitoring.

The average dose of Cylert is 37.5 milligrams per day, with a recommended upper dose of 112.5 milligrams or higher if clinically necessary.

Ritalin and Dexedrine are available in both short-acting and long-acting forms. Cylert is available only in a long-acting formula.

The average length of effectiveness for a short-acting dose of a particular stimulant is four hours, though for some patients it may be as little as two and a half hours and for others as long as five hours. Dose intervals should be determined based on observations made by the patient, his family, and, in the case of a child, his teacher.

Q: Ritalin in particular has received a great deal of media attention lately. Could you give us a little more background on this very popular stimulant?

A: Ritalin is a brand name for the prescription drug methylphenidate. It was developed in the 1940s and has been widely used since the 1950s to treat ADHD and other hyperactivity disorders (approximately 90 percent of today's ADHD patients receive the drug). In addition, Ritalin is often used to treat psychological, educational, or social disorders, as well as narcolepsy and mild depression in the elderly. It is also sometimes used to treat depression in cancer patients and to boost the action of antidepressant medication in treatment-resistant depression.

Methylphenidate is a mild central nervous system stimulant, which seems to activate the brain stem arousal system and the cerebral cortex. It has been shown to increase both the amounts of dopamine and norepinephrine (the chemicals that carry electrical messages from one neuron to the next) at the central nervous system synapses. It is not yet known, however, how this pharmacological effect brings about the improvement of symptoms in ADHD.

While most studies of the drug's efficacy have focused on improved behavior and classroom functioning, some studies have tried to focus more clearly on the actual attentional system. These studies design specific cognitive tasks that relate to the attentional system, and many have shown improvements resulting from Ritalin. However, even among these studies there is much variation and discrepancy as to what constitutes the focusing of attention and how to measure it, and it is often not clear if any two studies are measuring the same thing.

This lack of clarity in just what Ritalin is doing and how, and just which aspects of the underlying ADHD problems it actually affects, is yet another reason why close monitoring by the ADHD specialist is ideal.

The United States Drug Enforcement Administration (DEA) has classified Ritalin as a Schedule II controlled substance, which puts it in the same category as cocaine, methadone, and methamphetamine. Many parent groups, having seen the astounding benefits that can result from the use of Ritalin, are now lobbying to ease restrictions on the drug so that monthly visits to the doctor would no longer be necessary for a prescription renewal. Not surprisingly, the DEA—having noticed the increased black market sale of Ritalin—opposes such efforts, and has even enlisted the help of the International Narcotics Control Board, an agency of the United Nations that tracks drug production and consumption worldwide.

To remove the necessity of a patient's monthly review by a doctor, preferably an ADHD specialist, would also be a clinical mistake. As I will explain in succeeding chapters, a multimodal treatment approach involves a delicate balance of several different types of treatment. The ADHD specialist plays an indispensible role in coordinating this approach. By continually assessing the various inputs from home, school, etc., a specialist can more accurately manage a patient's medication and other forms of treatment.

Q: Is giving Ritalin to a child who shows symptoms of ADHD a good way to confirm a diagnosis?

A: No, it's not—though some doctors may insist otherwise. A detailed differential diagnosis that takes a close look at a child's physical, mental, academic, and behavioral history is still the best way to identify ADHD. Placing a child on Ritalin and then watching for relief of symptoms is a backward approach that can cause more harm than good.

If your child's doctor suggests Ritalin before making a clinical diagnosis, I'd advise getting a second and even third opinion.

Q: How widespread is the use of Ritalin in the United States?

A: As the number of children and adults diagnosed with attention deficit hyperactivity disorder has increased over the years, so has the manufacture and prescription of Ritalin.

According to federal studies, the rate of Ritalin use in the United States is five times higher than in the rest of the world. Researchers at Johns Hopkins University School of Medicine calculate that the number of youngsters taking Ritalin has grown two and a half times since 1990. In fact, among the estimated 88 million children between the ages of five and fourteen, approximately 1.3 million take Ritalin on a regular basis. As a result, sales of the drug have topped $350 million a year.

This astounding growth has caused many experts to suggest that Ritalin is overprescribed, and it can't be denied that many children currently taking Ritalin probably don't need it. Officials at the National Institute of Mental Health, for example, say they've heard of cases in which teachers have suggested Ritalin to the parents of very active children as young as preschool age. And many psychiatrists—myself included—have seen youngsters who were misdiagnosed as having ADHD and given Ritalin when, in fact, they have emotional problems that have been overlooked and denied.

However, it should be mentioned that the originator of a recent hearing on the alleged overprescription of Ritalin by the House Subcommittee on Human Resources and Intergovernmental Affairs was the Church of Scientology, which had circulated a pamphlet on Capitol Hill. The Church of Scientology opposes *most* medications.

Undoubtedly, there is some overprescription. Parents should certainly be aware of undue pressures to make their child conform and to raise grades that might lead them to seek medication for their children. They should also beware of managed health care's interest in sponsoring the least costly treatment. Some health maintenance organizations have made stimulant medication the prerequisite first line of treatment before they are willing to reimburse for behavioral or psychological treatments.

Q: How exactly do stimulants work to ease the symptoms of ADHD?

A: Ritalin and its stimulant cousins, Dexedrine and Cylert, appear to ease the telltale effects of ADHD by increasing the amount of one or both of the brain's two most important neurotransmitters, dopamine and norepinephrine. Each drug affects one or more of the many processes involved in the release, reuptake, breakdown, and autoregulation of these natural chemicals at the nerve ending, or synapse.

Ritalin decreases dopamine uptake and inhibits monoamine oxidase activity. Dexedrine, on the other hand, increases dopamine and norepinephrine neurotransmission by activating the release of dopamine at the synaptic cleft. And Cylert, which is completely different in structure from amphetamine, merely influences dopamine neurotransmission.

What does all this mean? Simply that the drugs, in their own unique ways, affect levels of dopamine and norepinephrine. This action correlates with the modification of disruptive behaviors.

But it's important to remember that though the improvements in a child's behavior and demeanor may be dramatic, none of these drugs is a miracle cure. And in very few cases is Ritalin, Dexedrine, or Cylert the only treatment needed. Most youngsters with ADHD also require individual and family therapy, behavior modification, and other strategies to keep their syndrome under control. Medication is just one small part of a successful approach for effective management of ADHD.

Unfortunately, it's very easy to develop an overreliance on Ritalin because it seems to do it all. A child's disruptive behavior lessens or disappears while he is under the drug's effects; he finds it easier to concentrate and learn, and his social skills may improve. For four hours he's a more loving, normal, pleasant child. Many parents, having struggled for years to discover exactly why their child behaves the way he does, come to think of Ritalin as a gift. That's understandable; throw a drowning man a rope, and he'll embrace it with all his might.

I mention this not to downplay the effectiveness or need for Ritalin. It's an extraordinarily useful tool in the management of ADHD, but it's not the only tool. Parents must realize that there's much more to caring for the ADHD child than merely placing a yellow pill in his mouth twice a day.

Q: Which aspects of ADHD are most improved by Ritalin and other commonly prescribed medications?

A: Thanks to ongoing research into the causes and treatment of ADHD, Ritalin, Dexedrine, and Cylert have become three of the most aggressively studied drugs ever prescribed, and researchers have found a wide range of benefits. They include the following.

- **Enhanced learning**. Numerous studies have found that commonly prescribed ADHD drugs help improve concentration, fine-motor coordination, impulsivity, and reaction time, all of which help children become better students. Students who had particular problems with inattentiveness seem able to focus on tasks for longer periods of time. Some children seem able to work faster and more accurately. Many patients on medication also report improved memory, which may translate into greater academic success. However, while there is definitely improvement in classroom attentiveness and activity, medication alone does not lead to improvement of overall achievement scores.
- **Improved behavior**. Children taking Ritalin, Dexedrine, or Cylert usually find it easier to control their hyperactivity, impulsivity, and other disruptive behaviors, which makes them much easier to be around in school and at home. Teachers often report that ADHD children are less distinguishable from their peers when on medication. Many parents are often reluctant to place their children on ADHD medication for fear that it will turn them into compliant zombies with no zest or energy, but this almost never occurs. Even on medication, ADHD children (and many adults) still have noticeably higher levels of activity and impulsivity.

- **Improved social skills**. Again, children on ADHD medication find it easier to control their hyperactivity, inattention, and impulsivity. This, in turn, makes it easier for them to make and keep friends. In one important study, students rated peers with ADHD as being more fun to be around when they were on their medication. However, other studies have found little or no change in aggressive behavior, antisocial behavior, emotional immaturity, and social miscuing.

- **Improved emotional state**. Medications such as Ritalin can have a strong impact on a child's mood, resulting in a much-improved state of emotional well-being. An improvement in grades and social life can also mean greater self-esteem and less anxiety and depression. Family members sometimes find youngsters on medication to be more reasonable and outgoing and less prone to fits of anger or aggression. However, if the ADHD child exhibits severe behavior and self-esteem problems, it is unlikely that medication alone will do enough to improve these.

An estimated 90 percent of ADHD children do receive some help from medication. In some cases the improvement can be remarkable, and sometimes parents do feel that it was one of the best decisions they could have made for their child. I have had college students tell me that stimulant medication makes their experience in a lecture entirely different. Suddenly they feel engaged and focused, can think more clearly and productively and can generally enjoy the academic experience much more.

One more important point: In a very small percentage of children, medication will have no effect at all or will result in side-effects so severe that medication must be discontinued. For these youngsters, other nonmedication treatments are the only option. I will discuss these in more detail in Chapters 5 and 6.

Q: How do I explain the need for medication to my ADHD child? She's reluctant to take Ritalin because she's afraid it will label her as different.

A: That's a very common problem, particularly among adolescents. Many are opposed to daily medication—especially Ritalin—because they are afraid it will confirm inner fears that they're abnormal, stupid, or crazy. I've had children tell me that they heard Ritalin was "for retarded kids." Very young children may associate the medication with "being bad." Others are reluctant to take medication because they're fearful that their friends and peers will find out and avoid them. And a few simply feel that they can manage their disorder without the "crutch" of medication.

It's vitally important that ADHD children understand why drugs such as Ritalin are so important to the management of their condition. They should also be aware that such medications are not a cure—they will help control symptoms, but they won't make the syndrome go away forever.

To this end, parents should explain how ADHD affects the brain and thus their child's behavior. Most children are aware of the problems their behavior causes and want very much to stop, but are unable to do so without outside help in the form of medication and other therapies. It is best to explain ADHD as a way in which the brain works and to explain it as a process, one that requires special treatment strategies. People who are short-sighted need glasses to compensate for how the shape of their eye lenses distorts their vision and to focus their vision. Similarly, in ADHD patients, the particular characteristics of the "wiring" in the brain mean that they need some special help to compensate. The medication is mental "glasses" used to focus attention. It is important to avoid any explanation that makes the child feel responsible for "bad" behavior. Focus your explanation on the underlying difficulties that give rise to the behavior, rather than the behavior itself.

It might help to have your doctor or ADHD specialist explain to your daughter exactly how Ritalin and related medications work to ease the symptoms of her condition. A doctor can allay her many concerns and detail in lay terms how medication will make her life easier, not more difficult.

Family support is also essential to the effective use of ADHD medication. A child should never be teased or made to feel different because she is on medication, and it's probably best not to make her medication therapy a topic of conversation with friends and family members in her presence. Such a focus will only make a child feel self-conscious.

Once your daughter realizes that her medication does, indeed, work and that she can study better and make friends more easily, she should have no complaints at all.

Q: Does Ritalin have any side-effects?
A. Ritalin is widely considered to be a very safe drug, but as with any chemical compound, certain side-effects may result. Many children, for example, experience a decrease in appetite while the drug is in their systems. That's why the first dose of the day is usually given with breakfast or immediately after. Because of this effect, many children are exceptionally hungry at dinnertime, when their second daily dose has worn off.

In addition, some youngsters experience a slight weight loss during the first few months they're on Ritalin. In most cases, weight stabilizes after a short period and then begins to increase again. If a child is overweight, this drop can be a good thing and very beneficial to his self-esteem.

Another common problem associated with Ritalin use is mild insomnia. This effect usually disappears within a few weeks. If it continues, reducing the second daily dose or giving it to the child earlier in the day may help. In extreme cases, a morning dose may be all that a child can handle.

Other possible side-effects include the following.

- **Headaches or abdominal problems** at the beginning of treatment. In most cases, these problems disappear within a few days.
- **Tearfulness and lethargy**. Some children become very emotional or overly subdued when on Ritalin, which suggests their dosages are too high. Very sensitive children often see dramatic improvement on a very small dose of the drug. Others require and are able to tolerate much higher amounts. In some cases, determining the proper dosage for a child involves close monitoring and more than a little trial and error. However, the side-effect of depression might also call

for a change in medication. Often Cylert or Dexedrine can have a very different effect.

- **A worsening of facial tics or other involuntary twitches**. However, many children find that their tics disappear when they're on Ritalin. Every child is different, and their reaction to the drug will be different too. If a child's tics worsen greatly, he should be taken off Ritalin and given an alternative medication, such as clonidine.
- **The development of psychosis**. Actually, this side-effect is so rare that it barely deserves mention. Only thirty cases of stimulant-induced toxic psychosis have been reported in the mainstream medical literature. Nonetheless, it's something your child's doctor should be aware of. Other extremely rare side-effects include alopecia (loss of hair) and hypersensitivity reactions such as fever, skin rash, dermatitis, angina, and erratic heartbeat.
- **An increase in sudden seizures**. Stimulants tend to lower a person's seizure threshold. The good news is that recent studies have found that stimulants and anticonvulsants can be given simultaneously with no reduction in effectiveness. However, blood levels of anticonvulsants should be checked frequently to prevent toxicity resulting from Ritalin's ability to boost blood levels of both drugs.

Because Ritalin, Dexedrine, and Cylert are all stimulants, many parents worry that their children will become addicted to the compounds much like someone becomes addicted to cocaine or methamphetamine. However, numerous studies have shown that Ritalin, especially, is not addictive when used as directed and under a doctor's supervision. In fact, many parents have the opposite problem—getting their children to take their medicine!

It's true that some studies suggest children with ADHD are at greater risk of developing an addiction problem later in life, but this is usually a personality disorder unrelated to Ritalin use in childhood.

Q: Are there any risks associated with using Ritalin or related stimulants in conjunction with other types of medication?
A: One should always be cautious when combining medications, and this is especially true of the drugs used to manage ADHD. Serious side-effects can result, which is why you should never mix medications without the knowledge and supervision of your doctor.

Ritalin and its stimulant cousins are reasonably safe when taken as directed, but there can be some dangerous interactions when combined with other drugs. Antidepressants containing monoamine oxidase inhibitors, for example, can result in a dangerous, even deadly, jump in blood pressure. And certain asthma medications, such as theophylline, can cause dizziness, heart palpitations, weakness, and agitation.

Stimulants may also interact with certain drugs in such a way that blood levels of both compounds become higher than expected. Ritalin, for example, is known to increase the blood levels of tricyclic antidepressants, anticonvulsants, anticoagulants, and others.

Sometimes stimulants can even block the action of a specific drug. Ritalin is known to inhibit the antihypertensive action of guanethidine, and Dexedrine slows the absorption of phenytoin and phenobarbital, as well as blocking certain beta-adrenergic antagonists.

Your child's doctor should tell you about all potentially harmful drug interactions resulting from the use of stimulants. If he does not or you still have concerns, don't hesitate to ask questions. And keep asking them until you're satisfied with the answer. It's always better to be safe than sorry.

Q: My eleven-year-old son has been diagnosed with ADHD and is now on Ritalin. His father occasionally shows symptoms of the syndrome and is thinking about taking a few of my son's pills to see if they'll help. Do you see any problem with this?
A: I see many problems, foremost being your husband's eagerness to pop pills that were not prescribed for him. As stated

earlier, Ritalin is reasonably safe, and chances are good your husband would suffer few ill effects from his little experiment. But there's always the possibility that he could suffer a potentially dangerous adverse reaction. That's why prescription medication should never, ever be taken without a doctor's permission.

In addition, there's a high probability that your husband does not have ADHD at all and that his "occasional symptoms" are something else entirely. If that's the case, you're just wasting your son's medication.

If your husband really, truly believes he may have ADHD, he should see a specialist for a definitive differential diagnosis. If it turns out he really does have the condition, then his doctor can place him on Ritalin (or some other stimulant) in the amount that is most effective for him.

Q: A friend of mine told me that Ritalin could stunt my child's growth. Is this true?

A: That's a very common myth based on some early studies. More recent studies have found that it is not generally a problem. Some children do experience a slight growth suppression, but this is usually cured by reducing the child's dosage. It's a short-term problem, and most children who experience it grow to a normal adult height.

In the past, it was common to discontinue the use of Ritalin at the onset of adolescence in the mistaken belief that the drug would permanently stunt a child's growth during this period. Now doctors know this is no longer true, and often all that's needed is a slight adjustment in a child's daily dose. Nonetheless, a child's growth should be closely monitored by his pediatrician or ADHD specialist.

Another common belief is that Ritalin and other ADHD drugs can lose their effectiveness when a child reaches puberty. This, too, is untrue.

Q: My eight-year-old son was recently placed on Ritalin and seems to be doing very well. However, he becomes irritable and a little hyperactive in the afternoon as his second dose wears off. Is this normal?

A: Yes, it's very normal. Your son is experiencing what's known as "rebound," and it should quickly disappear as his system adjusts to the medication. In the meantime, you may find it helpful to send your son outside to play, or encourage him to quietly watch television until he feels better. Most importantly, don't make a lot of demands on him during this period. If he doesn't outgrow the rebound effect, ask your physician about giving your son half a Ritalin after school to help him through the rest of the day.

I have sometimes recommended a small dose of stimulant after school to help a child organize and focus during homework time. In the case of Peter (described in Chapter 2), his ADHD symptoms worsened in the evening as he became tired, and it was often impossible for him to settle down and sleep. Sometimes as late as midnight, he would still be hyperactive and disruptive, or just pace around, unable to sleep or stay in bed. This, of course, could have meant that he was overstimulated by the Ritalin, as some children do have insomnia secondary to the stimulant medication. Careful evaluation is necessary when such a situation develops. In Peter's case an evening dose of Ritalin, around eight-thirty, actually helped him organize himself, settle down, and go to sleep at a reasonable hour.

Q: What are your thoughts on "Ritalin vacations"?
A: A Ritalin vacation is a period of days, usually a weekend, in which a child does not receive the drug. In the past, Ritalin vacations were encouraged under the assumption that a child's system needed a break from the drug to grow and function normally. We now know that this is no longer necessary.

However, sometimes a child can go a few days without Ritalin and still do well. If a child's biggest difficulties are impulsiveness and inattention in the classroom, for example, he may not need Ritalin on weekends or while on vacation. Many ADHD youngsters, however, have such extreme symptoms that they require Ritalin every day just to function.

Because Ritalin is not a cumulative drug, meaning its effectiveness doesn't increase or improve the longer you take it, a weekend or more without the compound should not result in any serious problems.

Q: Will Ritalin cause my son to become more aggressive? I've heard that's a common side-effect.

A: There are many myths surrounding the use of Ritalin and other ADHD medications, and that is one of the most common—and one of the most ill-founded. Let me reassure you: Ritalin does *not* cause aggression. In fact, it tends to reduce aggressive behavior in youngsters with ADHD.

One possible explanation for the aggression myth is the fact that some ADHD patients feel more edgy or irritable the first few days they're on Ritalin and may lash out when frustrated or angry. However, this phenomenon usually subsides pretty quickly as the body adjusts to the new medication.

Another possible answer is that the aggressive behavior parents sometimes see in their child is really the afternoon "rebound" effect discussed earlier. If that's the case, a tiny dose of Ritalin after school should keep it in check; ask your health care provider if this is appropriate for your child.

Another possibility is that the aggressive behavior is unrelated to the Ritalin and is part of your child's response to the chronic frustrations of his condition. Such aggressive behavior is a sign that an additional form of treatment, such as therapy or a better educational approach, may be necessary.

Q: Will my child have to stay on Ritalin for the rest of his life?

A: There's no way to accurately answer that question. As we've said repeatedly throughout this book, every ADHD patient is different. Some don't need medication at all; others require a heavy dose just to make it through the day. And some will "outgrow" the syndrome, while others will manifest symptoms throughout their lives.

Your son may be one of the lucky ones who will show diminishing symptoms as he matures, until he is "cured" and no longer in need of medication. Most doctors agree that a child's medication schedule should be reviewed every six months, with an eye toward weaning him off if possible. But many patients require some medication throughout their adult lives to keep the disruptive symptoms of ADHD under control. Try not to feel too badly about that. In most cases, the symptoms of ADHD tend to lessen with age, if they don't go away completely.

It is important to remember that medications only give symptomatic relief. They are not making any cumulative or permanent change, except insofar as the symptomatic relief allows more normal development and learning to occur. That is why a multimodal treatment approach is so necessary. Some of the other treatments, such as behavioral modification and psychotherapy (see the next two chapters), are aimed at bringing about more permanent change in the underlying cognitive and emotional mechanisms and skills. It is these that, in fact, may help make medication unnecessary in the future.

Q: I've seen reports in the news that Ritalin can cause cancer. This really frightens me. Should I take my daughter off the drug?
A: The reports you mention concerned studies made public by the Food and Drug Administration which found that Ritalin might cause hepatoblastoma, a rare form of liver cancer, in mice. However, FDA officials were very quick to note that there was absolutely no evidence of this effect in humans. In fact, a twenty-year analysis of Ritalin use in children and adults revealed no increase in the incidence of this particular type of cancer or any other.

In the studies, mice were fed extremely high doses of Ritalin—up to thirty times the typical human dose—for two years. Four male mice who received the largest doses developed hepatoblastomas, a slightly higher number than anticipated. In humans, hepatoblastoma typically afflicts children younger than four, and Ritalin is usually not prescribed for anyone under six.

Q: I read recently that Ritalin abuse is at an all-time high. Why would someone take Ritalin if they didn't have to?
A: In people with ADHD, Ritalin eases hyperactivity and inattention and makes it easier for the user to concentrate. But in people without ADHD, Ritalin in high doses can result in a heightened sense of awareness and even euphoria. It can also cause nervousness, irritability, and agitation.

Ritalin abuse is indeed at an all-time high, and authorities are doing all they can to stop it. Unfortunately, Ritalin is easy to find on the street, where it's commonly known as "Vitamin R," and fairly inexpensive to buy—about $1 to $5 a pill. The drug is either swallowed or crushed and snorted, like cocaine.

Some Ritalin abusers buy the drug directly from children and adults who receive it legitimately. Many youngsters are given several pills to take over the course of the day, so it's tempting for them to sell one or two. In some areas of the country, Ritalin abuse has become such a widespread problem that school districts now require students to deliver the medication in its bottle to school nurses, who keep it in a locked cabinet until needed.

Ultimately, children and adults who receive Ritalin for ADHD are cheating themselves when they sell their medication. And those who buy it from them are also asking for trouble. Several deaths have been linked to Ritalin overdose.

Q: Does Ritalin work on everyone with ADHD?
A: Ritalin has become the drug of choice in the United States for the treatment of ADHD, but it's not for everyone. Studies show that approximately 25 percent of ADHD sufferers don't respond symptomatically to Ritalin, experience serious side-effects, or are taking other medications that make the use of stimulants impractical. When that happens, doctors are forced to turn to what are known as second-order medications or non-drug treatments.

Q: What other medications besides stimulants are commonly used to manage ADHD and its resulting secondary conditions?
A: Tricyclic antidepressants, such as desipramine, imipramine, and nortriptyline, are some of the most common—and the most effective. These compounds are composed of a three-ring structure and have been found to block the reuptake of both serotonin and norepinephrine. Recent research has shown tricyclic antidepressants to have complex interactions with nerve-ending receptors. Some actually block the reception of serotonin, thus enhancing the action of norepinephrine. While different tricyclic antidepressants are very similar in structure,

they may have quite different effects according to which receptors are activated or blocked. Consequently, it may take some trial and error to find which one works for a particular individual.

Numerous studies have found that trycyclic antidepressants help improve mood and self-esteem and decrease hyperactivity, though their mild sedating effects make them relatively ineffective when it comes to concentration or other cognitive skills. Additional benefits include a longer therapeutic effect, which means they can be taken only once a day instead of in multiple doses, and little of the rebound effect often seen in stimulants. Their effect is cumulative, and it often requires a few weeks on the medication to fully assess its effectiveness.

Potential side-effects from the use of tricyclic antidepressants include decreased appetite, headaches, weight loss, dizziness, insomnia, and fatigue. However, the most worrisome side-effect involves the heart. In sensitive individuals, certain kinds of tricyclic antidepressants can affect the heart's natural rhythm, resulting in cardiac arrhythmias (irregular heart rate) and tachycardia (rapid heart rate). As a result, heart function should be closely monitored while these antidepressants are in use.

Nontricyclic antidepressants commonly prescribed for the treatment of ADHD in children and adults include bupropion hydrochloride (brand name: Wellbutrin) and fluoxetine hydrochloride, better known as Prozac.

Studies involving bupropion hydrochloride use in children found it fairly effective in managing the primary symptoms of ADHD. Bupropion is a unicyclic compound, and its biochemical action is unknown. It does not block reuptake of norepinephrine or serotonin, but is a weak blocker of dopamine reuptake. Potential side-effects include dry mouth, insomnia, headache, and nausea. A handful of seizure cases have also been reported, though these occurred in patients receiving extremely high doses. Some specialists now think that it may be one of the most useful antidepressants in the treatment of ADHD.

Prozac (fluoxetine) belongs to another group of antidepressants, which includes Zoloft and Paxil. This group is characterized by its main biochemical action, which is to inhibit the reuptake of serotonin, thus making more of the neurotransmitter available to the receptors. This has been shown to be a very effective treatment for some depressives and for obsessive-compulsive conditions. In fact, Prozac is currently one of the nation's most popular antidepressants. It has also received quite a bit of clinical study regarding its effects on ADHD, though the results have been somewhat confusing. One study showed significant improvement in eleven of nineteen ADHD youngsters who received the drug, while another study of twenty-four children found a worsening of symptoms among the three subjects who had ADHD. A third study, which analyzed the effects of Prozac and Ritalin together, found an improvement in depressive symptoms, as well as conduct, anxiety, and other problems associated with ADHD. Interestingly, the greatest improvement was seen in those youngsters with the most serious symptoms. Prozac looks like an effective supplemental medication for the treatment of attention deficit hyperactivity disorder, but more research is needed.

Another drug frequently prescribed for the management of ADHD symptoms is an antihypertensive compound known as clonidine. Studies suggest it is most useful in children who experience very high levels of hyperactivity, impulsivity, and aggression, as well as problematic secondary conditions, such as conduct disorder and oppositional disorder. By itself, clonidine appears to have very little impact on inattention, but it works well in combination with Ritalin or Dexedrine.

Benefits of clonidine use include better cooperation and compliance, greater tolerance to frustration, and improved learning. Potential side-effects include sedation, headaches, nausea, dizziness, depression, low blood pressure, and irregular heartbeat.

Venlafaxine, a new, structurally novel antidepressant, inhibits monoamine (norepinephrine) reuptake like the tricyclics, but it has no significant affinity for the other receptors that are thought to cause many of the side-effects of the tricyclics. A recent eight-week open trial of venlafaxine in the treatment of adult ADHD showed significant improvement in impulsivity and hyperactivity. It is thought that venlafaxine may make a safe, effective alternative to stimulants in the treatment of adult ADHD.

Then there are those drugs prescribed to help ease secondary symptoms of ADHD. Anger and rage are two common secondary problems that can be controlled with the use of mood-stabilizing medications such as lithium, carbamazepine, or beta-blockers such as nadolol and propranolol. Beta-blockers are also effective in reducing the anxiety that can accompany the use of stimulants such as Ritalin.

Obsessive-compulsive disorder, which occurs in a significant number of ADHD patients, can usually be eased with Anafranil (clomipramine), Prozac, or Zoloft. The last two have also been found to be effective in the treatment of severe PMS symptoms in women with ADHD.

FIVE

Other Treatments for ADHD

Medication is extraordinarily helpful in the management of attention deficit hyperactivity disorder, but it can only do so much. Many of the key symptoms and secondary problems associated with the syndrome are unaffected by Ritalin or other drugs, which is why a multimodal, interdisciplinary approach to treatment is best. In most cases, this includes individual and family education, psychotherapy, greater structure at home and school, and a variety of other important therapies.

Over the years, many alternative treatment modalities have been put forth, with varying degrees of success. Some are sound in scientific principle and quite well known for their effectiveness. Others are on the fringe and beyond and should be viewed with a cautious eye.

There is no cure for ADHD, at least not yet. The best we can do right now is manage the symptoms in an effort to help the patient lead a more normal life. If someone tells you they can cure your child (or you) of ADHD, be suspicious. And discuss all potential therapies with your physician or ADHD specialist. If something sounds too good to be true, it probably is.

In this chapter, we will discuss the many treatments that can make up an effective multimodal regimen for the management of ADHD. These include behavior therapy, biofeedback, and even exercise. Psychotherapy is also a very important part of the multimodal approach, but it will be discussed at length in Chapter 6. Educational and family approaches are discussed in later chapters.

Behavior therapy has been the main alternative to medication traditionally prescribed in ADHD. Many studies have shown a combination of behavioral approaches and medication to be more effective than either alone.

Behavioral modification techniques are based on principles of learning theory developed over the last fifty or more years. Essentially, these techniques are a way of isolating certain undesirable and desirable behaviors and associating them with unpleasurable and pleasurable consequences, respectively. These associations of behaviors with specific consequences are thought to reinforce learning behavior and thus help the ADHD sufferer learn to give up old patterns of behavior and to learn new and better patterns. Of course, a simple change in behavior does not mean that there is any real change in thinking or underlying coping mechanisms. However, if the ADHD sufferer's behavior begins to bring about better consequences, it is easy to see the related benefits, such as enhanced self-esteem and a sense of confidence gained by controlling his behavior.

Traditional behavior modification techniques have been based on the oldest types of experimental learning theory. You've probably heard of Pavlov's dogs. In these experiments, dogs were taught to salivate when stimulated by a bell as a result of repeated association of the bell sound with food. Other such experiments led to the development of techniques such as learning by association, reinforcement of learning by reward, and extinguishing behaviors by negative reinforcement, or unpleasurable experiences. The model for these theories was, in essence, a reflex, i.e., a certain stimulus can achieve a fixed reflexive response. In the field of learning, these old theories are currently being questioned. It is now thought that learning is much more complex, even in dogs. The internal thought processes need to somehow be included in any learning theory.

Unfortunately, the increasing sophistication of learning theory has not yet penetrated the rather mechanical approach to behavioral modification therapy. I believe this mechanical, limited approach has certainly contributed to the fact that in spite of behavior therapy, the long-term outcome for ADHD sufferers may not be much improved. In the discussions below, I will outline some of the behavioral methods that can be used. However, I stress the importance of understanding your child, of seeing his behavior in its specific context, of being flexible (often advised against in traditional behavior therapy), and of talking with your child to help him learn how to control his behaviors.

Q: Our nine-year-old son has responded fairly well to Ritalin, but there are still many issues that cause serious problems in our family. The most frustrating is our son's unwillingness to do what we ask of him. He's often abusive and loathe to take a bath or pick up his clothes, and we end up in a big fight almost every day. Our ADHD specialist has recommended behavioral modification therapy as a way of regaining and maintaining control. Do you think this will work?

A: Behavior modification therapy has proved almost as effective as medication in the treatment of many symptoms and side issues that can accompany ADHD. Therefore, physicians and ADHD specialists have traditionally recommended it as a way of altering a child's disruptive and troubling behaviors.

Behavior modification is especially helpful to the estimated 30 percent of youngsters with ADHD who don't respond well to medication, as well as those who still need help with inappropriate academic and social behaviors. Many times Ritalin and other medications will alleviate hyperactivity, inattention, and impulsivity, but a child will still behave inappropriately at home or at school. This may be because of the secondary gains his behavior awards him, such as more attention from his parents. But it may also be that the underlying ADHD dysfunctions, such as impulsivity or distractibility, constantly impair his ability to control his behavior. Behavior modification may help "train" the child to consider the consequences of his actions so that he behaves in a more socially acceptable way.

Q: Is there only one type of behavior modification therapy? Considering the wide range of inappropriate behaviors commonly seen among children with ADHD, I find it difficult to believe that a single approach would work for everyone.

A: Clinicians typically divide behavior modification into three types: clinical behavior therapy, direct contingency management, and cognitive-behavioral intervention.

Clinical behavior therapy involves training parents and, in some instances, a child's teacher to carry out contingency management programs when an ADHD child acts up. Contingency management programs involve such things as a reward system for good behavior, and time-outs or loss of favors for bad behavior. Teachers are taught how to quickly end disruptive behavior in the classroom and usually provide parents with a daily report card so they can see how their child is doing and reward good behaviors at home.

In most cases, a handful of specific behaviors are defined, such as completing homework, paying attention in class, and not disrupting others. These target behaviors are then broken down into small, reachable goals, and the child is rewarded for achieving them.

This is an effective form of behavior modification, but it often takes a while to get going. Quite a bit of monitoring and modification is required, and the child may balk at the concept when first assigned. However, several studies of this approach have detailed significant improvement in behavior at home and at school, though it's seldom a cure-all.

Direct contingency management is similar to clinical behavior therapy, but with greater intervention by a trained professional. Usually this form of behavior modification is done in a treatment facility or specialized classroom, where doctors and teachers can closely monitor its implementation and effects.

In most cases, direct contingency management incorporates time-out strategies, a simple reward system, or a response/cost program. For example, a child may lose something important to him, such as free time or a chance to play videogames, if he refuses to work or doesn't do what he is told. This is especially valuable in managing a child's behavior in the classroom, though it can also be an effective tool at home.

A reward system for good behavior can help control inappropriate behaviors to a certain degree, but several studies have shown that negative consequence—a verbal reprimand from the teacher or a loss of privileges—works even better. This is especially true when introduced at the beginning of treatment rather than later in the program.

Of course, the goal of behavior modification is to teach an ADHD youngster to monitor and control his behavior himself, rather than have it controlled through outside influences. Cognitive-behavioral interventions can help a great deal toward this goal.

In a nutshell, cognitive therapy promotes self-control by enhancing specific strategies, such as verbal self-instruction, self-evaluation, and problem-solving techniques. With the help of a therapist or ADHD specialist, a child is taught to evaluate a specific situation, contemplate his actions and possible consequences, and then react accordingly. When taught properly, cognitive therapy can stop bad behavior in its tracks.

As I will show in Chapter 6, I feel that the goals and techniques of therapy should be broadened beyond simple behavioral control. When a family tries to set in motion a behavioral modification program at home, an essential part should be the quiet talking that can go on between a parent and child at a time when the child is not behaving disruptively. Then a parent can nonjudgmentally encourage a child to talk about a particular episode of disruptive behavior, to reflect on what brought it about, and to consider what might be alternative responses to a situation. This talking can take place after a child calms down from a disruptive episode, but it may also take place at other quiet interludes. In fact, I think the parents of ADHD children should make an effort to have quiet one-on-one time with their child, away from siblings and chores or other expectations, on as regular a basis as possible.

The goals of these talks are multiple. They give the parent a chance to better know how their child is feeling and what he is going through. They encourage their child to begin to think about himself, his feelings, and his behavior. Doing this with his parent enables a child to learn the important skill of using language internally to think about himself and to reflect on his behavior, his experience, and his feelings. Not only does this allow him to think of alternative responses for the future and to understand better the consequences of his behavior, but the very act of beginning to think about himself is giving him the beginning tools to control his impulsivity, to think rather than to act.

Q: Does behavior modification work better when used in conjunction with stimulant medication?
A: Yes, it does. Several studies have concluded that a combination of the two modalities is far more effective at altering disruptive behavior than either alone.

There's also a cost benefit. Because stimulants can inhibit certain symptoms of ADHD, such as hyperactivity and impulsivity, the scope and degree of behavior that needs modifying is much smaller. As a result, the cost of therapy is less. In addition, some studies have found that ADHD patients often require less medication when it's combined with behavior modification therapy.

Q: Could you give us some specific behavior modification techniques for use at home? Professional therapy is well and good, but my husband and I need something concrete that we can turn to when our thirteen-year-old son acts up.
A: The most effective behavior modification starts at home—for both the ADHD child and his family.

I mention this because behavior problems are seldom the sole province of the ADHD patient. In most cases, a child's disruptive behavior will have a ripple effect that causes difficulties family-wide. His parents may disagree on how to handle the problem behavior, resulting in fights between themselves, fights with the problem child, and ineffectual discipline across the board. His siblings, noticing that bad behavior is a good way to get attention, may also become disruptive. His grandparents, not realizing that ADHD is the core problem, may put in their own two cents, resulting in anger, resentment, and still more arguments. The result is a continual cycle of problem behavior that adversely affects all concerned.

The most effective behavior modification always begins with the parents. They must make a decision to do what's necessary to stop this cycle, no matter how difficult. Firm but kind consistency is extremely important in order for the child to learn from this technique. This usually means strong, behavior-altering discipline and a unified front. The parents must work together so that the ADHD child cannot use guilt or threats to play one against the other.

One of the most common complaints I hear from parents is that their ADHD child ends up running the household. The parents grow weary of the constant yelling and fights and tune out or ignore the child's disruptive behavior. Or, worse, they schedule their lives around his demands because they don't want to spark yet another altercation.

It's a sad way to live and detrimental to all concerned—especially non-ADHD youngsters who may be living under the same roof. But there are many easy and useful techniques you can employ to stop disruptive behavior and thus make your child more amenable to other helpful approaches at school and at home.

First, take a moment to closely evaluate your family situation. Look for harmful patterns in your life that directly result from your ADHD child's poor behavior. Make a list of these dysfunctional patterns and the many problems they cause. Then make a vow to end them starting immediately. Talk privately with your spouse about your child and your family situation, and promise each other that you will work as a team to turn your child's behavior around. Agree to uniform discipline and how it will be carried out. Then sit down with your child, and explain to him that you have to work out a plan to make your family life easier. Explain to him that his behavior sometimes makes life for everyone in the family difficult, including himself. Reassure your child that you love him, but you cannot tolerate his behavior. It is his behavior you are having a problem with, not him.

Of course, your ADHD child may react by becoming even more abusive, belligerent, aggressive, and recalcitrant. It's his way of pushing the limits, and it will no doubt strain your patience. But be strong, stay unified, and try not to back down. Even one backstep can keep problem patterns in motion. Very soon, however, your child will realize that he can't win and his bad behavior will not be tolerated, and he will start to face the prospect of change for the better.

Most parents find that their children's poor behavior falls into three categories: physical abuse (striking a sibling, damaging property), verbal abuse (swearing at a parent, calling a sibling names), and noncompliance (general uncooperativeness, refusing to pick up clothes or do homework). Once you've identified the behaviors you want to change, take a moment to analyze what typically occurs prior to an outburst, and record any patterns you discover. Many behavior problems can be controlled quite easily, such as providing a small dose of Ritalin after school to eliminate rebound or making sure that the child eats on a regular schedule.

If your child's behavior problems aren't so easily fixed or your child seems intent on maintaining them, the next step is establishing a corrective plan. The most effective, I've found, is defining the specific behaviors that you want him to achieve and the specific behaviors that must be changed, and designing rewards that he will earn when successful. Imposing a reasonable punishment, or consequence, or a loss of privilege each time "bad" behaviors occur is also possible. I do find that the positive reinforcement, for example, a reward system, is usually preferable and more likely to succeed. Once you've worked out the plan, introduce it at a family meeting, and make sure all the children are involved.

The key to success here is rewarding good behavior and withholding privileges for bad behaviors. It's also important to have preplanned responses so that the child can't sabotage the program with surprises. Consistency is essential. Once the plan is in effect, it ought to be followed as consistently as possible.

You may find it helpful to write down unacceptable behaviors and post the list where the child can read it. Define these behaviors as clearly as you can so that the child understands exactly what is expected of him.

One effective option is to reward good behavior during a

Other Treatments for ADHD

specific period with points, or stickers on a chart, and punish inappropriate behavior with the removal of points. Once a certain number of points has been achieved at the end of a specified time period—one day, one week, or whatever—the child should receive a reward. This can be whatever you deem fit. A movie rental, perhaps, or an extra hour playing video games. Something very special, such as a new bicycle or baseball glove or a trip to the zoo, can be a very good incentive for long-term behavioral change.

If the specified number of points has not been achieved in a given time, explain to the child that his reward is being withheld because of his poor behavior, but that he will be given another chance. Pretty soon the child will realize that there's more to be gained by being good than being bad, and his behavior will improve accordingly.

Having outlined this plan, it is important to remember that a child may have a very hard time responding to these changes and challenges. I've found it best to start small and work your way up. Too many failures and not enough successes can be very detrimental, so try to maximize your child's chances of success at the very beginning and let him grow towards the bigger challenges.

In addition, while creating a unified front, parents should agree that there are some things that simply aren't worth fighting over. Learn to be flexible and use understanding to help mold your child's behavior into that which is more socially acceptable. Your child is not a simple reflex machine who will change at the snap of your fingers. A change in behavior is a complicated process that requires as much understanding from you as it does from your child.

Finally, try to include your child in every phase of the planning. Sit him down, and say, "Look, we all know your behavior is causing problems. It's not fun for us, and it can't be fun for you either. We know you must feel bad about it, and we want to help you find a way to control it." This integration of responsibility allows the child to feel that he has a hand in helping himself get better and not that "treatment" is being forced upon him.

Behavior modification techniques were an important part of the treatment of Peter, who I first described in Chapter 2, and who I will discuss in much more detail in the next chapter. I helped his parents and teachers set up behavioral strategies and systems to work with Peter. These included sticker charts for step-by-step behavior in the classroom, time-outs when necessary, reward and punishment systems at home for many different targeted behaviors, and even a sticker-chart system for his encopresis. Peter would earn stickers towards a toy he wanted by exhibiting positive behaviors, such as cleaning himself up when he had an accident or trying to defecate in the toilet. He would be rewarded with several stickers when he actually succeeded in defecating in the toilet. This program was quite successful, although when his parents became inconsistent with its application, so would Peter's response become inconsistent.

Q: In my day, all it took was a scolding or a spanking to change a child's behavior. Why doesn't that work with children who have ADHD?

A: Spankings may have been popular when you were a child, but current opinion tends to be against corporal punishment. Using violence and force to resolve problems is the wrong solution for a child with ADHD, who may already be prone to violent or abusive reactions to problems. And scoldings tend to have little effect on children with ADHD. Many "zone out" when they hear a lecture coming, while others quickly forget what they have been told.

Children with ADHD tend to crave attention, both good and bad. They prefer to be praised for their actions, but they'll settle for the angry attention that comes from disruptive or inattentive behavior. As a result, many such youngsters act up because they feel it's the only way they can get their family to notice them. And when a parent shouts at or punishes them, it means they've succeeded.

One effective way to put a stop to this destructive cycle is to ignore disruptive behavior whenever safely or reasonably possible. If the child tries to get his way by throwing a temper tantrum, for example, merely turn your back and pretend he's not there. Do not make eye contact or acknowledge him no matter how loudly he screams.

Once the child realizes his tantrum isn't getting the desired effect, he'll stop. At that point, invite him to rejoin the family activity—but don't say anything about the tantrum. Act as if it never occurred.

On the other hand, I often tell parents to make the most of happy, quiet times with their child, to give him the attention that he craves without his having to ask. Often this is best done by a parent having a special one-on-one time with that child, away from siblings and the hustle and bustle of family life. This could involve picking the child up after school and going out for a snack; a special trip to the library or to a movie on the weekend; or perhaps just a walk in the woods or down the avenue, with no particular agenda other than being together.

While this one-on-one time may not be part of a behavior chart, it is likely to be an important behavioral learning experience for the child. He learns that when his behavior is under control, his parent wants and likes to be with him. And getting this attention at these times may lessen the push to seek attention through disruptive behavior. It also gives the parent an invaluable opportunity to better understand this child, his emotions and experience.

These quieter times together may also help your child gradually learn to think and talk about himself, an invaluable tool in controlling his impulsivity and behavior. You can aid this learning process by talking about yourself, thus modeling how someone can think and reflect on his own experience. Also important is your interest in your child's experience, accepting how he feels, even when you feel he is misinterpreting events or reacting inappropriately. It is possible to validate a person's feelings even as one tries to show them another way of looking at something.

Q: Are time-outs really an effective technique for changing bad behavior?

A: I believe they are, when used consistently and properly.

The goal of a time-out is not to punish, but to make the child think about his behavior and why it is wrong. Sending a child to his room won't accomplish anything if he's got books, television, and video games to entertain him, so choose a location that is not fun.

If you decide that time-outs will be part of your behavior modification program, outline at the very beginning those behaviors that are so bad or disruptive that they demand special attention. These might include physical abuse, foul language, or persistent refusal to do as instructed. Tell the child that these behaviors will always result in a time-out and that the time away from family and fun should be spent thinking about what he did and why it was wrong.

A time-out of ten to fifteen minutes should be sufficient for small children. Older children and adolescents may require thirty minutes or more. When a time-out is ordered, set a timer and tell the child that he is not to come out until the timer rings. If he emerges before the specified time or engages in another disruptive outburst during the time-out, the timer should be set to zero and the time-out started again. After a few lengthy time-outs, the child will associate his negative behavior with this form of punishment and try to avoid repeating it.

Q: What should we do if our child acts up outside of home, such as in a restaurant or store?
A: As stated earlier, a consistent approach to discipline is essential. This means that poor behavior is unacceptable at any time—at home or out in public. Every outburst must be dealt with immediately.

If the behavior would have resulted in a time-out at home, then it's okay to enact a time-out wherever you are. For example, if a child behaves inappropriately in a restaurant, take him outside and let him spend the time-out in the car. You should stand nearby and within the child's line of vision for safety reasons and so as not to terrify your child. After fifteen minutes or so, ask the child if he understands why what he did was wrong. If he does, let him rejoin the family.

Children may act up outside of the home because they believe that their parents will acquiesce to their demands to avoid a public confrontation. Every incidence of bad behavior should be dealt with immediately so that the child quickly learns what is and what is not acceptable. If you make a threat to return home or leave early if a child misbehaves, you must do so when challenged. Empty warnings send a confusing message to the child and will not help his behavior.

Again, I would stress the importance of talking with your child about these events. Once you've returned home, join the child in his room for a chat. Bring up the most recent incident of poor behavior, and ask him what prompted it and how such outbursts can be avoided in the future. Let him talk, even if all he does in the beginning is blame others. Try to keep the conversation on the issues at hand, and gently encourage him to talk about alternatives to screaming, hitting, or name-calling.

If the child says he erupted because his brother was picking on him, acknowledge the problem, then ask what else he might have done to correct the situation, besides striking out. Try to talk with your child in such a way after each incidence of bad behavior until your child starts to review his actions, their consequences, and potential alternatives on his own. In time he'll start to reflect before acting, and his behavior should improve accordingly.

Q: My twelve-year-old son is a perfect gentleman in school or while visiting with his friends, but he turns into a monster the moment he comes home. Is this a common phenomenon?
A: Yes, it is. Many parents are amazed to discover that their ADHD child is an angel in school or while visiting peers and becomes a terror only around his parents and siblings.

One possible explanation is that your child's medication keeps him under control throughout the day and his disruptive behavior is the result of a late-afternoon medication withdrawal. Another explanation could be that your child is holding in his anger and frustration so as not to get in trouble in school or in social situations; he lets it out only in the safe confines of home. Regardless, his disruptive behavior should not be tolerated.

If you haven't instituted the behavior management strategies discussed above, you should seriously consider them. You'll be amazed at the peace they can bring to your family.

Q: My husband and I are trying desperately to help our son cope with his ADHD and, at the same

time, change his abusive behavior. Our doctor gave us a list of tips that are supposed to make things easier, but they're not very realistic. What should we do?

A: Unfortunately, many of the coping techniques suggested by ADHD specialists sound good in theory, but are next to impossible to enact at home. For example, parents may be told that their ADHD child needs a quiet place to study, one with few distractions. But most normal households would be hard put to find such a place, especially if they have other young children. Or they may be told to stick to established routines for the sake of the ADHD child—a near impossible task for today's modern, on-the-go family. As a result, adjustment and behavior modification can take months or longer to show results.

You need to raise these important issues with your physician and ask for additional help in changing your son's behavior. Explain the realities of your family situation, and ask him for information that's more pertinent to your specific needs. Every family is different, and their approach to easing the problems of ADHD and changing disruptive behaviors will be different. Nothing related to the treatment of ADHD is set in stone.

Q: Our daughter was diagnosed with ADHD a year ago and is doing pretty well on Cylert. However, we're still having a great deal of difficulty getting her to do her chores. Any advice?

A: Youngsters with ADHD often find chores boring and balk at every request. The result: an ongoing power struggle and a lot of fighting.

Dr. Larry Silver, in his book *Attention Deficit Hyperactivity Disorder*, has some unique suggestions that you might want to try if all else fails. He calls one "maid service." Tell your daughter that if she doesn't do her chores by an assigned time, you will do them for her—and deduct the cost from her allowance. Picking up her clothes, for example, might cost fifty cents. Taking out the garbage, another fifty cents. Keep a running tab, and when it comes time for her to receive her allowance, present her with a bill detailing the deductions. If the deductions exceed the amount of her weekly allowance, tell her the balance will come from next week's allowance. Once she realizes that you mean what you say—and she finds herself with less and less money to spend on herself—she should be more than willing to do the chores you assign her.

A technique he suggests for changing the behavior of children who fail to pick up after themselves is to establish a "lock box"—a room or storage area where items left lying around will be held for a given period of time. Tell the child one final time that he must pick up his things when he's done with them, or you'll do it for him. From that moment on, all toys, sporting equipment, videotapes, and video games left lying around will be placed in the lock box for one week or whatever period you deem sufficient. After a few days without his most prized possessions, the child should start picking up after himself with very few reminders.

Again, I would caution you, however, to not get too caught up with details and to choose your battles. ADHD children are struggling with many issues and are very often truly hampered by their condition when it comes to organizational skills. Your goal is to teach them skills and strategies to get around these difficulties, not to create a situation of anger and poor self-esteem because your child cannot reach the organizational standards of the rest of the family.

Your child may need more structuring input than others. For example, you may have to help your child with a system or organization, such as labeling boxes or helping her find easier ways to organize her school papers, books, and homework. And you may have to relax your own standards somewhat. When choosing chores to assign to your child, try to choose things that she will be likely to succeed at.

Q: Our ADHD son is fairly well behaved, thanks to medication and other management techniques, but he still has a great deal of difficulty getting things done on time. He's always late for school or family trips because he gets distracted while taking a bath or getting dressed. This situation is starting to cause serious problems in our family, and we're at our wits' end. Any suggestions?
A: This behavior tends to result from the inattention so common in ADHD children, but there are ways to teach a child

to be on time for school, dinner, and family outings. First, I would try techniques such as giving a child more warning time and giving him a structured plan of what is about to happen. ADHD children often have great difficulty changing activities, and in shifting attention from one thing to another. A usual routine that is predictable and makes sense to the child often helps; for example, helping the child lay out his school clothes and pack his backpack the night before. Make sure that you, the parent, have a reasonable routine in the mornings, and have his breakfast ready at the same time. In many households everyone is rushing around frantically in the mornings, trying to get ready for work and school, and it is no wonder that the ADHD child either gets frantic and hyperactive or "zones out" the overstimulating household by losing himself in television cartoons, toys, or a book. So I would begin with your own routine. Is everyone else in the household frantic, rushed, and anxious in the mornings or when changing activities? If so, then the first step would be to change that. This may mean getting up a bit earlier and getting yourself ready first, before waking your child. Or this may mean more careful planning around family activities and routines, trying to minimize anxiety and hassle.

Then I would recommend that you help your child develop a routine. For example, if the problem area is getting ready to leave for school on time in the morning, I would sit down with your child and work out a time schedule, itemizing everything that needs to be done in the morning. Make sure to allow time for a little playing or reading. If he needs that time right after he wakes up, before his stimulant begins to work, then suggest he get up in time each morning to take his medication and then play for fifteen minutes with the dog or in his room or even watch cartoons for fifteen minutes, if this helps to organize his activity and calm him down. *No* child enjoys being rushed, and many find it anxiety-provoking when the rushing also involves a separation from parents and home, such as going to school in the morning. An anxious, rushing household can only undermine the coping strategies of an ADHD child.

If you have instituted a calmer transition between activities and an expected routine and your child is still having difficulty, I would suggest trying specific behavioral measures. Perhaps a sticker chart with target behaviors would help make the process more concrete and manageable for the child. Break down the behaviors into several smaller parcels at first. For example, to help with your child's morning schedule, include a separate line on the chart for each of the following: getting up when asked, taking medication with no hassle, getting dressed, washing, brushing teeth and hair, eating breakfast on time, and, finally, leaving the house on time. Eventually you can work up to just focusing on leaving the house on time, but at first your child will need this structured help at every step along the way. At the end of the week, earned stickers can be traded in for a reward. The chart should be kept in a place where the child can see it and watch his own progress.

It is essential that you be patient and at all times remember you are working with the child against his behaviors. If these measures fail and if your child's ADHD seems well controlled in other circumstances, it is possible that the family struggles surrounding these transitions have become somewhat emotionally gratifying for the child. In these circumstances, it is important to break the cycle of battles that go on between you and your child. And an effective way to do this, if the above measures don't succeed, is to let the child see that only he is going to pay the consequences of his actions. But again, it is imperative that you don't overwhelm the child with anxiety. If the problem with these transitions is an unresolved anxiety about separation and loss, then it is imperative that this be taken up in psychotherapy.

If the child is older, such as a teenager, and capable of taking more responsibility for himself, then it would be reasonable to sit him down and explain to him that from now on, he is completely responsible for being on time. You will no longer remind or nag him, and if he's late, it's his loss.

Say, for example, your ADHD child is chronically late for breakfast. Tell him the hours breakfast will be served every morning; then let it go. If he arrives late, tell him the kitchen is closed and he'll have to go to school hungry. After a few days, he'll get the message.

If your child is often late for the school bus because he

can't get dressed on time, let him miss the bus and pay the consequences. Of course, with a younger child or when there is no other means of getting to school, this may not be a feasible approach. With an older child, it may mean walking to school or taking public transportation. Also, having to deal with the school about that lateness himself may reinforce his learning about the consequences of his behavior. If your child is unable to attend school because of his lateness, make sure he spends the day in his room, reading or studying. It's not a vacation and shouldn't be treated like one. This means no television, no video games, and no playing.

If your child is perpetually late for family outings, consider going without him. If he's too young to be left alone, have a babysitter on standby. Again, I would not do this lightly. If the child is suffering separation anxiety or fears about sudden changes, having his family go out without him may be an overwhelming experience. But for more secure children, leaving them with a familiar sitter while the rest of the family goes out may be a significant learning experience. Once the sitter has been called, stand firm on your decision, even if the child races to get dressed. After a few missed movies and dinners out, the child will almost certainly be on time every time.

The key to these programs, as heartless as some of them may sound, is to make a child aware of his actions and the fact that his parents will no longer bail him out. They may be effective ways to change problem behavior, as long as they do not increase anxiety and fear in an already insecure child. Your ADHD specialist, after the full diagnostic evaluation, will best be able to guide you in terms of which techniques are likely to be helpful with your child and which might be counterproductive.

Q: Every time I mention to someone that my daughter has ADHD, they all tell me I should eliminate sugar from her diet. I thought researchers found that sugar has no bearing in hyperactive behavior.

A: It doesn't, but that hasn't stopped uninformed people from continuing to believe that it does.

Over the years, several theories have been put forth on how

refined sugars might promote adverse behavior in children. One theory suggests that sugar affects brain neurotransmitter levels and thus the activity level of a hyperactive child. Another common theory is that carbohydrate intake affects blood levels of fatty acids, which are essential for the synthesis of the hormone prostaglandin in the brain. This theory makes sense because insulin is required for this synthesis, and blood sugar levels can influence insulin production.

However, as intriguing as these and other theories may sound, only a small handful of clinical studies have found any evidence that sugar can influence behavior. Most studies have found no correlation at all.

In one well-known study, researchers analyzed the relationship between sugar intake and conduct disorders, learning disabilities, and attention deficit hyperactivity disorder. Youngsters with these disorders were given sucrose, fructose, or a placebo, and their behavior and classroom activity was evaluated. After all the data was analyzed, however, the researchers were unable to tell the difference between the normal effects of increased energy intake and sugar effects. As a result, they could not accurately conclude that any disruptive behavior was caused by the consumption of sugar.

Another study of hyperactive children came to almost the same conclusion. The researchers placed newspaper ads seeking youngsters diagnosed with ADHD who, according to their parents, experienced an increase in hyperactive behavior after eating a sugar-rich snack. However, absolutely no difference in hyperactive behavior was observed by the researchers after the children received a high dose of fructose, glucose, or a placebo.

A related study questioned whether the hyperactive behavior reported by parents might be the result of high blood glucose levels and not the intake of sugar. To find out, researchers gave ADHD children one of three breakfasts: one that was high in carbohydrates, especially refined sugars; one that was rich in protein; and one that was high in fat. After finishing their meals, the children were given glucose, fructose, or a placebo.

The researchers found an increase in hyperactive behavior only when the children received glucose following a high-carbohydrate breakfast. This suggests that refined sugars may increase a child's hyperactivity if his blood sugar level is already sufficiently elevated, possibly due to consuming a very sugary food over a long period of time.

What all this means, ultimately, is that the amount of sugar found in most foods isn't enough to affect a child's behavior, and restricting normal sugar intake will have no effect in controlling hyperactivity.

Q: Can artificial sweeteners have an adverse effect on youngsters with ADHD?

A: Yes, they can. Recent studies have found that products containing aspartame (such as Equal or NutraSweet) can increase noncompliant or aggressive behavior when consumed in large quantities.

Q: Is there any connection between ADHD and food additives?

A: Some researchers believe so, though there is little clinical evidence to support this theory.

One of the most vocal advocates of the food additive concept is Dr. Benjamin Feingold, who suggested, more than twenty years ago, that the behavior of many children with ADHD is directly influenced by specific food additives. The result of his work was the Feingold Diet, a complex and difficult-to-maintain dietary regimen that excludes all food additives, as well as artificial flavorings, colors, and preservatives.

Many parents of ADHD children have embraced the Feingold Diet and swear it helps reduce the syndrome's telltale symptoms. However, few studies have been able to confirm this effect, so if the diet works at all, it's probably on a very small percentage of children with ADHD.

Q: Have researchers been able to determine a correlation between allergies and ADHD?

A: Pediatricians and other experts have long reported a higher incidence of allergies among children with attention deficit hyperactivity disorder, though there has been little scientific study of this phenomenon, and no treatment has proved 100 percent successful.

One true believer of the allergy/ADHD connection is Dr. Doris Rapp, who has proposed in various books that hyperactivity is connected to food or other sensitivities. She has identified a wide variety of potential allergy-causing items, including milk, peanuts, corn, pork, and eggs, and recommends completely eliminating these foods from your child's diet and then adding them one at a time to see if any cause a change in behavior. Environmental sensitivities, such as mold or the chemicals found in new carpet, can also affect behavior, Dr. Rapp notes.

Few studies have been able to confirm Dr. Rapp's theory, and many researchers have found fault with her approach and conclusions. As a result, a great deal of her work regarding food allergies and ADHD remains very controversial. If you suspect your child may be the victim of a food sensitivity, he should be examined by a trained allergy specialist who is familiar with the child's ADHD history.

Q: A member of our ADHD support group brought up the subject of amino acid therapy. Does this treatment have merit?

A: Again, this treatment is based on a theory that makes some sense, but researchers have been unable to confirm any positive results in clinical studies.

Amino acid therapy is based on the plausible hypothesis that ADHD is the result of a deficiency in the amino acids necessary for the production of certain important neurotransmitters in the brain. This concept might seem to make sense, because some amino acids cannot be manufactured by the body and must be obtained through a healthy diet. However, no studies have been able to prove a therapeutic link between amino acid supplements and ADHD. If someone tries to sell you on this approach, walk away. There are much better ways to spend your money.

Q: Can megadoses of vitamins and minerals help alleviate the symptoms of ADHD?

A: It's true that a vitamin deficiency can result in serious health problems, but both the American Psychiatric Association and the American Academy of Pediatrics stress that there is no clinical evidence that large doses of vitamins and minerals have any beneficial effect on ADHD.

More importantly, massive doses of certain vitamins can actually be dangerous, especially to children, so consult your physician before starting any kind of megavitamin therapy.

Q: I've been hearing more and more about biofeedback as a way of easing the symptoms of ADHD. What can you tell me about this approach?

A: Some researchers speculate that ADHD is actually a secondary symptom of a neurological disorder that produces abnormal brain wave patterns.

Neurofeedback is a type of EEG biofeedback that theoretically trains ADHD patients to increase beta-wave production and slow theta-wave production so they can concentrate more easily. It sounds like science fiction, but studies with other physiological functions, such as pulse rate, show that biofeedback methods can indeed influence physiological functions not usually under conscious voluntary control. However, a great deal more research must be done before this technique can be considered genuinely effective. There have not been any characteristic brain wave patterns found in all ADHD sufferers, and as yet little is really known about what biofeedback can do to cognitive and other brain functions. Thus, I would suggest using biofeedback under the close supervision of your ADHD specialist and only in conjunction with other modalities, such as medication, behavior therapy, and psychotherapy.

Q: Is integrative sensory training the same thing as biofeedback?

A: No. "Sensory integration" is a phrase first coined by occupational therapist Dr. Jean Ayres to explain the brain's ability to organize stimuli based on information derived from all five senses.

Dr. Ayres theorizes that many of the symptoms of ADHD are the result of the brain's inability to integrate this flood of information. The result is an information or stimulus "overload'' that can cause problems with attention, learning, speech, behavior, and coordination.

This concept is difficult to dismiss. ADHD children often exhibit many of the problems Dr. Ayres mentions, including clumsiness, inattention, and learning disabilities. Many ADHD children also complain of tactile overstimulation, or extreme skin sensitivity. This could explain why many ADHD children hate to wear tight-fitting clothes and shoes or dislike the sensation of water on their faces while swimming or bathing.

The answer, according to Dr. Ayres and others, is what's known as integrative sensory training, in which the nerve-cell connections are stimulated through various techniques to help the brain organize itself. It is an intriguing concept, but there have not been enough clinical studies to prove whether the technique has any lasting benefits. I suspect it is too simplistic.

Q: Is it possible that my child's attention deficit hyperactivity disorder could be caused by something as simple as a yeast infection? My sister read about this in a book, but I find it hard to believe.

A: The theory that many of the symptoms of ADHD might be the result of a yeast infection run wild was brought into the mainstream by Dr. William Crook, author of *The Yeast Connection*. Crook offers no explanation of how this phenomenon supposedly works, but claims that many of the symptoms of ADHD can be brought under control through a special yeast-free diet, yeast-controlling medication, and an allergy-free environment.

Dr. Crook and his advocates report great success in managing ADHD through this approach, but again, there is no convincing evidence that yeast is a potential cause of ADHD or that Dr. Crook's treatment regimen is the answer.

Q: Our sixteen-year-old son has been on Ritalin for nearly six years and has responded well to the medication. He's still a little forgetful and hyperactive, and his temper flares up now and then; but all in all, he's much improved. He recently started a daily exercise regimen to get

in shape for high school football, and we've all noticed a marked improvement in his ADHD symptoms. Could exercise be the miracle cure we've been looking for?

A: "Miracle cure" is probably a little strong, but there's some scientific data and a lot of anecdotal evidence suggesting that exercise can play a valuable role in controlling the symptoms of ADHD.

Many people with the syndrome report that they can concentrate and focus more clearly after a vigorous workout and that they're less prone to inattention and impulsivity. In many cases, the beneficial effects of exercise last three hours or more.

Researchers have only begun to investigate the potential benefits of exercise on ADHD, but the work that has been done so far is impressive. For example, people who exercise regularly have shown a marked decrease in depression and anxiety and a greater ability to handle daily stress. There is also a small but noticeable improvement in certain types of learning and memory.

At first, researchers thought such benefits were the result of an endorphin rush similar to that experienced by marathon runners. But the real answer appears to be an increase in the production of the neurotransmitters dopamine, serotonin, and norepinephrine—a boost quite similar to that caused by stimulant medication. In other words, exercise does naturally what stimulants do chemically.

Adding credence to this theory is the fact that the enzymes necessary to produce dopamine have been found to be significantly higher in a part of the brain called the caudate nucleus following regular exercise. This is an important discovery because the caudate nucleus is responsible for our ability to pay attention and is known to be quite different in people with attention deficit hyperactivity disorder.

For Leslie (discussed in Chapter 3), intense exercise was essential in boosting alertness and ability to concentrate. She also needed exercise to help her sleep; if she didn't work out, she suffered terrible insomnia. The endorphin rush that came from exercise was no doubt helpful, but I also suspect that in this particular case, exercise helped the patient focus her attention and reduce the anxiety that exacerbated her ADHD symptoms.

With Peter (discussed in Chapter 2), I found that he became anxious and upset when forced to remain inactive (such as sitting in a chair in a doctor's office). I quickly discovered that it was easier to treat Peter while engaged in some sort of physical activity, so we would often take brisk walks through the woods near my country office while we talked. There was something about the exercise and the lack of physical restraint that allowed for greater organization of thought and helped Peter speak and communicate better. This was true in school too. For some reason, Peter could function much better when unrestrained.

No doubt further research into exercise will uncover additional benefits to ADHD. In the meantime, encourage your son to continue his regular exercise routine, and don't forget to discuss his improvement with your doctor or ADHD specialist.

SIX

Psychotherapy and Its Place in a Multimodal Treatment Plan

So far I have discussed the medications and behavioral treatments traditionally used to treat ADHD. Medication, especially Ritalin, has very often been the first, and often the only treatment recommended to the ADHD sufferer. Sometimes behavior therapy has been used in combination with the medication, and studies have shown that the combination is more effective than either treatment alone. However, as I have already stressed, the long-term outcome studies have shown that ADHD sufferers continue to have symptoms well into their adult lives in spite of these traditional treatments. In addition, in severe cases, their academic, emotional, and social developments have been severely interfered with by their lifelong disorder, leading to significant problems in all spheres of their lives as adults.

Q: Besides medication and behavior modification, what can be done to help ADHD sufferers?
A: In this chapter I will discuss psychotherapy, which I see as a significant part of the multimodal approach to ADHD. I believe this treatment method has great potential in altering the outcome of ADHD. The National Institute for Mental Health (NIMH) is now overseeing a long-term prospective study of a multimodal treatment approach to ADHD that includes psychotherapy. The study is taking place at six different

sites, with children of a wide age range, starting with children as young as four. In this chapter I will explain why it makes sense that broadly informed psychotherapy can and should make a significant difference to the study outcome.

Previously, psychotherapy has been underutilized as a treatment method in ADHD and has only been seen as necessary when the individual is suffering from very severe secondary effects, such as depression, anxiety, suicidal behavior, and despair. In the discussion that follows, I will show why I believe that psychotherapy is almost always of enormous potential benefit to the ADHD sufferer. I will describe in some detail my individualized approach to therapy with a person with ADHD, discuss how it works and illustrate with examples. In addition, I will discuss how psychotherapy fits into the whole multimodal treatment plan.

Q: Just what is psychotherapy?
A: Psychotherapy is a treatment method, sometimes referred to as talking therapy, that involves a patient speaking with a therapist about his problems. The goals of psychotherapy include gaining insight and knowledge about the self and its emotional states and personal life history. The ultimate goal is to change ways of reacting to and dealing with situations that have caused trouble previously. So the goal is not just one of changing behavior, but rather of changing emotional responses, thinking patterns, and coping strategies. Behavioral change will follow on from that.

As long as people have had the gift of language and have lived in communities, they have undoubtedly found it helpful to share their thoughts and worries with a person whom they trust and esteem. While a sympathetic ear and supporting friend can go a long way, people seek therapy when, in spite of such support, they are not able to change their emotional state or recurring maladaptive behaviors and when they are not able to carry out the advice that friends and advisors may give. The particular techniques used in psychotherapy and the understanding of the human mind upon which they are based have only developed over the last hundred years, starting in Europe with the work of people like Freud, Jung, and their associates.

In psychotherapy, the therapist is a supportive, intent listener who tries to remain neutral toward the patient, especially in terms of opinions about actions the patient should take and in terms of morally judging the patient. In this way the therapist differs from a friend, who may have very strong opinions and may try to persuade or coerce the person to do certain things. Another important skill of the therapist is to not only listen very carefully to the patient, but to listen very carefully to her own reactions to the patient and to make sure that her interventions are in the patient's interest only and not entangled with her own needs or desires. This is much harder for family members or friends to do, partly because their lives are necessarily entangled with the patient's.

The intent, trained listening of the therapist makes it possible for her to hear patterns, underlying issues, hidden emotions, and conflicting feelings that the patient may be unaware of and to begin to bring her observations to the patient for his own conscious examination. To have such a trained, objective, sympathetic outsider focusing all her attention on just what one is experiencing and why can open up a whole universe of understanding and make it possible for the patient to begin to see, feel, and do things very differently.

Psychotherapy differs from the other treatments discussed in this book (i.e., medication and behavior therapy techniques) in two significant ways: First, its efficacy depends on the development of a trusting, consistent, and ongoing relationship between the therapist and the patient. Second, it is a talking therapy, and the role of language is crucial not only to the process of communication in therapy, but also to the healing mechanisms themselves.

Q: I've heard there are many different kinds of therapy. How do I know which to choose?

A: It is true that there have been many contributors to the field, and many different branches of therapy have developed. Consumers may find themselves faced with a dizzying array of therapies and not know how to choose between them. It may be reassuring to know that all these competing therapies have evolved from common roots and that the most important factors in the success of the therapy are the level of training and competence of the therapist; her personal qualities of empathy, maturity, and intelligence; and her ability to draw on a broad and eclectic (from many schools of thought and theories) background to tailor a program of therapy to the needs of a particular individual.

The kind of therapy that I will describe is a combination of techniques. This combination incorporates elements of supportive psychotherapy, analytic insight-oriented therapy, cognitive-behavioral therapy, and language remedial therapy, as well as elements of family therapy and sometimes group therapy. In this chapter I will focus on my approach in individual therapy.

Q: How does the therapy proceed?
A: As I have said, the first requirement in psychotherapy is for a relationship, a working alliance, to develop between the patient and doctor. To ensure this development and the unfolding of the therapeutic process, the therapist and patient must meet at least weekly over a period of months. The sessions are usually forty-five to sixty minutes in duration. In these sessions the patient talks about his thoughts and feelings, events in his life and his earlier life, and, in whatever way possible, shares his consciousness of his own mental life with the therapist.

How this proceeds will obviously vary from treatment to treatment. Young children most often express themselves freely in play, so play materials, games, and storytelling are all a part of their treatment. Adolescents may need more indirect ways of communicating, such as talking about others or sharing homework assignments, and may require more help to be able to open up. Adults are more likely to be able to at least identify with the task of sharing their thoughts, even if it is not always easy.

The degree to which I structure the sessions will also vary from person to person. With some I may focus their attention repeatedly on symptomatic behavior and feelings, while with others I will adopt a more open-ended approach, with the belief that we will learn most if we don't prematurely limit the topic of focus. Some of these choices will of course depend on how widely a patient's ADHD has affected his development and personality.

Q: You said that psychotherapy uses the relationship between the therapist and patient, as well as the nature of what is spoken between them. How does the relationship help psychotherapy work?

A: As I have explained, psychotherapy takes place within the context of a secure relationship between a therapist and a patient. The therapist utilizes this relationship in many different ways to help her client. Certain aspects of the relationship itself are very important to why the therapy is helpful. These include the support inherent in having a consistently available, accepting, empathic person focusing all her skilled attention on the ADHD sufferer's experience. For many, this is the first time they have had such undivided attention. Then there is the possibility of using the therapist as a role model. The therapeutic relationship may be experienced as replacing a lost relationship, and in this sense the therapist can indeed become a very important adult in a child's life. The therapeutic situation can be a uniquely calm, soothing, safe, and tolerant atmosphere in which the troubled person can begin to heal and grow. In other words, the therapeutic relationship provides a haven away from school or work, family, and peer relationships—situations where an ADHD sufferer's symptoms have already caused failure, rejection, anger, and frustration.

In addition, the therapist remains as objective and neutral toward the patient as possible. This is very hard for someone directly involved in the patient's life to do. Because of the therapist's neutrality, she is less likely to become personally upset by a patient's actions or difficulties. Likewise, the patient can feel less inhibited about sharing the full range of his emotions and thoughts, knowing that the therapist has a basic respect for him and an unswerving alliance with the part of him that wants to "get better." This neutrality allows the therapist to have a relatively objective viewpoint from which she listens to what the patient reports about his feelings, thoughts, and daily actions. She can then offer her objective observations and possible deductions about them for the patient to consider.

Q: Then how does the talking part of the therapy work to help?

A: It is difficult to describe the elements of therapy that are specific to what actually goes on in the sessions, to the language that is spoken. To appreciate the full impact of therapy's enormous potential, we have to think about the meaning of language. It is obvious to us that language is a tool we use to share our experience with others. But language is much, much more than that. Language gives us a complex and liberating way of ordering our minds and experiences. Language is intimately involved in the nature of memory. And language is a tool of self-knowledge, control, and mastery.

In addition, and of obvious relevance to ADHD, is the fact that language and thought give us an alternative to action. Language and thought allow for a processing of perception, for a delay between stimulus and response. By stimulus, I mean a perception, originating from within or from without, or a feeling, sensation, memory, or thought. Language and thought are not synonymous, and this is certainly a hot topic of study in psycholinguistics, i.e., how do we think if not in words? But it does seem to me that language is more than just a tool to communicate between people. I think language actually facilitates the internal processing of experience. Using language allows an individual to take a stimulus and to work with it in some reflective way. The input can be compared to memory traces, can be subjected to judgment and reasoning, and can be tested against other generalized situations. This allows for understanding the stimulus in a more complex context, for a delay in response, and for a greater repertoire of responses.

I stress this because I believe that psychotherapy works precisely because it has the potential of strengthening the individual's ability to use language both internally and as a tool in communication. Therefore, psychotherapy may actually be able to bring about enduring structural change, not just temporary relief, as Ritalin may do, or behavioral substitution, as behavioral therapy may do.

As a therapist, I facilitate this strengthening of language in many ways. First, by encouraging the medium of speech over action and by modeling this with my own behavior, a goal is set for my patient. I try to clarify my patient's experiences by asking questions and by offering descriptions of what I perceive about him and about what he describes, all the while offering him ways in which to think about and describe his feeling states. I may use descriptions of my own reactions and feelings that arise in the treatment to both model the use of language in this way and to help him to begin to structure his perceptions of what other people feel and how other people react to him. I may confront him verbally when he is being evasive or defensive or when he is misinterpreting his perceptions. And I may interpret the underlying issues that are appearing in his associations or behavior as we become more familiar with his patterns of response, feelings, internal conflicts, and distortions of the emotional reality.

Q: Is insight into the meaning of one's problems also important in getting better?

A: Definitely. But insight and self-knowledge are dependent on the ability to think about oneself, i.e., to have a well-developed ability to use language internally. This goes hand in hand with an ability to delay action, to tolerate frustration, and to tolerate and hold on to intense feelings, including sadness and anxiety. Consequently, psychotherapy must be focused on enhancing the development of that internal language and the ability to think about oneself.

Only then can psychotherapy further its other curative mechanisms. These are to foster insight and self-understanding; to understand the maladaptive patterns that have developed, perhaps in response to originally traumatic situations; and to understand how one misperceives events and communications. Such understanding allows the individual to work through past traumas, rejections, misunderstandings, and conflicts. As a person begins to feel sympathetic toward his own suffering, he is then able to begin to understand and empathize with others. These processes help to lessen guilt and enhance self-esteem, as well as open up the potential for more satisfying and successful relationships.

Q: How does psychotherapy address the difficulties specific to ADHD?

A: This is a very important question. By the time the ADHD sufferer first presents for treatment, his difficulties are likely to have spread widely throughout all spheres of his life: work, school, family, and personal relationships. In addition, the underlying problems of his ADHD may have already affected his personality development, affecting his self-concept and esteem, moods, sense of hopefulness, ability to empathize with himself and others, ability to tolerate feelings and to find solutions to conflicts within himself and with others, and so on. Many of these widening effects are discussed earlier in the book, in Chapters 1, 2, and 3.

Obviously, the more severe and widespread the difficulties are, the more urgent a need for an intensive psychotherapy treatment as part of the multimodal treatment plan. It has been common practice to prescribe some form of psychotherapy when the ADHD sufferer also demonstrates severe psychiatric symptoms, such as depression, severe anxiety or suicidal thoughts, and helplessness. Psychotherapy has been thought of as a treatment for the secondary effects of severe ADHD.

However, I believe that psychotherapy should also be a very important component of the treatment of the primary symptoms of ADHD, that is, the hyperactivity, impulsivity, and inattention. In Chapter 2 I described how the presence of the primary biological defects of ADHD in infancy must affect the child's earliest development, especially the early development of the infant-parent relationship and of language. I will describe those effects here in a little more detail, in order to explain why psychotherapy can be so helpful for the basic ADHD symptoms.

It is in the context of that earliest relationship that the infant begins to learn to structure his inner experience, to delay response, and to feel assured of being calmed and soothed. He also begins to learn of the separateness between himself and his mother, of the entity that constitutes himself. He needs to experience reassurance and consistency in that relationship. He needs to experience his mother's growing ability to soothe him and meet his needs before he is totally overwhelmed with pro-

Psychotherapy in a Multimodal Treatment Plan 137

longed distress. Only then can he learn to integrate his inner mental states. At first, these are just organismic states of pleasure or distress, but they gradually differentiate into more complex states, with learned associations, such as with the presence or absence of mother's breast or her voice. And gradually these states are integrated into a sense of himself as a unified being, separate from his mother.

The acquisition of language is crucial in these developments. The infant's growing ability to use language gives him a new tool with which to structure his experience and probably affects the way in which memory is recorded. It allows for a richness in mental associations and processes, which rely on the symbolizing nature of language and on the fact that it codes and categorizes experience. Of course, the structure of language must reflect an innate tendency in the human mind to organize, store, and process experience. In fact, modern linguistic science has shown that there is an innate and universal ability to create a grammatical language if the correct early environment is provided. Language is like a sentinel, standing at the gateway of human mental experience, modifying what comes in, structuring what goes on within, and organizing and making communicable what comes out.

Language can only develop in the context of a human relationship. No children who have been left alone as infants and not spoken to have learned to speak (there have been some tragic cases of such "feral" children described). This development of language begins in the earliest days of life, as the infant gazes into his mother's face, as he begins to learn of repeated structured experiences. For example, he soon learns that when he cries out, his mother appears or when he moves his arm, a little hand appears in front of his eyes. As he becomes more mobile, he begins to learn from repeated experience that his actions on the environment can have predictable responses, such as shaking a rattle in his crib to produce a sound he likes. The infant is a scientist, eager to experiment and learn, and this early experience begins to structure his mind, with the help of his mother's response.

From the earliest such explorations and discoveries, his mental experience becomes organized. Important to this organization is the ability to repeat the action and to receive the same response; the ability to pay attention to the details of what is happening; and the calm, soothing sharing of the experience by the mother. These experiences are laying down the structure of language, for they are imposing some order on the world that the infant is beginning to perceive.

This order is enhanced greatly by the naming and symbolizing function of language. At first, the infant babbles and cries, and each sound will bring a different but predictable response from the mother. Soon the mother will begin to provide particular sounds for particular experiences or will respond to the baby's own initiated sound with a differentiated response. For example, when a baby first says "Mama," his mother will respond in a way that will make it clear that this is a special sound to be repeated often, and soon the baby will use it to signify his desire for his mother.

As language develops, other psychological functions also become enhanced and more complex. For example, the ability to structure inner experience linguistically will help the baby learn frustration tolerance and learn to tolerate intense feeling states. This will be associated with a shift toward thought as opposed to action. The overwhelming physiological states of infancy will gradually be replaced by more structured reactions, by organized responses. The infant will gradually develop a larger repertoire of responses, and the enhanced ability to think about oneself and to communicate will allow the infant to move away from impulsive and disorganized responses. It may well be that the early development of effective inner language skills also enhances memory and attentional functions.

But it is clear that many things can interfere with this development, and it follows that this interference will have enormous consequences for later psychological development. Further study is needed into just which biological deficits in ADHD are present at birth. But certainly retrospective reporting suggests that these infants are more irritable and perhaps are hypersensitive, i.e., are subject to more intense and disrupting sensory impressions. This tendency frequently interferes with the calm, alert, and comfortable satiated states that are so important for the early learning and explorations of an infant.

Psychotherapy in a Multimodal Treatment Plan   139

In addition, it appears that when these infants are in a state of physiological arousal—in other words, when they have become fussy, stimulated perhaps by hunger, bodily discomfort, or sensory overload—they are much more resistant to comforting than non-ADHD children. For some reason, probably of a biological nature, their neurophysiological systems don't respond to the usual parenting methods with organization and reduction of arousal level.

For parents, this means their infant is more likely to get upset and will be distressed both more intensively and for longer. Such parents experience the repeated distress of being unable to calm their child, of feeling incompetent or a failure because their baby won't be soothed. Such stress can lead to frustration and anger and even rejection of the baby, which of course can only compound the problem.

For the baby, this state of prolonged hyperarousal and stress means a reduction in the calm, alert states essential to learning. It also means a disruption of the empathic, mirroring bond between mother and child that facilitates the structuring experiences I have spoken about above.

Conversely, some of these infants have a stimulus hunger. Perhaps they need more stimulation to achieve the same degree of arousal, interest, and attention. They may be described as "good" babies, sleepy and quiet. But they may be missing out on the level of focused arousal essential to the kind of learning I have spoken about. As they get older and are more motorically independent, they may seek the more intense stimulation they need by increased motor activity and by an urgent rush from one stimulus to another. This too interferes with the ability to fully benefit from the kind of repeated structuring experiences I have spoken about that take place between an infant and mother in the earliest months.

Whatever the intricate mechanisms may be, I have seen again and again in my practice that ADHD sufferers of all ages have some interference in their ability to use language and thought to tame their inner experiences and to modulate their perceptions and responses to the outside world. As I have explained in answer to the previous question, it is precisely the inner language that psychotherapy begins to strengthen. It is the ADHD sufferer's poor ability to use thought—both to control inner mental states and as an alternative to immediate responsive action—that can be addressed and helped through psychotherapy. Thus, psychotherapy offers the possibility of altering the most profound underlying effects of ADHD.

Frustrated parents often say to their ADHD youngster, "Why don't you think instead of act?" or, "If only you would think before you act!" And yet it's so difficult for that youngster to do precisely that. It is just this difficulty that psychotherapy begins to address.

Behaviorism teaches delaying techniques, such as counting to ten before acting or drawing up a list of alternative actions before taking any one action. Medication offers a chemical restraint to try to slow down reaction. But psychotherapy works by modeling and training through practice experiences in the sessions, where talking and reflecting replace action. It also works by providing a safe, accepting, sympathetic relationship in which the patient can begin to tolerate his inner states and then to name them. Further, it assists the person in developing his own internal language and way of thinking about himself and his feeling states. In this way, those "dangerous" overstimulated states that lead to impulsive action can be replaced by knowable feelings that have a context and a reason for arising and can be reflected upon, understood, and resolved.

The clinical examples that follow show how psychotherapy can perhaps play an important role in healing some of the underlying effects of ADHD. In subsequent chapters, I will talk about how the family and school and other professional helpers, such as remedial education specialists, can support and further the work that is begun in psychotherapy and how all can work together, in a multimodal approach, to make truly lasting changes in the outlook for the ADHD sufferer.

Q: Is it possible for psychotherapy to help preschoolers with ADHD?

A: Yes. With the very youngest children and, of course, with those who do not yet speak, I would work with the mother and child together. Here the goals would include incorporating the mother into the facilitative work with the infant to help the introduction of language, especially complex inner and emotional language. But another goal would be to help the mother learn to find ways of soothing the baby, of maximizing the possibility of calm, alert states in the infant. This would mean educating the mother about the difficulties ADHD is posing for the normal development of her youngster and developing strategies with her to work around those difficulties. Thus, we would be working to maximize the possibility of successful experience between the mother-infant couple.

Once a child is three or four, I recommend that we begin individual sessions in addition to the facilitative work I do with the parents. I will describe the family work in more detail in the next chapter. Let me illustrate this individual work with a preschooler by telling you about Peter's therapy. I have already described Peter in Chapter 2, as an illustration of the manifestions of ADHD in a three- or four-year-old.

Peter, a four-year-old preschooler

I initially saw Peter and his parents on several occasions and soon had a picture of severe ADHD symptoms, worsened by emotional issues in his family and by some traumatic events that had led to increased anxiety in Peter. I also wondered whether there weren't specific learning disabilities that could add to his school problems. So I recommended pediatric neurological examination and neuropsychological testing to complete the assessment. I spoke to his pediatrician about his general medical health, and I spoke to his preschool teacher, who agreed to give me regular reports on his progress in the classroom. I recommended that he begin individual psychotherapy at least once a week, though preferably more often, and that his parents have a counseling session every two weeks. Both due to his young age at the time and due to his parents' strong feelings against Ritalin, I did not recommend medication until several years later. I will here focus on how the individual psychotherapy transpired and in the next chapter talk about my work with Peter's parents and the very important role they played in the multimodal approach to Peter's significant problems.

Peter rapidly became devoted to his weekly sessions, asking

if he could come more often, running from the car to my office and often bringing things from home to show me. At first, his constant activity and loud, nonstop speech made any interventions on my part seem to go unheeded, except when I had to intervene in his activity for safety's sake. When I tried to control his hyperactivity in the office or to talk directly to him about his behavior or feelings, he would become more anxious and often break off from his play and engage in disorganized, wild activity.

I soon learned that if I could structure our sessions so that Peter did not have to lower his activity level, his anxiety level remained lower. This was important because my imposing restraints on his physical activity not only interfered with his ability to discharge anxiety through activity, but also because he experienced my restraints as a disapproving attitude. Not having to constantly restrain him allowed me to be in a more neutral position and allowed him to feel more accepted and respected by me. This enhanced the possibility of my engaging with him and ultimately of being able to use speech in a direct communicative way with him.

So we began having our sessions outside when weather allowed, often walking down to my garden, even to a nearby pond, where he would try to catch frogs. Peter loved nature; therefore, what we saw and found interested him greatly enough for us to be able to speak about it. So here we had a medium, nature, through which we could begin to use language to think about and talk about the immediate experience. This was how we began to slow down the action and begin to convert the impressions into language. Whether it was a frog or plant, a particular vegetable in my garden or the way a tree had blown down, we could speak about our shared perceptions, relate them to other memories and knowledge (of which he had an enormous fund), and gradually relate them to other times and situations in Peter's life.

Often Peter filled our inside meetings with fantastic play, using action figures or Lego vehicles and men to wildly enact plots filled with violence, destruction, chaos, worlds ending, volcanoes erupting, ships sinking, nuclear warfare, and so on. Here, too, it was essential for me not to impose halts on this activity, but rather to enter it with him and to use it as a medium to develop a narrative about our shared here-and-now experience. So I could play along, but my characters would talk about the events and about themselves. I would describe their reactions to what was happening, and I would ask him questions, trying to encourage him to talk about the action too, rather than just enact it.

Gradually, I could discern how the themes of his play reflected his own emotional states and experiences. For example, as his mother's new pregnancy became more obvious and the birth of his second sibling approached, his games were full of space outposts running out of food, of people dying inside spaceships, and of a cruel dictator blowing up the whole world. From meetings with his parents, I knew that his mother's pregnancy had been met with very angry feelings from Peter and that he had adopted many babyish behaviors, trying to get his mother to care for him like a baby, including sucking a pacifier again. In his fantasies in the sessions, he always played a totally invulnerable character who could manage great physical feats and could choose to either save the world or destroy the world. The theme of Mount Vesuvius would often return, and he would describe his great prowess in blowing up volcanoes and rescuing cities.

But at this stage of the therapy, when I tried to relate our talk or play to real events and feelings in his life, he would shut me out, heighten his disruptive activity, and, on occasion, even refuse to come into my office. He could not yet tolerate any awareness of his threatening affects, so as yet I could not use words to describe what I knew about him. However, I could use words to describe our shared experience, and this introduction of language into our games gradually began to play a significant role. Soon he allowed his characters to speak as part of the play. This meant a temporary inhibition of activity while the story of our play was carried along by words, such as the threatening speech his tyrant figure might make to my poor slaves from another galaxy. And gradually he did not seem threatened when I let my characters speak about feelings of fear and loneliness, frustration with their abilities, wishing to be invulnerable, and so on. Gradually I began to step back out of my characters and talk about them with Peter, rather than only speak as if I was one of them. And gradually he began to respond and add his conjectures as to the characters' experiences. However, he would soon always say, "Let's get back to the game!"

It was a long time before Peter and I could use words to talk about *his* emotions about the very important things in *his* life. But already he was responding to the support inherent in our relationship. He was responding to the possibility of a calm situation where he could begin to use talking about his current experience as a way to structure his inner experience and as a way to begin the process of forming a more secure internal narrative of himself.

I remember well the first time he used language to speak of his own state. This was nearly a year after we began working together. One day he raced into my office, impatient to get started, but in a distracted way started jumping on my sofa. Before I said anything, he said, "I'm really hyper today." Unwittingly, he had announced a major shift in his internal abilities. He could now, at least in a rudimentary way, observe something about his state, think about it, label it, and communicate it. In fact, as he made that observation, he climbed down off the sofa, grinned at me, and began to arrange our armies of Lego people and spaceships. It was as though the act of labeling his own state had given him some control over it. I said to him that he had shown me with his action very clearly how he felt and then he had been able to tell me in words. And maybe now that we had a word for that feeling that makes him jump around sometimes, we could start to be detectives about it and see what else we might discover about it. Did he have any ideas just what it might have been that made him hyper today?

Of course, it would have been too much to expect that on that first day he could have articulated just what events had upset him earlier. But this was the beginning of a new way of our working together. For example, a few weeks later, he again arrived in an extremely distracted and hyperactive, impulsive state. As he ran to my office, his mother said angrily to me that she had just announced to him that he would be punished with no TV for the weekend because he had hit his sister that morning. This then gave me the opportunity to suggest to him that perhaps he was "hyper" because he was upset about his mother being angry with him and punishing him. He acknowledged this indirectly by angrily defending himself, accusing his sister of being mean to him. But he did calm down a little. Gradually, over time, these connections we made between his states and possible feelings about real situations gave him more ability to think about his situation and his emotions.

His play remained an important outlet for him, as well as a way of symbolizing some of what he felt. However, as he began to think more about himself as someone with his own continuous story, his impulsivity began to diminish, as did his general activity level, both in the sessions as well as in other situations. He could begin to use his newfound language skills and self-observations to talk about things that were troubling him, like his siblings and their demands on his parents or their taking his toys or breaking up his complex Lego constructions. Other things were much more difficult to talk about, like his sense of humiliation at school or his feeling that other children did not want to be his friends.

Eventually, however, it was possible for me to talk with him about his fears, his sense of vulnerability, his need to believe he was so strong that nothing could possibly hurt him and his fears of his own emotional states and their consequences. When he was in first grade we added Ritalin to his treatment in order to help him be in more control in school. It seemed to help him control the volume of his motor activity and possibly to focus his attention on an academic task. His parents also felt he was often less emotionally unstable and more likely to listen to them when he was medicated. This did help pave the way for academic successes. He was gifted in math and science, and successes in these areas certainly had a needed positive influence on his self-esteem. All of this work went hand in hand with work that his parents did with him at home and his teachers at school, as I will describe further in the coming chapters.

Peter and I worked together for several years, during which time there were many ups and downs in his life. His struggles to be accepted by peers and to develop interests and skills to share with potential friends, his difficulties with his younger siblings, and the increased demands made on him by academic expectations were all part of what we had to deal with. Ideally, the psychotherapeutic work should have continued into his adolescence, but many factors made that impossible. However, other aspects of the multimodal treatment were able to be continued.

The success that we did have in helping Peter develop a way of thinking about his experiences and communicating about them—rather than being forced into unreflective, impulsive, continual action—certainly helped in his beginning to make some friends, and in his family life. His parents were able to continue the work of helping him verbalize, and at the time he left treatment, they were obtaining a computer for him so he could express himself in writing without being hampered by the small motor problems that made handwriting and drawing such arduous tasks for him. Our work in identifying his fears, traumas, and his defensive ways of dealing with these also enhanced his sense that he could trust others and lessened his anxious sense of vulnerability. He seemed more hopeful of success for himself and more willing to expect that relationships could be positive and helpful.

Q: Is psychotherapy really necessary for an older elementary school-age child whose ADHD symptoms are not as severe as Peter's?
A: Yes. Even in the child whose ADHD has not been diagnosed until he or she is well along in grade school, the effects on development, though subtle, have also been widespread. If not addressed, these effects can lead to persistence of ADHD into adulthood, as well as relationship problems throughout life.

I will illustrate this by talking about my treatment of Stephanie, whose symptoms were previously discussed in Chapter 2 with regard to the manifestation of ADHD in a grade-school–age child.

Stephanie, an eight-year-old third-grader

In Chapter 2, I described how Stephanie was a much less severely afflicted case than Peter. She was brought for assessment because her teacher was worried about her tendency to daydream and not pay attention in class. While not a behavior problem, I soon found that she did have some hyperactivity, distractibilty, and attentional problems and already suffered from low self-esteem and an intolerance of her own affect states. These she attempted to control by replacing with a kind of "as if" self. She would fabricate stories about herself and her feelings and focus intensely on the emotions of those about her.

While, for Peter, language became a route for urgent explosive discharge, language for Stephanie became something to swallow whole, to copy and to reproduce with great skill. But her words and demeanor did not truly reflect her authentic inner experience. It was easy for her to talk about feelings in the sessions with me, but they weren't her feelings. So I had to backtrack with her.

We began to play with small doll figures and furniture, each time setting up a large house and continuing a story of a large family of children. Rather than confront her with the falseness of her stories about herself, our play encouraged her to displace these stories onto the characters. Through long sagas that she directed, which included dinosaurs and earthquakes threatening the house, the adoption of many more children, the persistent absence of the father at the "war" and the emergence of one daughter doll who was the heroine, I began to verbalize the possible emotions of the characters. Often these were quite contrary to what she would insist. For example, she asserted that the heroine was not scared of the dinosaur. This then allowed me to talk about how the heroine may be very brave, but almost certainly would feel afraid too. Thus I could talk about what are expectable emotions in certain situations, as well as address the need for defensive denial in the face of fear, or other strong emotions. Giving emotions names and talking about them in the context of our relationship, in which Stephanie felt safe and accepted, was a way of letting her feel that her emotions were also acceptable.

I could direct the play to introduce situations that I knew were akin to her own. Then I would suggest the characters felt certain things that I knew were often stirred in her but remained unrecognized, hidden by her false narrative about herself. When I knew of specific events in her life that had upset her, I would bring them in for discussion, trying to help her to articulate what she truly felt. At first, this often met with more implausible elaborations. At times I would communicate my own reactions to her to try to make our narrative of our shared experience as true as possible.

As she became more willing to apply her language skills to her own emotions and to communicate them, it became essential to begin to talk about and understand the fears that created her anxiety about her own inner states. These had to do with her fantasies about her father, who had died in her infancy; her anger at feeling unable to pull away and be more separate from her mother; her fear of losing her mother; and her feelings of inadequacy in school and socially. But this was a very slow process because of Stephanie's lack of trust in the safety of being aware of her inner states. It was as though she had no confidence in being soothed and as though she feared those around her, and most especially her mother, would be as overwhelmed by her emotions as she was. She attempted to exert rigid control on herself, only finding release in the safety of daydreams and stories. Gradually she learned, in the safety of our sessions, that these inner states could be tolerated, that nothing terrible would happen and that they could be talked about, thought about, and understood.

In addition to her therapy, it was important to find ways of molding Stephanie's environment to her special needs. We wanted to maximize her successes and thus to boost her self-esteem and give her the courage to begin to know herself. To achieve this, I worked closely with her mother and with her teachers. As she entered higher grades, we also began math tutoring because by then her inattention and her visual spatial problems had significantly interfered with her learning basic math concepts.

Q: How does psychotherapy differ with a teenager with ADHD?

A: As I have discussed in earlier chapters, ADHD can impact on the teenager's life in many ways. Sometimes teenagers are diagnosed for the first time when they are in high school. This may be because of significant academic problems, but sometimes may be because of behavioral problems. This may be because teenagers are now more independent of parental guidance and can in a sense get into more trouble than when younger. I would like to illustrate with two examples from my practice: one is Rebecca, and the other is Colin.

Rebecca, a sixteen-year-old high-school student

I have previously described Rebecca, in Chapter 2, as an illustration of the manifestations of ADHD in adolescence. There I described her as a sad teenager who was sent for assessment and treatment by her parents and school guidance counselor due to her chronically low academic performance and her apparent lack of motivation or interest.

In the therapy it was very important to help Rebecca begin to understand the roots of her low self-esteem, of her sense of hopelessness about ever being able to be passionately interested in something and about ever being really good at something. She felt angry and misunderstood, but had no understanding herself of how things had "gone wrong." She had learned to not expect much of herself or of life. But first we were faced with her inarticulateness. She blanked out in the face of intense emotions. She did not understand them, feared that they were a sign of her weakness or craziness, became sleepy and hypoactive, and even went so far as to medicate herself with street drugs. While this was clearly an attempt to be accepted by peers, it was also an expression of her need to numb herself and to substitute an altered state for her own confusing inner states.

Medication was helpful for her, but when I heard of her contacts with drug dealers, I felt she was at risk of being approached to have her Ritalin sold as a street drug, so we changed her medication to Prozac, an antidepressant that also seemed to help with her energy and focus.

Our work was slow, but it was possible to see how the acquisition of an internal story, a way of thinking about her feelings and about how she had arrived at her current situation, began to give Rebecca tools of reflection. We went about this in several ways. At first, she had very little to say: she "did not know what to talk about"; there was "nothing on her mind." Sometimes patients will claim there is nothing on their minds when they are determined not to share their thoughts. This certainly happens often enough with a teenager who feels she has been forced to go to therapy due to "bad behavior." But this was clearly not the case with Rebecca.

In the face of intensely unpleasant inner feelings, she succeeded in blanking out, in not knowing what was happening within her or even what she was reacting to in her external environment. So, to begin with, I had to help her tolerate turning inward enough to even be aware of her thoughts. I needed to communicate unconditional acceptance of her feelings, opinions, and behavior and to help her feel that therapy was a safe and confidential place. It was clear that she did not need me to tell her what was appropriate behavior. Her parents were already angry, frustrated, and making rules and regulations in vain to try to control her. I will describe in the next chapter how I worked with her family.

I asked her many questions and encouraged her to talk about the details of her day. In this way I began to help her recognize reactions and feelings and put them into words. Gradually she could tolerate more difficult affects. She could begin to acknowledge her sense of despair and self-hatred without needing to immediately expunge her consciousness with sleepiness, drugs, or impulsive, self-defeating actions like skipping school or staying out all night. I acted as an objective voice for her with which she could identify and then begin to wonder how and why she came to feel this way. My own acceptance of her and obvious respect for her would stand in contradiction to her self-hatred.

So even a question of mine such as "I wonder why you feel so hateful of yourself?" would introduce the possibility to her that maybe others don't see her as so hateful. Such a question also introduces a mental process, an internal thought-action that can interpose between the unpleasant feeling and some impulsive external action. She was able to become more curious about herself and to begin to put together the story of how her ADHD had affected her. This alleviated her terrible sense of guilt and inadequacy. But maybe just as importantly, having an internal narrative, a way of thinking about herself and of explaining her emotional states to herself, gave her a tool. It helped her tolerate difficult affects long enough to be able to begin to engage with difficult tasks and to develop skills that she did not know she had. She began to do better both academically and socially.

Q: What about an adolescent boy with ADHD who has the serious behavior problem known as conduct disorder or even oppositional defiant disorder? Is psychotherapy applicable in this case?
A: Absolutely. However, it may be much more difficult to engage such a boy in therapy, for he may already be very untrusting of adults. He may seem quite unmotivated and uncooperative, and may need an approach that is very intensive and includes many modes. As I have explained earlier in the book, it is quite possible that severe ADHD can interfere very profoundly with the earliest development of trust and empathy, as well as the ability to understand social and emotional cues and to modulate responses in the interpersonal sphere. Let me illustrate some of these concerns with Colin, a seventeen-year-old boy I worked with and whose symptoms I described in Chapter 2.

Colin, a seventeen-year-old boy

As I described in Chapter 2, Colin was sent to boarding school from overseas by his parents, nominally to place him in a safer environment due to political unrest at home. But it was also clear that they were hoping that the structure of boarding school would help in a long history of academic failure, behavioral problems, and symptoms of ADHD.

Psychotherapy was one part of a very intensive approach to this boy, which included Ritalin, tutoring, and behavioral management at school. In addition, he had regular meetings with his advisor, both to speak about social and behavioral issues and to receive regular feedback from his teachers on his performance. It was a stormy course, and many times his privileges at school were withdrawn.

In the therapy, I confronted his inauthenticity and manipulativeness by trying to convey both basic respect for him and an unwavering interest in the truth, including the truth of his own emotional experience. Often I told him I did not believe what he told me and that I suspected that, in fact, he felt quite differently. I had to be careful to not simply supply him with another story that he could use to outwardly comply with me, yet still keep me at a distance. I also had to be the voice of reality, informing him of my concern for his disregard as to the consequences of his behavior and discussing with him information about his problem given to me by the school. It was a fine line to walk, trying to help him feel worthwhile and accepted, while at the same time letting him know that I would not be fooled and that my interest was in his authenticity and, ultimately, in him knowing as much as possible about himself.

Unfortunately, his behavior and academic performance led to his not being invited back to the same school the following year. However, the therapy and academic remediation had made quite a difference in his motivation, his beginning ability to control his impulsive action, and in his willingness to work more closely with adults who could help him. He transferred to a school that specialized in ADHD and learning disabilities and included psychotherapy, as well as remedial education, as part of its approach. I saw him for several followup sessions after he began at the new school and was very pleased to see the very real changes he had begun to make in all spheres of his functioning.

Q: We have heard that ADHD continues into adulthood. Is it too late to hope that psychotherapy can make real changes in how the person thinks and functions when he or she is already an adult, out of school, and trying to make it in the world?

A: No, it is not too late, and perhaps it is even more essential, because by adulthood so many more layers have been added to the problem. As I have described in Chapter 3, by the time the ADHD sufferer reaches adulthood, they have already experienced repeated failures academically, socially, and personally. They may have suffered consequences of maladaptive behavior problems that have interfered with relationships, school, and jobs. By this time they may feel they can't expect

Psychotherapy in a Multimodal Treatment Plan 153

much out of life for themselves. They may have made limiting decisions and choices based on their low self-esteem and on years of guilt, shame, and self-blame. Or they may be so jaded and angry at the world that they totally externalize all the blame and don't at all perceive the role they play in their ongoing difficulties.

Adults with ADHD often go unrecognized and so don't seek help. Others may suspect it in themselves when they have a child or other family member diagnosed with it. And occasionally an adult may go to a psychiatrist or psychologist for help with depression or anxiety, and only then, and often not at first, will the ADHD be finally diagnosed. I will illustrate such a case with Leslie, whose symptoms and background were first described in Chapter 3.

Leslie, a twenty-eight year-old woman

In Chapter 3, I described how Leslie had wandered, unattached and unhappy, for the ten years since her mother had died. When she came to see me at age twenty-eight, she felt lost, alone, and unloved and had no interests and no sense of direction or commitment. She suffered overwhelming mood states of anguish and anxiety and felt unable to understand why she felt this way. She saw no connection between the moods and events in her life and, in fact, was unable to communicate any cohesive narrative about herself and her life story.

My initial conclusion was that Leslie was severely and chronically depressed. I suspected she had totally repressed her enormous grief at her mother's death and that her wandering over the last ten years represented a numbed searching for her mother or for someone to mother her. I understood her behavior in therapy to indicate not only her severely depressed state, but a wish that all she had to do was sit in my office and show me her anguish and that I would then do the mental work to make her feel better—as though she didn't need to think about herself at all. For her, talking meant showing me her anguished state.

Sometimes her words did not hang together in a logical

progression or in complete ideas. Rather, they seemed to merely demonstrate the intensity of her emotions, like an infant crying and thrashing in distress. This made it very difficult to put together a cohesive history of her life.

I soon realized that her severe difficulty in describing her inner states, as well as her inability to find ways to soothe herself or to modulate her overwhelming affects were part of a total picture that included severe impulsivity, a poor academic record, and a lack of interests. This difficulty with using language to talk about herself went beyond a defensive not knowing to protect herself from painful or conflicting emotions. I was able to see how the kinds of difficulties that ADHD presents to early development could account for many of Leslie's difficulties as an adult. In addition, it became clear she still suffered from anxiety, enormous hyperactivity in the form of restlessness, and severe attentional difficulties and problems with concentration and memory. I confirmed by hunch that she had severe previously undiagnosed ADHD with psychological testing.

I prescribed Ritalin, but Leslie did not find it helpful, partly because she found any physiological awareness of medication in her system made her intolerably anxious. But it may also be that so many of her disturbing symptoms were of the kind that stimulants cannot help. She did receive some help from antidepressants in very small doses. She could not tolerate anything larger.

I began to concentrate on helping her understand the nature of her difficulties, including how they may have accounted for many of her terrible self-esteem problems and difficulties in school. I focused on her inability to describe events in her life or her mood states and began to encourage her to connect her affect states to particular events in her day. I did this by modeling, by questioning, and often by guessing and hypothesizing with her as to what might have upset her. I thus communicated a tireless interest in the details and an unwillingness to be thwarted by her agitated, distressed exclamations of lifelong despair. In this way, she began to learn that it was possible to tolerate these feelings and to think about them. She began to exercise her mental faculties in thinking about herself as she went through her day. As she began to speak about things she did or people she interacted with, she seemed to become more engaged with them.

I maintained an unswerving attitude that things could be talked about and ultimately understood. I tried to impress on Leslie that overwhelming states were really feelings that had been aroused in a context—usually involving feelings about another person, perhaps in the present and often in the past—and that these feeling states could be tolerated and thought about. These feeling states wouldn't destroy her, and in fact, beginning to know what the states were about would ultimately give her a freedom from them. Other helpful aspects of the therapy included the structure our relationship lent to her life, the clarification of her feelings and experiences, and the support and respect she felt from me. In the beginning of therapy, these supports were more significant in helping her than the content of what I said.

I do think these therapeutic processes are similar to what is happening when a mother empathetically soothes an infant, allowing the infant to learn that those states of pain and frustration are manageable, soothable, and have a name. As I have described in Chapter 2, this is precisely one of the earliest developmental steps that is seriously interfered with by ADHD.

Leslie was often overwhelmed by excited states, as well as her despairing states. In these states of excitement, she would suddenly make decisions or act in a way that she later often regretted. These decisions or actions would center around things like buying clothes or choosing a job or an interest. She would passionately insist she had found the answer, only to be despondent by the next day and wonder why on earth she had thought she could ever be interested in that. Her relationships with men were similar. She would fall overwhelmingly in love, only to have her feelings change overnight, leading her to either angrily discard the man or continue in a bitter, dependent way. She would then feel trapped by her need for this person, who she was now convinced was not right for her. To think through her excitement, to try to apply judgment, self-knowledge, and questioning were foreign to her, and she would at first resent my attempts to interpose thought before action, just as she resented my questioning the onset of an intensely despairing mood. If I asked whether something might have happened yesterday to set off the mood, she would angrily retort that I just didn't understand that she had felt this way ever since birth.

She did indeed experience her states as global and permanent and seemed unable to remember that she had felt entirely differently the day before. In a similar manner, I noticed that often she seemed to have no recollection of what had transpired between us when we met the next time, even if it happened to be the next day. It was as though she went through her life totally at the mercy of her mood states, as though she was unaware of her own identity, of her own course through her day, as though one moment was not connected to the next. It was as though she could not learn from one experience and use that learning to inform the next experience.

This was very slow and difficult work. The first outward sign of her improvement was that she was able to begin an interest, which she turned into a business that rapidly became rather successful. It was a terrible struggle for her, however, and as her business became more successful and grew, the demands on her emotionally, organizationally, and cognitively were at times overwhelming. It became clear that her true talents lay on the entrepreneurial, creative side. However, the day-to-day running of her business—the handling of bookkeeping, sorting out problems with clients and dealing with multiple problems and complicated issues, often requiring the assimilation of enormous amounts of information at one time—was incredibly stressful for her.

Improvement in the interpersonal sphere was slower in coming. Here she was not only troubled by her cognitive difficulties and attentional problems, but also by her poor self-esteem, her longing to be mothered, her intolerance of painful affects, and her need to act rather than to feel or talk. All these interfered with her ability to sustain intimacy. Again the approach in therapy was to slowly help her tolerate the painful loneliness and her fear of rejection so that she could talk about her experiences and begin to understand them. I sometimes referred to her experience of her relationship with me to illustrate some of the important issues in her interactions. Often I encouraged her to speak of her family and childhood, to try to put into a historical context some of her feelings and fears. This was very important in order to show her how often she blindly repeated experiences from the past in her present life.

As she became better able to tolerate and think about her feeling states, to postpone action and to use internal language to reflect, it became possible for her to begin to explore her own history and to understand more fully some of her experiences. Once again we began to look at her experience of her mother's illness and death and how she had blocked off her awareness of grief and anger. As she remembered with sympathy her aloneness and neediness in the years after her mother's death, she could begin to integrate the sadness and loss. We explored how she continued to fear attachment due to a conviction that she would lose the person she loved. She also began to talk of her own conviction that she would die young.

This was a far cry from her initial sessions, filled with crying and anguished activity. But those states often returned, when she was particularly upset about something. However, we could now more quickly contain them through talking about them and putting them in some understandable context. It was clear that our work would have to continue for a long time. She would continue to need my practical interventions to help her sort out the reality of her everyday experience and sometimes to actually help her problem-solve and study practical situations she was faced with. Our goals were to eventually give her confidence in herself and her own coping skills and an internal continuous narrative that included an understanding of her own strengths and weaknesses and an historical understanding of how these came to be. This she could then use as her base to integrate and to cope with new experiences.

SEVEN

The Family's Role

Medication, psychotherapy, a healthful diet, and behavior modification are all essential components of a multimodal approach to the management of ADHD. However, none of these modalities can be fully effective if the patient's family isn't behind him 100 percent in his struggle to live a normal life.

Adults with ADHD often have long-standing family difficulties. If married, their ADHD symptoms may well lead to frustration, anger, blaming, and poor communication in the marriage. Frequently, they become less than effective parents, and their impulsivity, short fuse, and emotional liability may lead them to be inconsistent, punitive, and even violent with their children. It is essential that any treatment approach to the adult sufferer include the education of his family about his condition and their involvement in helping to change some of the patterns of behavior and communication within the family.

It is just as vitally important that the family of an ADHD child be involved in his treatment. Parents of a child with ADHD must feel empowered to become their child's strongest advocates. Once a thorough workup confirms a diagnosis of ADHD, parents must become superbly educated consumers, capable of taking charge of their child's treatment, education, and other necessary support systems.

Various professionals in the child's life may focus on the need to modify the child to better fit into his environment, and drug therapy may be the mainstay to this approach. But it's also important for the child's parents to focus on the need to sometimes modify both the home and school environments to better suit the child. This may involve the following.

1. Insisting on a thorough workup and diagnosis and gathering all the information they can find from all sources regarding their child.
2. Becoming a vigilant and energetic supporter of their child in the community, which may mean making a fuss at school and elsewhere. It may also mean taking a hard stand against their insurance carrier or HMO to guarantee coverage of the medical care their child will require. This can be extremely difficult because managed care companies often set strict limits, such as one medication visit every six weeks, which many providers erroneously claim is the only care necessary for attention deficit hyperactivity disorder.
3. Having the insight to question the emotional climate at home—how the family works together, what stresses may impact on the ADHD child, how the siblings interact, the state of the parents' marriage, the consistency of their discipline, the kinds of role models they provide and so on.

In my practice, I usually find it necessary to work closely with families of ADHD children in helping them understand their child's difficulties and the impact the syndrome can have on the lives of every family member.

The families of adults with ADHD must also strive to achieve a sense of empowerment as they work to help the patient deal with his condition. A great deal of understanding and support is essential here, especially in the first few weeks following a clinical diagnosis. It's often difficult for the patient to come to terms with his disorder and even more difficult for his family. Everyone involved must work extra hard to help the patient make the necessary adjustments.

In this chapter, we will discuss the family's role in the management of ADHD, the importance of parent support organizations and common mistakes that families make in dealing or not dealing with attention deficit hyperactivity disorder.

Q: Our thirteen-year-old son was recently diagnosed with attention deficit hyperactivity disorder, and we're stunned and overwhelmed at how this is impacting us as a family. Could you give us some insight into what we should expect?

A: A diagnosis of ADHD can be both a blessing and a curse. The blessing is finally knowing for certain just what has been affecting your son—and that it can be managed. The curse, many parents have found, is trying to cope with this diagnosis as a family unit; struggling to bring your son's condition under control through medication and other modalities, and dealing with the ignorant and uninformed at school, in the community, and elsewhere. It can be a grueling, exhausting, and demanding job, but at least you'll have the comfort of knowing your son's future will be brighter because of your hard work and loving efforts.

As I'm sure you've realized by now, the family's role in the management of ADHD covers many areas. When I first meet with the parents of a child with ADHD or with an adult with ADHD and his family, there are two immediate agenda items. One is to educate the family about ADHD. The other is to begin to examine the way the family operates. This is both to ascertain how much the ADHD sufferer's problems have impinged on the family and to what degree family problems are making things worse for the ADHD sufferer.

Educating the family about ADHD is extremely important. There are so many misconceptions about it. A full understanding of the underlying disorder and how it has impinged on their child's life and development from his earliest infancy is essential to empowering parents to be the best advocates for their child. Understanding can also help families to not lay needless blame on their child or themselves, but rather to begin to see the layers of the disorder, how they interact with all aspects of the sufferer's environment, and how to best plan a therapeutic approach.

In these early meetings, I try to review all aspects of the

child's life and the impact his disorder has had on others. In working with your ADHD specialist, you should be as open and straightforward as you can regarding the feelings you have toward your son (both good and bad), how your family life and relationships have impinged on your son and perhaps contributed to some of his difficulties and how his ADHD has affected your family's life up to that point.

This can take a great deal of determination because very often the strongest emotions felt by the parents of an ADHD child are guilt and anger: guilt over the thought that their child's problems may have been caused by something they did or did not do as parents and anger at the way their child's bizarre behavior has upset or adversely affected their family's well-being.

By talking with a counselor or specialist at length and from the bottom of your heart, you will learn how to come to terms with these overwhelming emotions, how to keep your family on track, and how to facilitate your child's journey toward wellness. There will be tremendous ups and downs, but always remember—you're not in this alone.

My third agenda in meeting with the family is to develop the multimodal treatment plan. It is absolutely essential that parents of children with ADHD be instrumental in planning this with the specialist. This is not a matter of a simple prescription. It is essential to gain as much information as possible as to the child's functioning in the various aspects of his life and to then design the treatment strategies according to that child's particular needs. Many of the treatments are going to need very close supervision by the parents, particularly the medication and behavioral strategies to be implemented at home. The parents are also going to be responsible for arranging tutoring or therapy appointments for their child, transporting him, regular conferencing with their child's teachers, and so on.

Q: Is psychotherapy always a part of the management of attention deficit hyperactivity disorder?

A: Unfortunately, psychotherapy has often not been part of the management of ADHD. I have explained in the previous chapter why I think some form of psychotherapy should almost always be an integral part of the multimodal treatment plan. Very often, I will recommend family therapy, either in addition to individual therapy, or by itself, as a way of facilitating the well-being of the ADHD sufferer and his family.

Very often, family therapy is recommended when there are detrimental family issues to be examined, such as poor communication, or when it's obvious that family members need to reexamine how they live together as a unit. Through regular meetings, a therapist can see how the family operates, how the children relate to each parent, how the parents relate to each other, and how various patterns have developed.

In my practice, I've found that some of the most common family problems include sibling rivalry, blame-placing, tension between parents, and parents taking sides with one child against the others. Sometimes these issues are independent of the ADHD, whereas sometimes they may be secondary to the long-term stresses the ADHD has placed on the family's functioning. Regardless of etiology, the ADHD always further exacerbates family tensions or maladaptive patterns.

Once a therapist has had a chance to spend time with the family of an ADHD sufferer and see how family members interact, she can pinpoint problem patterns and suggest ways to relate and communicate that are more constructive for both the family and the ADHD patient. The methods a family therapist may use include clarifying the troubled patterns, confronting family members as they fall into old patterns, and interpreting interactions and behaviors. The therapist aims to help the family members to improve communication with each other, to step outside the repeated behavior and communication patterns, and to develop new strategies. This may be done by role-playing, by teaching specific negotiation techniques, and by direct intervention and suggestion by the therapist when impasses are reached. As much as possible, the therapist becomes a neutral advocate for the family system. She will work to help family members understand each other's point of view better and will try to correct misunderstandings and misinterpretations. Most especially, she will interpret and explain how the family has come to react to and even use the ADHD sufferer's symptoms to express family tensions.

I will illustrate this with an example from my practice.

Philip, a thirty-eight-year-old man

Philip called me for an appointment for himself and his wife, Audrey, saying it was urgent, things were very bad between them and he feared their marriage was about to break up. When I met them, they sat far apart on the sofa, and at first, Audrey let Philip do all the talking. In fact, she said, she didn't see that there was much hope in coming to talk to me, since she had been asking him to change for years and things had just gotten worse; he never seemed to understand or listen.

They had been married twelve years and had a nine-year-old daughter. Their marital tension had led to Philip staying away from the family as much as possible, his business giving him plenty of excuses for long hours and frequent business trips. In fact, as he had become more successful, his business required more and more time. Audrey explained that this was partly because he ran it in such a disorganized way, there were constant crises he was having to spend hours, days, or weeks to sort out. Often he had to undo harmful actions or business decisions he had made. "He's the creative, entrepreneurial type, but hopeless at following through. He's just impossible to live with. It's like having another child in the house."

Philip shrugged his shoulders, not disagreeing with her complaints. He turned to me and said, "You see. That's all she does, complain about me. And she gets our daughter to join in. Sometimes I don't even want to come home. I feel they don't want me there. It doesn't even feel like it's my home. I just pay the bills."

Things had obviously gone pretty far by the time they came for help. But I decided to proceed with some marital therapy even as I further investigated Philip for the possibility of ADHD. Psychological testing in fact showed significant attention problems and distractibility, and when I met with him individually to take a careful history of his childhood and school experiences, it became clear that he had long-standing, previously undiagnosed severe ADHD.

The first task for the therapy was to help both Philip and Audrey understand the impact his ADHD had on their lives. This required educating them as to just what the syndrome was. We discussed it at length, and I recommended some reading. Then we began to look at the behavior patterns in the home and to understand how the ADHD was involved. At first, Audrey was reluctant to accept that Philip wasn't in control of his behavior. She felt he was "copping out" and it was just another example of his being passive and not contributing more actively to family life. She was so angry that it was very difficult for her to empathize with his difficulties.

She spoke of how rejected she had felt when he seemed to ignore her requests and tune her out. As she cried, she talked about how she had hoped he would be someone who could nurture her and how, instead, she had ended up running the household completely and taking care of him as though he were a child. Once again she was caring for everybody, just as, in her own family, she had had to raise her younger siblings. Her mother had abandoned the family when Audrey was thirteen, leaving an overwhelmed husband and three children.

I interpreted her feelings toward his ADHD problems to be just like the lack of nurturing and love she had felt as a child. I added that maybe some of the anger she had felt at her parents and had never been able to express had found a route of expression in her marriage. Maybe, in a way, Philip was taking the rap for her parents. She agreed with this. And when Philip began to talk about how he feared his constant feelings of failure and frustration had made him opt out and tune out so much of the time and how badly he felt about how that had hurt Audrey, I could see that they were on their way to a new way of communicating.

Philip decided he was willing to attempt a trial of Ritalin therapy, and they decided to work together with me to develop some problem-solving strategies on the home front. They also decided to bring their daughter to two meetings so that I could help them explain to her about ADHD and how it had affected her father and help her begin to verbalize to her parents her frustrations and anxiety about the tensions at home.

Q: I'm intrigued by the many different kinds of patterns that can develop within an ADHD family unit. Could you elaborate on this concept?

A: Every family, no matter how large or small, develops relationship patterns. In healthy, functional families, these patterns work to the advantage of the individual as well as the family unit. The concept of "self" is emphasized, especially with children, but everyone works toward the success and happiness of the family group. Love and nurturing are strong bonding agents.

In families with an ADHD child, however, a different set of patterns may occur—especially if the child's behavior is extremely disruptive or hurtful. Many of these coping patterns are detrimental to all concerned, but they've become so well established that no one really notices. It's just life as usual.

One of the most common patterns is that of the ADHD child as scapegoat. Everything that goes wrong within the family is blamed on the ADHD child, and gradually the family unit starts to gang up on him at every opportunity because they simply don't know how to cope with his disorder. The ADHD child, feeling abandoned and unfairly targeted, frequently fights back with even more aggressive and disruptive behavior, causing the cycle to worsen.

Another common pattern is for parents to ignore their healthy children and spend all their time and attention on the ADHD child. This can create tremendous feelings of jealousy and rage among the normal children, who come to hate their ADHD sibling because he seems to get love and attention simply by being bad.

It's also common for the brothers and sisters of an ADHD child to feel that the disorder is merely an excuse for their ADHD sibling to slack off and not carry his weight within the family. This is understandable, since there are no outward signs of ADHD, as there are with many other disorders. The child looks completely normal, but behaves badly, and Mom and Dad don't seem to mind. This is often a difficult situation for children to comprehend, and it's made worse when their parents dote on the ADHD child without giving equal love and attention to the others.

Detrimental patterns can also develop between the parents of an ADHD child. Often parents find themselves in frequent fights because one wants to indulge the ADHD child, while the other feels that extreme discipline is the answer. It's also common for one parent to become completely enveloped in the whole ADHD scenario, while the other ignores it entirely.

None of these patterns is good for the family, and certainly they do nothing to help the ADHD child get better. But as mentioned earlier, these patterns often develop so slowly and insidiously that the family isn't even aware of them until they're pointed out by a therapist. Not surprisingly, these patterns are very difficult to break. It takes a lot of commitment, patience, and love to move from dysfunction to a healthy and productive family union.

Q: How can we as a family make sure that we don't fall into these harmful patterns?
A: One very important step is education. Every member of the family should know what attention deficit hyperactivity disorder is, how it manifests itself, how it can be controlled—and that it's no one's fault. Children who understand that their brother or sister is the victim of a very real but invisible medical condition will almost certainly be more understanding when problems arise. In addition, education is essential if parents are to join forces for the well-being of their ADHD child and themselves.

It's also vitally important that parents spend equal time with all of their children. The needs of an ADHD child can be very demanding, but for every hour you spend with him, an hour should be scheduled with your other children. In this way, no one feels ignored or unloved, and your healthy children will be less likely to feel jealous or angry toward their ADHD sibling.

Finally, if you feel your family is starting to develop unhealthy patterns, consult a therapist—and listen to her. No one likes to have a mirror held up to them, but it's a therapist's job to notice patterns and try to correct them. What you're told may be painful, but it's also the first step toward recovery.

Q: How can I find an ADHD specialist in my area?
A: The best place to start is with your child's pediatrician. If he's not well versed in the management of ADHD himself, he

may be able to put you in touch with a qualified child psychiatrist or other ADHD expert. Another option is to contact one of the many support groups and referral organizations listed in the back of this book. It's their job to put the parents of ADHD children in touch with specialists who can help them.

If you live near a large medical school with a department of psychiatry, call and ask for a recommendation. Or consider a central agency, such as the American Psychiatric Association or the Academy of Child Psychiatry, for a local referral.

However, keep in mind that if you have insurance, your carrier may require a referral from your primary physician before it will pay for treatment by a specialist.

Q: You mentioned the need for parents to become strong advocates for their ADHD children. One area in which I'd like to help my ADHD daughter a bit more is the social arena. She desperately wants to make and keep friends, but her behavior makes this difficult. How can I help?

A: Most normal children make friends by getting involved in school life. They learn to negotiate their way through the school culture by meeting with teachers, discovering support systems with peers, and finding gratification through academics or sports.

However, this scene can be a source of deep frustration and depression for youngsters with attention deficit hyperactivity disorder. They want desperately to be a part of their peer group, but their inattention, hyperactivity, aggressiveness, and immaturity can be off-putting. Their peers find them strange or frightening and want nothing to do with them. As a result, ADHD youngsters are often the butt of cruel jokes and taunts, which only compounds their poor self-esteem.

Adding to the problem is the fact that children with ADHD are frequently subjected to difficult impulses and feelings they don't know how to modulate, and they often have trouble reading social cues. There may also be an overpowering need for impulsive action and a difficulty in focusing attention, all of which makes it hard for them to succeed on a play date. However, play dates are important because they are a way of learning how to deal with people and manage in the world later in life.

Parents can help arrange friendships for their ADHD children, but it must be done delicately and sensitively. The first step is to look at the lay of the land in terms of your young child's peer group. Look for a child who might be sympathetic in playing with your child, then facilitate their interaction. Invite the child over for a play date, and be part of it. Be watchful for your child's need to change activities, and take quick control so that the other child doesn't feel disrupted. If you notice that your child is becoming restless or aggressive, change the venue. Go out for ice cream, or take the children to the beach or a park, where they can run around to their hearts' content.

Of course, if you're dealing with a child of preteen or teen age, parental involvement must be done even more sensitively. Obviously, you can't call up schoolmates and make a play date for your teenage daughter, but there are other ways to facilitate peer experience. Go out of your way to take your child wherever her schoolmates enjoy hanging out, for example, or invite others over for dinner and perhaps a movie. And while school is a very good place to find potential friends for your child, don't forget church groups and other social environments.

It may also help to "coach" your ADHD child on certain essential social skills, such as making eye contact when talking with someone, letting someone finish talking before speaking, respecting physical boundaries (i.e., not hugging or touching everyone they meet), interpreting body language, initiating a conversation and, perhaps most important of all, coping with rejection. For most of us, these skills are just second nature. Strangers become friends with very little effort. But social skills can be a foreign language to children with ADHD. Coaching them now will enhance their chances of making friends later on.

All of this requires involvement, diligence, and a major investment in time. It can be very hard to maintain, especially if you have other children—but the payoff, in terms of your child's self-esteem and emotional growth, can be spectacular.

Q: I know it's important that I talk to my son about his ADHD, his emotions, and behavior, but this is usually easier said than done. He doesn't reveal much, and when he does open up, what he says doesn't make much sense. Do you have any advice?

A: One of the biggest difficulties ADHD children face is being able to articulate, to themselves and others, their emotions and feelings. They have trouble talking about themselves and their problems, which is why they often have catastrophic reactions. They don't have a way of thinking through and analyzing things when under pressure or anxiety.

One of the best things parents can do is continue the work started in therapy—set specific times when the child is encouraged to discuss his emotions and experiences. It's best to do this during calm periods, when a child is better able to verbalize his feelings and thoughts. Avoid extended conversations when the child is upset or distressed.

Chat periods may require a lot of patience on your part. Many children with ADHD have trouble organizing their thoughts internally and linguistically and have equal difficulty telling a story from beginning to end in a coherent way. Regular relaxed and informal periods of conversation will help them do this.

For best results, start simply. One excellent way to stimulate conversation is to watch a movie or read a book together and then talk about it. Ask questions about a character's feelings and emotions, and use that as a springboard to talk about what your child may be feeling. The goal of all this is to help your child develop an internal language, to develop ways of thinking about himself and his experiences, and to begin to see himself and others more objectively. These skills will then enable your child to begin to think before acting, to control his impulsivity, and to use insight and language to develop better coping skills. Once the door to communication is open, it can have a dramatic impact on how your child feels about himself, his condition, and the world around him.

Q: In what ways can I be my child's advocate at school? After I drop her off each day, what more

The Family's Role

can I do to ensure that she's getting all she should from her teacher and the school system in general?

A: Foremost, you must educate your child's teachers and other school officials regarding your child's special needs as dictated by her ADHD. Very often, teachers have had no experience with ADHD youngsters and are unsure how to handle the various problems that can result. In addition, they may be unfamiliar with the different ways that ADHD children can be taught for maximum learning. It's your job, as a parent, to supply information and materials about ADHD and to ensure that your child's teachers understand why she behaves (or misbehaves) the way she does.

You may encounter difficulties within the school system itself. Many schools are unwilling to offer individualized schooling for children unable to handle a mainstream program. They feel that bringing in children with special needs will lower the school's academic record or adversely affect the more normal students in a classroom. Again, it's up to you to inform the uninformed and ensure that your child receives the education to which she is entitled. Very often, a letter or phone call from your ADHD specialist can help educate school officials about how they can best approach those children who have it. Be courageous, and don't settle for a simple no, especially if you feel you're being railroaded by school officials who simply don't want to supply the extra effort your child may require.

Sometimes it's worth it to fight the system; other times it's better for all concerned if you withdraw your child and place her in another school better suited to her special needs. That's a decision only you can make. Turn to Chapter 8 for a more in-depth look at the school's role in helping youngsters with ADHD.

Q: I want to make sure that my husband and I do everything we can for our ten-year-old ADHD son, and I feel the best way to do this is to learn from others who have been there before us. With that in mind, what are the most common

mistakes made by the parents of children with this condition?

A: From my experience, I'd have to say the most common mistake is not dealing with the disorder after it's been diagnosed. In most cases, this results from not taking the time to understand the disorder, how it affects a family, and how it can be managed. The more parents educate themselves and understand the condition, the better equipped they are to become advocates for their child.

Sadly, some parents dismiss their ADHD child by believing that the problem is the child's temperament and that there's nothing they can do about it. Rather than invest time and money in trying to bring the condition under control, they focus their attentions on the children who do not have ADHD. There is a kind of fatalistic feeling in the face of the difficulties being posed, but it's important that you always remember that ADHD can be controlled and that most children who have it can grow up to be normal, healthy adults. Think of it this way: If your child had diabetes and required insulin shots and a special diet, you would meet these special needs. It would be a huge commitment, but you would do it for the health and well-being of your child. It's exactly the same with ADHD.

Another common mistake made by the parents of ADHD children is assuming that the diagnosis explains everything. These parents use it as an excuse for their insensitivity to the complexities of the child's life. They blame everything on ADHD and believe that Ritalin will take care of it. They don't get more deeply involved in the disorder and its impact, and that can cause big problems.

One reason for this is guilt—parents feel responsible for their child's problem. Receiving a diagnosis of ADHD may offer some relief, but it can also close off further inquiry of the child's experiences. The disorder has impacted on the child's emotional, academic, and social development, but the parents don't get a true sense of what has occurred.

This can be especially problematic if a child has difficulty communicating his emotions, which can be overwhelming and very confusing. His parents, believing all his problems are ADHD-related and easily solved with Ritalin, make no effort to answer the child's emotional needs. It must always be re-

The Family's Role

membered that Ritalin is only part of the solution to managing ADHD.

Another common mistake among families with an ADHD child is poor communication in relation to the disorder. Attention deficit hyperactivity disorder is too quickly blamed for strange or disruptive behavior, and parents don't stop to think that there may be other causes.

Children may jump up and down and scream because something is genuinely wrong, not because they have ADHD. Parents must remain alert to the specificity of a new situation and not assume that everything is related to the syndrome. Something traumatic may have occurred that requires parental compassion and understanding, not a stock answer of "It's only the ADHD."

A good example of this is Rebecca, discussed in Chapters 2 and 6. Rebecca's parents and their teenage daughter had become estranged and had very little understanding or empathy for each other. Her parents were willing to consider that ADHD was to blame for all this. However, they did not see the complex family problems that had interwoven to make their daughter lose faith that they had her interests in mind or that they could help her.

Rebecca's father was frustrated with her apparent lack of motivation and poor grades. His own difficulties in his professional life and his sense of failure in not meeting his own ambitions became subsumed under his angry frustration with Rebecca's lack of success. Similarly, his growing alcoholism and difficulties in his relationship with his wife became hidden behind the angry family arguments about Rebecca's latest transgressions. Family meetings with Rebecca's parents and family meetings that included Rebecca were invariably oriented around the latest crisis, and I was cast, by the parents, in the role of attempting to bring Rebecca under control with medications and strict rules.

But the more her parents tried to control her, the worse the situation became. Despite screaming fights at home, which occasionally became physical, Rebecca would leave the house without permission and sometimes stay out all night. Sometimes she did not go to school for days at a time. She had terribly low self-esteem, felt unattractive and unlovable, and was despairing about her father's disapproval of her. All of these factors pushed her into the wrong social cliques, staying out at night, and experimenting with drugs and sexually.

It soon became clear that to work with Rebecca in sessions with her parents was counterproductive, due to their insistence in turning the sessions into accusations and attempts to control her. I began to meet with Rebecca individually in psychotherapy and continued to meet with her parents. They would not come in regularly, but only around big crises. However, I began to use those sessions to try to get them to look at some of the other family and personal issues that were interacting with Rebecca's problems and were resulting in their loss of empathy for Rebecca and the breakdown in communication. Eventually they were able to see that there were significant issues in the family that needed addressing, including the role of the father's alcoholism, and they agreed to begin regularly scheduled sessions with a couples therapist I referred them to.

The lessening of the scapegoating of Rebecca had immediate beneficial effects for her. She began to feel some hope that she could buckle down and catch up academically and try to find friends who were not on drugs.

Q: Several friends have told my wife and I that we should join an ADHD parent support group. Are they really helpful?

A: Support groups are an excellent way of acquiring essential information regarding the management of ADHD, especially for parents who do not have easy access to an ADHD specialist.

Most support groups are composed of parents who have experienced the nightmare of ADHD and are anxious to help other parents in a similar situation. Many times, such groups also provide literature and other materials that may not be readily available within the community.

Because the family's role of helping a child with ADHD is central and ongoing, parents can benefit greatly from other families' mistakes and successes. Just hearing the details of how others deal with day-to-day life can be indispensable in developing new and effective ways of coping with the myriad factors of ADHD.

Support groups are also a great way to come to terms with certain emotions. If parents feel guilty, for example, they may respond to that emotion in ways that are not best for themselves or their child. They may become withdrawn or project their guilt onto their child. They may become depressed and anxious. Having others to talk to can make parents realize that they are not alone and that difficulties similar to theirs are shared by other parents. All of this can help parents become more effective in the management of their child's ADHD.

Q: Our insurance carrier is giving us a hard time regarding the medications and doctor visits recommended since our daughter was diagnosed with ADHD. It's as if they don't consider ADHD a real medical condition.

A: The insurance industry doesn't cover mental health very well at all, so I'm not surprised by the trouble that you've been experiencing. It's also undeserved, considering that ADHD is one of the most commonly diagnosed mental disorders in childhood and that it's recognized by the American Psychiatric Association.

It might make things a little easier for you if your primary care physician wrote a letter to your insurance carrier explaining the importance of a referral to an ADHD specialist, who will prescribe a specific treatment plan. Very often the insurance problems experienced by the parents of ADHD children result from incomplete medical information or from going against the rules established by the insurance carrier.

Keep in mind, however, that no matter what you do, you probably won't get full coverage. Many aspects of your daughter's treatment will be covered under your plan, but very few insurance companies pay 100 percent when it comes to ADHD.

The only other advice I can give you is to work closely with your physician and take a firm stand with your insurance company if it doesn't comply. If your company continues to refuse coverage and it has an arbitration board, have your physician supply the arbiter with all pertinent information regarding your daughter's medical needs. And if you're in an ADHD support group, ask other members how they've approached the insurance situation.

Q: My family is rather large, with lots of aunts, uncles, and cousins spread across the country. Is it necessary to tell everyone that my daughter has ADHD?

A: What goes on in your household is no one's business but your own. However, it might be a good idea to tell your immediate family, including parents, grandparents and close aunts and uncles, because they'll probably find out anyway. Besides, hiding the fact that your daughter has ADHD makes it sound shameful, which it isn't, nor is the fact that she takes medication for her condition. If your daughter had diabetes, would you hide the fact that she had to take insulin?

There's no need to send out a newsletter regarding your daughter's condition but, similarly, there's no need to treat it like a deep, dark secret. As mentioned earlier, education is an important part of the multimodal approach to management. By being honest and open, you just might be opening the door for another family member with ADHD to get the treatment he or she needs.

Q: My wife and I are trying very hard to help our son manage his ADHD, but he seldom listens to us. It's as if he doesn't trust what we tell him simply because we're his family. Any suggestions?

A: Young people with ADHD often refuse to listen to advice from family members because they don't feel the advice has merit. You're just Dad, not a doctor, so your son places little trust in your counsel, no matter how sound.

One answer is to solicit the help of an outsider whom your son trusts, such as your primary physician, ADHD specialist, or therapist. Have this person echo the advice you've been trying to offer. After a while, your son will realize that you really do know what you're talking about and will listen to you more closely.

It is very important to let a teenager feel he has some autonomy and control. He is very vulnerable to feeling incompetent and humiliated in relation to his parents. This is especially so for boys with their fathers. Hence, perhaps there are ways you can find to offer advice where it seems to come from a joint effort, rather than from a position that you know best. When there is some problem that you would like to help him with, try brainstorming *with* him. Let him know that you think he can probably come up with a good solution himself and that you would like to work with him to find solutions. Similarly, he should definitely be part of the planning of his multimodal treatment plan, and be present at conferences with the ADHD specialist.

Don't take this situation too personally. There's not a teenager alive who isn't convinced his parents are clueless when it comes to certain matters. But as he matures, he may come to realize that your experience has tremendous value.

Q: How do I control the anger I sometimes feel toward my nine-year-old son? He's a good kid, and I love him dearly, but sometimes I become so angry at his behavior that I have to leave the room to keep myself from lashing out. Is this common among parents of ADHD children?

A: Parents, despite the tremendous love they feel for their children, are only human, and they tend to react in very human ways. Anger is a common and understandable reaction to a child's chronically disruptive behavior, so don't punish yourself for your feelings.

Appreciate the positive side of the situation, which is that you know to leave the room before lashing out at your son. You understand that his behavior is beyond his control, caused by his ADHD; he's not a bad child any more than you're a bad parent. Spanking or striking him will not change his behavior; it'll only increase his frustration and anger and end up making you feel guilty.

If your son has been receiving a stimulant medication for his condition but his behavior still has not improved, he might need a medication adjustment. It could simply be that his dosage is not high enough. Consult your doctor or ADHD specialist, and ask him about this concern. If your son is receiving the correct dosage, it might be time for some behavioral therapy. See Chapter 5 for some helpful tips.

Make sure you discuss your bouts of anger with your spouse and your son's ADHD specialist. It could be that you're trying to carry too heavy a burden and that it's time to delegate some responsibility to other family members.

Therapy may also be of help, especially if your bouts of anger are becoming increasingly frequent or they're having a detrimental effect on your relationship with your ADHD son and other family members. A qualified psychotherapist can help you come to terms with these feelings and offer effective coping strategies. Family therapy may also help to change some of the patterns of family interaction that result in your anger.

Q: I never know what's going to set off my fourteen-year-old son, who was diagnosed with ADHD four years ago. Every day it's something different. What are the most common causes of conflict in an ADHD family?

A: ADHD specialists typically call these conflict triggers "crisis points," and they're as individual as the people who have ADHD. Some children have only one or two, while others seem to have a dozen.

From my experience, the most common areas to provoke family conflict include getting dressed and ready on time, completing schoolwork, completing homework, doing chores, keeping track of school materials, playing indoors, sitting still for meals, relating to siblings, taking a bath, and getting ready for bed. Not surprisingly, some children experience several different crisis points within each of the descriptions mentioned above. In most cases, the problems can be boiled down to the three primary manifestations of ADHD: inattention, impulsivity, and hyperactivity.

Q: Our thirteen-year-old son has absolutely no interest in extracurricular sports, which is a major disappointment to my husband, who was a jock in high school. Is there any way we can get our son interested in these endeavors?

A: Youngsters with ADHD typically don't do well in team sports because of their disorder. Most have trouble concentrating during the course of a game, and their chronic impulsivity and hyperactivity makes it difficult for them to wait their turn. In addition, many children with ADHD have balance and control problems that make them clumsy and unskilled on the playing field.

However, many find that they enjoy individual athletic endeavors in which there is a lot of one-on-one interaction between student and instructor, such as karate, judo, tai chi, or dance. Better yet, there is less competition in activities such as these, so the child can experience greater personal success. Ask your son if any of these activities appeal to him, but don't push him if he appears uninterested.

Exercise in general can be very helpful to the ADHD sufferer, so it is a good idea to encourage it. However, it does not have to be an organized sport at all. An ideal way for a family to be together with their ADHD child is through some active pursuit, such as hiking, bike riding, playing ball in the yard, and so on. So encourage your husband to engage in physical activities with your son. Just try to remove the competitive aspect. Walking, running, or swimming together could help cement a close understanding between them that will be enormously important for your son.

Q: Our eight-year-old daughter has mild ADHD and has responded very well to medication. Our biggest problem is getting her to follow our instructions and to do what we ask of her. Any suggestions?

A: One of the most common mistakes made by the parents of ADHD children is phrasing instructions as a question rather than as a statement. For example, you might ask your daughter, "Is your homework done?" when you really mean, "It's time to do your homework." Phrasing statements in a question offers a child too many options and doesn't clearly state what you want her to do.

It's also a good idea to look your daughter directly in the eyes when you're telling her something. This helps keep her focused on you and what you want her to do. If you're unsure she's listening, have her recite the instructions back to you two or three times until you're satisfied.

In addition, be sure that the requests you make of your daughter are within her capabilities. Too often parents ask an ADHD child to perform a task that is completely beyond their skill level. The result: more frustration and anger for both of you.

It may be helpful to consider some behavioral strategies, such as outlined in Chapter 5. In these, the family often plays the most crucial role. It is at home that so much behavioral learning must take place, and only the parents can control the child's environment enough to allow a behavioral modification plan to be carried through. A simple chart with expectable behaviors may be the way to begin, with a supply of rewards or tokens, such as stickers, which will earn a reward when accumulated. Young children often love participating in these reward charts.

Your ADHD specialist can advise you on how to set up such a program, but remember to include your child in the planning. Have them help you make the chart and decide on the colors of stickers or on the rewards and so on.

Q: Our eleven-year-old son enjoys school, but has trouble studying or completing his homework. Nagging only makes both of us feel bad. Do you have any advice on how to make this situation easier?

A: The completion of homework is one of the most problematic situations in families with ADHD children. The disorder can make studying difficult for a variety of reasons: the child doesn't read well, the child suffers from extreme inattention, or hyperactivity makes it difficult for the child to sit still for any length of time.

There are things that you can do to make studying a little easier. First and foremost, make sure your son's study area is well equipped, quiet, and away from other family members. The fewer distractions your son has to cope with, the better. This means no windows, no television, and no radio (unless your son is one of the many ADHD children who actually study better with background music). For most children this would mean being in their own room, alone. However, some children may work better at the kitchen table. It may take some experimenting to find the best setting, but take into account your child's tendency to be distracted easily, his difficulty sustaining focus, and his need to have things structured for him.

Check on your son's progress often. You might even want to sit with him while he studies or completes his homework assignments to be sure that he's focused on his task. This isn't to say that you should do it for him, but sometimes having a parent present is a good way to ensure that everything is being done as it should be. Review his work when he's finished to make sure it's complete and readable. If not, have him do it again. (This shouldn't be perceived as punishment, but it's important that he understand why he has to do it over.)

If your son frequently forgets his schoolbooks or homework assignments, ask his teacher to write down what he's supposed to do, and make sure he gives you the note every evening. Pretty soon he should start remembering on his own. It may be helpful if you set up an organizational system for him, such as filing cabinets for his papers and so on. He may also need periodic help in sorting through masses of papers and books and getting organized again. Of course, if you do it constantly for him, he may never learn to manage this himself. However, if you leave him totally alone, the chances are that he will get further and further behind and will just begin not to do the work because he feels so helpless about how disorganized and behind he is. If his school has a study skills teacher or a remedial teacher, ask her how best to help your child with study skills and organization at home.

Many ADHD students excel at certain subjects and do poorly in others. If your son needs help, consider hiring a tutor to help him over the rough spots. If your son's hyperactivity and inattention seem a particular problem in the evening, when he should be doing his homework, you might speak to your specialist about medication after school.

Q: We have three children, two boys ages seven and fifteen and an eleven-year-old daughter. Our oldest son was recently diagnosed with ADHD, and his younger brother and sister seem

to be having a difficult time adjusting to this situation. They're angry all the time and sometimes behave as badly as their older brother. My husband and I are struggling to hold things together. Any advice?

A: Sibling conflict is very, very common in families with an ADHD child. Conflicting emotions run rampant, fights and screaming matches occur almost daily, and everyone seems to be on edge.

First, have your other children tested to make sure they don't have ADHD too. The chances are good that they don't, but sometimes the disorder can crop up in more than one child.

If the diagnosis comes back negative, sit everyone down for a long family meeting. Explain that certain patterns and problems have started to crop up and it's time to nip them in the bud. Ask each child what's been bothering him or her, and let them talk without interruption. Don't be accusatory or condescending; everyone, no matter what their age, has a right to their feelings and emotions.

Explain to the younger children about their brother's condition, what it is and how it affects his behavior. Tell them they must try to be a bit more understanding and that his bad behavior doesn't give them the right to act up. Next, ask your children for ideas on how difficult situations can be more easily resolved. This is also a good time to reassure them that they can come to you if they have any problems and that you'll do all you can to make sure everyone is treated equally and fairly.

It's essential that all of your children feel loved and respected. Very often, the child with ADHD will get the majority of parental attention, making the others feel left out. It could be that your younger children are fighting and misbehaving because they feel it's the only way to get your love. Frequent reassurances from you and your husband should go a long way toward eliminating any feelings of jealousy and resentment.

Sometimes it is helpful to have some family sessions with the ADHD specialist. She can observe and clarify patterns that are occurring and bring them to the family's attention. She can also help the family to better understand ADHD and to learn

The Family's Role

new negotiation and communication skills, which can make giving up old behavior patterns possible.

Q: My sixteen-year-old son was diagnosed with ADHD when he was eleven. He's always had a terrible temper, but lately it's been getting a lot worse. I'm terrified that he's going to hit me, his father, or his younger sister in a fit of anger. He's basically a good kid, but I have to admit that I'm frightened of him. What should we do?

A: Aggression is a common side effect of ADHD, but most young people are able to keep it under control, especially if they're receiving multimodal therapy. When a mother becomes afraid of her teenage son, it's time to take drastic action.

I suggest that you talk immediately with your family doctor or ADHD specialist and ask him to reevaluate your son to determine the cause of his aggression and what can be done about it. It's obvious that the boy's condition is getting the better of him and that he needs help before someone gets hurt. Individual psychotherapy may be necessary to find the cause of his deep-seated anger and to teach him how to keep it under control. If the problem is largely one of family communication, family therapy may be preferred.

Similarly, it is important to investigate all other aspects of your son's life, i.e., his academic and social life, to ascertain whether something is causing him to be chronically upset and distressed. Unrecognized academic problems could be fueling his distress. Drug use could also be involved in his increasing loss of control.

In the meantime, if your son does seem out of control, do what you must to separate yourself from the situation. At all costs, avoid situations that you know will provoke him.

If his father is not so involved due to work or the way your family has been structured, now is the time for him to engage his son. He will need to put in a lot of time, and it may be stormy at first. It may well be that your son's aggression is being fueled by his formerly close relationship to you, his mother. It becomes very hard for sexually mature teenage boys to remain close to their mothers during the early and middle teenage years. Often they need to pull away and may do this angrily and even violently. It is helpful to have a father on hand to become a close friend, advisor, and companion for his son at this time. Of course, in the relationship with his father, there are likely to be issues of competitiveness, humiliation, and conflict. For a boy with ADHD, these emotional and developmental issues are often heightened, and he does not have healthy coping skills or interpersonal skills to deal with them.

Q: Our nine-year-old son is begging us for a dog, but my husband and I are concerned that his ADHD makes him a poor candidate to own a pet. Should we risk it or wait until he's older?
A: The answer to your question depends on your son's maturity level and how his ADHD most commonly manifests itself. If he's prone to forgetfulness and inattention, then you and your husband will probably end up taking care of his new pet because he'll never get around to it. However, if your son is fairly mature and good about doing what he's told, a dog might be an appropriate companion.

If you do decide to get a dog for your son, sit down with him first and explain in detail exactly what will be expected of him regarding the animal's care. Make sure he understands that the dog will be his responsibility and that he will have to feed and walk it every day (even when it's raining) and bathe it when necessary. Many times, pet ownership is an effective way of instilling a sense of maturity in youngsters with ADHD.

If you feel that your son isn't quite ready for the responsibility of owning a dog, you might want to consider a pet that's a little less trouble, such as a hamster or a guinea pig. These are gentle animals that enjoy playing with people, but don't require a lot of day-to-day care. Once your son has proven himself responsible in this way, you can reconsider his request for something larger.

In my experience, ADHD children who have significant self-esteem problems and difficulties with social relations often feel very comfortable with animals and develop devoted relationships to them. The pet can then help the child to deal with upsetting incidents; in other words, help the child learn to soothe himself. This ability is extremely important in overcoming the tendency to impulsive action brought on by intense emotional states. Similarly, the unconditional love of the pet for its young owner can be very enhancing to the child's self-esteem. And as the child learns to care for his pet, it helps him to develop skills of empathy for others. In fact, so much benefit can be obtained by the experience of having and caring for a pet that I think you might want to consider it, even if your child may need reminding and help in caring for the pet.

Q: It seems that every waking moment is spent caring for our eight-year-old ADHD daughter, and it's starting to drive a wedge between my husband and me. We barely spend any time together, and we haven't made love in months. Please help!

A: It's very easy to become consumed by all that's involved in rearing an ADHD child, and that can place a serious strain on any marriage. The answer is obvious—you *must* schedule some time so that you and your husband can be alone. A regular night out each week or even a lunch during the workday can work wonders. It certainly is too easy for a couple to let the concerns of their family life and children's care replace the necessary caring they should do for each other. Then they may reach a point of not expecting much from each other or of only seeing the other as a resource in managing the stresses of the family, but not as a fun partner with whom they wish to do things.

Some families are lucky to have extended family willing to help with the children, and this can make a night out or even a weekend away an easy reality for the parents. If this is not available, then it would be a good idea for you to begin to familiarize your child with a babysitter who they can feel secure and comfortable with. Once you and your child are comfortable with the person, a regular night out can be both a necessary refueling for you and your spouse, as well as an event to be looked forward to by your child, who may enjoy some special activities each week with the babysitter.

EIGHT

The School's Role

Making sure that a child receives adequate love and support at home is only half the battle in managing ADHD. Parents must also ensure that their children receive equal support and compassion in school.

Until recently, many teachers knew little about ADHD. They did not understand the cause for the behavior of hyperactive, impulsive children, and these children were often labeled as troublemakers. More importantly, many teachers did not know how to work with these children in the classroom.

Fortunately, this has changed significantly. Today your child's school and teachers play as important a part in the overall multimodal plan as do his medication and other approaches. Most teachers, especially those beginning their careers, are well aware of ADHD and its symptoms. In fact, very often it's a concerned teacher who first recognizes the condition in a child and brings it to the attention of his parents.

Teachers are frequently very active in making sure that an ADHD child receives the special attention and instruction he requires in the classroom for effective learning. And most teachers are more than willing to work with parents and a child's specialist to help implement a multimodal approach to ADHD that guarantees consistent ADHD management in school and at home.

Sometimes, however, a teacher or school administrator is

less than supportive when it comes to managing a child's ADHD or making sure that he receives the instruction to which he is entitled. Classrooms are packed, teachers are overworked, and administrators have more to worry about than a single hyperactive or inattentive child. In situations like this, parents may have to become more active advocates for their child and play a role in educating teachers about their child's needs. Intervention by your ADHD specialist may be helpful to alert the school to your child's special needs and to engage the cooperation of administration and faculty.

The long-range role of teachers and school administrators comes in assessing academic strengths and weaknesses and providing support. Teachers should be aware that ADHD and related learning disorders can cause children to fall behind in their schoolwork. They should be prepared to institute remedial action at the first sign of academic difficulties. This is vitally important because failure in school sets up a vicious cycle of anger, frustration, and poor self-esteem. Worse, it can discourage a child from future academic achievement and life potential.

In summary, then, your child's school and teachers can play a very important role in many facets of ADHD management. These include the following.

- Diagnosis.
- Helping to dispense and assess the use of medication.
- Providing special classroom approaches to help your child academically, socially, emotionally, and behaviorally. In particular, the classroom environment may need to be adjusted to minimize the impact of the ADHD child's hyperactivity, attentional problems, distractibility, and impulsivity both on himself and the rest of the class.
- Assessing special academic problems and providing special educational approaches or remediation.
- Recommending tutoring and working with outside educational professionals.
- Being active participants of the multimodal team, providing feedback to parents, the ADHD specialist, and

other professionals involved and being willing to adjust their approach according to feedback from other members of the team.

In this chapter, we will discuss in more detail a variety of important issues regarding the school's role in the management of ADHD, including choosing the best school, designing an educational program specifically for your child, and the role of medication.

Q: I know that teachers are often the first to notice that a child has ADHD. What I don't understand is how a parent could miss the telltale signs of this condition. What does a teacher notice that a parent does not?

A: Parents often miss the obvious signs of ADHD because they are with a child all the time. The child's behavior may be odd, but the parent may not notice because the child has always acted that way. The parent comes to believe that it's just the child's nature or his personality and doesn't give the occasional disruptiveness, hyperactivity, or inattention another thought.

Teachers, however, are more attuned to what is normal behavior and what is not. The ADHD child usually stands out from his classmates because of his inability to complete desk work, his unwillingness to pay attention, or his constant distractibility. This is not typical behavior, and most teachers pick up on it right away.

If a teacher is concerned that a student has undiagnosed ADHD, she may suggest special testing to confirm her suspicions. The most common tests, such as the Wechsler Intelligence Scale for Children (WISC), compare the intellectual potential of a child with his academic behavior and achievements. They also compare different areas of cognitive functioning to see if there is a wide scatter in abilities, which sometimes points to learning disabilities. The teacher may also address obvious distractibility and attention issues. If ADHD is strongly suspected, the teacher may suggest a differential diagnosis by a doctor or ADHD specialist.

Parents should never ignore the concerns of their child's teacher. Her observations and conclusions usually have merit, and it's in the child's best interest to take a teacher's recommendations seriously. Left undiagnosed, ADHD can adversely affect a child's ability to learn, make friends, or develop fully as an individual.

Q: What important issues should parents consider regarding school once their child has been diagnosed with ADHD?
A: The first question parents should ask themselves is: "Is this the right school for our child?" Most schools will do all they can to accommodate an ADHD child, but some schools are better than others. It's up to the parents to make this evaluation.

One important factor is the student-teacher ratio. The smaller the ratio, the better, because the needs of an ADHD child can become lost if a teacher must divide her attention between twenty or more students. ADHD children need a lot of individual instruction and support, and it can be difficult for a teacher to provide that and still give her all to the rest of the class, especially if she has little assistance.

Equally important is the flexibility of the school's teachers and administrators. Are they willing to modify the teaching environment for a child with ADHD? This can be difficult to assess. Talk with your child's instructors and school administrators to see how much they're willing to work with your child so that he can learn around his disorder.

Another consideration is the classroom environment. Many newer schools provide open, unstructured classrooms with multiple teachers and mixed grades. This situation may work well for normal children, but it's not the best environment for a child with ADHD.

Students who are disruptive or inattentive tend to do better in a more structured, formal school setting—particularly ADHD children who are easily agitated. An open classroom with younger and older students and multiple activities can be very distracting. Many educators applaud this type of learning environment, but I feel it's inappropriate for students with ADHD because it causes more problems than it solves.

Q: Do all children with ADHD have learning disabilities in addition to those that characterize the syndrome?

A: Many do, but not all—a phenomenon that illustrates well the individual nature of ADHD. Among those who do experience learning disabilities, the most common problems include the following.

- **Visual perception disabilities**, such as dyslexia, in which certain letters or words appear to be reversed or jumbled.
- **Auditory perception disabilities**, in which common words sound strange or confusing.
- **Integration disabilities**, in which the brain has difficulty recording and organizing the information it receives.
- **Memory disabilities**, in which information is quickly forgotten. Most children with this form of disability experience short-term memory problems that make it difficult for them to remember their lessons from one day to the next.
- **Output disabilities**, in which the student has difficulty answering questions asked of him. It may be a verbal disability (an inability to recite an answer when questioned) or a motor disability (an inability to write down an answer).

Don't be upset if your child is diagnosed with a learning disability; most of these problems can be easily corrected with the appropriate therapy. But it's essential that treatment coincide with the management of a child's ADHD. Otherwise, his behavior may improve, but he will continue to do poorly in school.

Q: How are learning disabilities diagnosed?

A: In most cases, it's a teacher who first suspects that a child has a learning disability. She may notice that the child appears intelligent and eager to learn, but that he does poorly on tests or classwork despite his best efforts.

Typically, the child is seen by a doctor or educational specialist, who conducts a series of studies to compare the child's intellectual potential with his current level of academic achievement.

If there is a marked difference between the two, another set of studies is conducted to determine the specific area of difficulty. As mentioned earlier, it could be a problem of visual or auditory perception or an information integration problem. Each of these disabilities is treated by a specialist in that area, whether it be a speech pathologist, an auditory expert, a remedial education specialist, or a learning disabilities specialist.

The parents of ADHD children with learning disabilities should meet with their children's teachers often to discuss the course and effectiveness of treatment both at school and at home. A little trial and error may be necessary before the most effective treatment regimen is perfected.

Keep in mind that learning disabilities aren't a school-only problem; they affect a child twenty-four hours a day. A youngster who has difficulty reading in the classroom will have equal difficulty reading at home, and the resulting frustration can dramatically affect a child's personality and behavior. Be understanding and compassionate, and do all you can to facilitate the treatment process and boost your child's confidence and self-esteem.

Often youngsters with significant learning disabilities will need tutoring outside of school, as well as special help in school. The educational specialist can also advise parents how to continue this valuable work at home. It may be necessary for parents to be very involved with the child as he or she does homework. In addition, the parent may have to make available special study aids, such as tape recorders or computers, and particular software, such as dictionaries, encyclopedias, or a thesaurus. Children with expressive difficulties, such as enormous difficulty in writing, may be better able to type at a keyboard or may even need to dictate some of their work and have a parent type it for them. Younger children may need to be drilled on numbers or facts and have their homework explained to them in detail.

It is extremely important that parents work closely with the educational specialists involved, including their children's teachers, to provide the necessary academic structuring, support, and enhancement.

Q: My eleven-year-old son must take Ritalin twice a day to control his ADHD symptoms. Should I discuss my son's medication schedule with his teachers?

A: Absolutely. Medication issues should be discussed at length with all of your son's instructors, as well as the school administrators. This is important because most schools now have strict policies regarding student medication. Some schools store all students' medication in the school clinic, where it is distributed by the school nurse. In other schools, individual teachers take care of it. These policies may sound overly strict, but they serve two very important functions: making sure ADHD students receive their medication on time every day and discouraging medication abuse.

In talking with your son's teachers, make sure they're aware of the drug's effects, including potential side-effects. They should also work closely with you in determining the best time for your child to receive his medication, such as when academic demands are greatest.

Many youngsters are embarrassed by the fact that they take Ritalin or some other medication for their ADHD. They fear ridicule or harassment from their fellow students and are concerned about being perceived as "different." This is a valid concern and should not be taken lightly. To avoid potential embarrassment, parents and teachers should work out a way for a child to slip off to the school nurse without drawing undue attention to himself. If a child is younger, the teacher will need to be more involved. But if a child is older, he may be able to visit the school nurse between classes or during his lunch period. Or if he's mature enough and it doesn't violate school policy, he may be able to keep his medication with him and take it per a prearranged schedule.

Teachers should closely monitor the effects of an ADHD child's medication and offer regular feedback to his parents. Does it help curb disruptive behaviors? Is the child less hyperactive, inattentive, or impulsive? Does he learn better after the drug has taken effect? These are important questions that help support a child's medical treatment.

One option is to have the teacher complete a special classroom behavior rating scale every day or every week and have the child return it to his parents. Reports like these provide valuable information to the child's parents, as well as his ADHD specialist, and can help determine which therapies are effective and which are not.

A typical example is the Conners' Abbreviated Teacher Rating Scale. The teacher is asked to rate a list of ten behaviors according to the scale of "not at all," "just a little," "pretty much," and "very much." These behaviors are described as follows.

1. Restless or overactive
2. Excitable, impulsive
3. Disturbs other children
4. Fails to finish things he starts—short attention span
5. Constantly fidgeting
6. Inattentive, easily distracted
7. Demands must be met immediately, easily frustrated
8. Cries often and easily
9. Mood changes quickly and drastically
10. Temper outbursts, explosive and unpredictable behavior

Q: How often should my wife and I meet with our son's teachers? Is twice a year sufficient?

A: I'd suggest a more frequent schedule, perhaps every month or two if possible. The important thing is to stay in close contact with your son's teachers so that everyone is kept well informed.

Parents should use these regular conferences to notify teachers of any changes in a child's treatment, medication, or home life, as well as any difficulties in getting the child to do his homework. Teachers can use the time to inform parents of any changes—good or bad—in the child's classroom behavior, learning skills, or social situation.

Unfortunately, many parents find it difficult working so closely with their child's teacher. They may feel intimidated or put off by the instructor, who is often forced to do a massive job under extremely difficult circumstances.

Teachers, too, may feel uncomfortable with this relationship. They may feel intruded upon or intimidated, especially if parents are overly strident in their efforts to make sure that their child is receiving everything to which he is entitled.

This is a sensitive alliance that works best when developed and nurtured at the beginning of every school year. The more parents can get a teacher to understand their child, the better off the child will be. But everyone must take into consideration the feelings and opinions of others. Remember: You're a team working toward the same goal. As such, compromise and understanding make up half the battle.

Q: What techniques do teachers commonly use to help ADHD students with extreme distractibility?

A: Distractibility is one of the most common symptoms of ADHD and one of the most troublesome when it comes to learning. Children with this problem have a great deal of trouble paying attention to their teacher or completing seat work because their attention is everywhere but on their lessons.

What makes this situation so maddening is that the smallest things can distract a child, from another student walking by the door to a plane flying overhead. When the student finally returns to the task at hand, he may find that several minutes have elapsed and the teacher has proceeded without him.

One answer is to position the child so that he witnesses a minimum of distractions, such as in front of the teacher's desk, where she can keep an eye on him and bring him back if his mind starts to wander. However, this can actually worsen the situation if the teacher's desk is a site of high traffic flow. The easily distracted student should also be placed away from windows and doors, though often this is easier said than done.

If the distractible student is older, the teacher should ask for his input regarding the situation. Where would he feel least distracted and most able to focus on his lessons? Most adolescents know what works best for them, and their teachers should consider their suggestions.

Ultimately, a teacher may have to experiment a bit with classroom seating arrangements to determine how best to overcome an ADHD student's distractibility problem. Keeping the child away from other disruptive students is always a good idea, as is close monitoring by the teacher to make sure the student is paying attention when he should be.

It may also help to pair the distractible student with a friend who has good classroom study habits. This gives the distractible student someone he can turn to for help and input besides the teacher. The buddy can check to make sure the ADHD student has done his in-class work properly, knows what his homework is and has the books he needs, all without bothering the other students. And if the distractible student has any questions once he's home, his study buddy is just a phone call away.

Less helpful is cluster seating, in which students face each other all or part of the day. Face-to-face contact with fellow students is the ultimate in distraction and seldom works with ADHD children. If used at all, it should be only for limited group activities.

Some schools have even resorted to special barriers and partitions to separate distractible students from those things which cause their minds to wander. However, there's a downside to this solution—partitions can't separate the child from the distractions in his own head that result in daydreaming, doodling, or other nonproductive activities. That's why close contact with a teacher or assistant is best.

The teacher can also attempt to structure tasks for the ADHD child so that there are fewer distractions for him. If the children are to have a free-form activity that involves moving around the room and using their own initiative, the teacher might decide to give the ADHD child a more structured choice. Otherwise, the lack of structure may result in more distractions and hyperactivity. For example, if the assignment is for the child to choose any book from the library shelf to read and write a report about, the teacher or aide may accompany the ADHD child and help structure his decision, such as ask him what he is interested in, make suggestions, and so on, to prevent him from roaming around the library in an unfocused way.

Q: Our fourteen-year-old daughter has ADHD and suffers from serious attention problems. As a result, her grades aren't as good as we would like them to be. Could you suggest some simple classroom changes that might make learning a little easier for students with attention deficits?
A: Stimulant medication, such as Ritalin or Cylert, can work wonders in easing the attention difficulties that afflict many youngsters with ADHD. Because of this benefit, some teachers try to arrange demanding academic activities so that they coincide with a student's peak periods of concentration. For some students, it's immediately after their first dose in the morning. Other students find they're at their best in the afternoon, following their second dose. Every student is different, so a teacher should work closely with the ADHD student's parents and ADHD specialist in making this determination.

Greater one-on-one instruction from the teacher can also help students with attention difficulties. If a classroom has more than one instructor (or an instructor and one or more teacher's aides), then the team can work out a schedule in which one member is able to spend more time with the ADHD student while the others take care of the rest of the class.

Sometimes a child with severe attentional problems needs time out of the general classroom. Many schools have a resource room, with a special education teacher who can work one-on-one with students for a part of each day. This may be very helpful and can sometimes be teamed with special instruction in a subject that the child has particular difficulty in.

Other helpful strategies include the following.

- Repeating verbal instructions several times. ADHD children often have trouble keeping instructions in their minds because of classroom distractions, and they frequently need to be reminded to remain on task. Or they may have short-term memory problems that make holding sequential information in their minds difficult. Letting the student take notes while the teacher is talking, or writing all instructions on the blackboard can also be helpful. It is essential that the teacher give all instructions very clearly, that they be composed of precise and simple steps, and that not too many steps in sequence are given at once. It may be necessary for a teacher or aide to check specifically if the ADHD student was able to receive and record all the necessary information. With younger children, after speaking to the whole class, the teacher may go and stand next to the child and perhaps even lay a hand on his shoulder to draw his attention while she repeats the instructions privately for him. With an older child, the teacher may work out special strategies with the child and his or her parents, such as checking a list of homework assignments at the end of the day to ensure that the student received all the necessary information or even providing written instructions for the more complicated assignments.

- Letting students with ADHD record their teacher's lectures in order to listen to them again at home. Taking written notes is difficult if not impossible for many ADHD children because of poor fine-motor coordination. The result of their efforts is usually a scribbled mess that the best cryptographer would find difficult to decipher. Tape-recording lectures lets students listen to them again in the quiet peace of their bedrooms or study areas.

- Allowing the use of laptop computers for note-taking and other classroom activities. Even though handwriting is often difficult for ADHD students, many are able to use a computer keyboard with ease. As a result, a growing number of high school and college instructors are allowing students with ADHD to type their lecture notes rather than write them by hand.

Q: Could you recommend some useful strategies for helping teachers cope with an ADHD stu-

dent's hyperactivity or impulsivity in the classroom? I have two such students in my fifth-grade class right now, and their behavior makes it extremely difficult to effectively teach the other students.

A: Two students with hyperactivity and impulsivity can be a real handful, and you're to be commended for helping to keep them in the learning environment.

The first thing you should do is find out if these students are receiving stimulant medication, which can work wonders in calming hyperactive youngsters. If they are on medication, see if you can talk with their doctor or ADHD specialist to make sure their dosages are correct.

It is also important to assess whether there is something in the classroom that is stimulating these students' bad behavior. Are they out of their depths academically? Do they need more support or special education help? Are there social factors in the classroom that require intervention? Is low self-esteem and a sense of repeated and inevitable failure fueling their disruptive behavior? Perhaps separating certain children would help or moving the hyperactive children to less distracting seat placements. Maybe the class routines could be more structured. Writing up the schedule for each day on the board, as well as anticipating ends of class periods and other changes, can be helpful. And trying to help the child find activities he can be successful at is essential.

In addition, I would also suggest the implementation of some behavior modification techniques in the classroom, as discussed in Chapter 5. These can include time-outs, a simple reward system, and a lot of positive reinforcement for appropriate academic and social behavior. It's important that you include the hyperactive/impulsive students in the planning of these strategies and that you offer a contract clearly outlining the rewards for good behavior (such as tokens that can be redeemed for special privileges) and the consequences for disruptive behavior.

Behavioral planning must be combined with a consistent approach at home. Parents and teachers should work closely together and reinforce each other's actions, which is why frequent communication is so important.

As a teacher, you should recognize that the more positive reinforcement a student receives, the better. Try to get away from penalties and chastisement by setting up tasks that are likely to be successful, then gradually striving for bigger goals and harder tasks. The more successes a student has in the beginning, the more he will be motivated to achieve greater success. The results: better discipline, improved grades, and greater self-esteem. The better the self-esteem and belief in the possibility of his own success, the more the ADHD child is going to be motivated to control his hyperactivity and disruptive behavior.

Q: Our thirteen-year-old son was diagnosed with ADHD four years ago and has done pretty well on Ritalin. He's a good student except for math, which has always given him difficulty. We'd like to get him a tutor to help him with this one subject. Should we consult with his teacher before proceeding?

A: Your son's instructor will certainly be able to advise you and may even recommend a qualified outside tutor or at least assist the person you choose so that your son receives the kind of instruction he needs most.

As discussed earlier, everyone involved in the management of your son's ADHD is part of a team, and that also includes tutors. Clear communication between team members is essential so that you don't have four or five people working independently and at odds with each other. For best results, the tutor you choose should be in frequent contact with you, your son's instructor, and your son's doctor or ADHD specialist.

Q: I can't seem to get my daughter's teacher or school administrators to acknowledge that she has special needs in the classroom. They try to completely mainstream her, and as a result, she's doing poorly academically. What should I do?

A: If you feel that your daughter's school is not effectively addressing her ADHD, consider asking for a group meeting

The School's Role

with her teacher, the school's principal, and your ADHD specialist. An expert in the field can explain exactly what your daughter's condition represents and how it affects her ability to learn, as well as offer various strategies her teacher and others can implement to make learning a little easier.

Very often, teachers are unaware of just how severely ADHD can affect a child's personality and classroom ability. They assume that the problem child will eventually just change for the better, but as we know, that seldom happens. Education and advice from an expert in the field can often work wonders in improving their attitude toward and understanding of ADHD.

You might also want to contact your school's Parent Teacher Association (PTA) or similar organization and ask if there are any support groups in your area for the parents of ADHD students. Other ADHD families may be able to provide tips and information on getting your daughter's school to respond better to her unique academic requirements.

Another option is to seek assistance within your local school system. The mother and father of one of my ADHD patients approached the handicapped student division of the local department of education and got permission to have special in-class help for their child. This help came in the form of a part-time aide whose role in the mainstream classroom was to work with their child, helping him focus and follow instructions, keeping distractions to a minimum, and providing support and guidance socially. These agencies take many forms across the country, but most school systems have one, and they can be extremely helpful in cutting red tape when it comes to getting help for ADHD children. Often they can even help arrange for a part-time special aide or one-on-one instruction.

As parents, you have the right to expect your daughter's school to become actively involved in meeting her special needs. Be assertive without being obnoxious, and don't be intimidated by the school's cool response to your requests. By providing information and advice, you can help the school help your daughter, just as the school can help you become a better parent.

Teachers are usually grateful when parents become involved

in the education of their ADHD child because it makes the teacher's job easier. The more parents work and show willingness to help, the more teachers are willing to give special attention.

Don't be afraid to ask for help.

Q: Under what circumstances should an ADHD child be transferred to a private school or a special school?

A: It's my belief that children with ADHD should be integrated with other students as much as possible. But sometimes the symptoms of ADHD can be so severe that a child cannot learn in the traditional school environment and would be better off in a private school designed for his special needs.

Such schools typically emphasize more personalized attention, with a smaller student-teacher ratio and more instructors and aides per class. The teachers may be specialists in ADHD instruction or well versed in the many facets of a multimodal approach to ADHD management. They know how to motivate their students to learn and how to keep disruptive behaviors, such as hyperactivity and impulsiveness, under control.

Private schools also often have equipment, such as computers, that make learning easier for children with ADHD—something that is not true for all public school systems.

Before making this very important decision, you should have a long talk with your child's ADHD specialist, his teachers, and, most importantly, your child. Many youngsters are uncomfortable with the notion of going to a "special school," while others welcome it because they've had such difficulty in the traditional classroom setting.

Q: Everyone keeps talking about student rights. Are the rights of a student with ADHD different from a child who does not have the syndrome?

A: Every child has the right to be educated, and that sometimes means the educational process must be altered slightly to meet the special needs of the individual. No child should be forced into a classroom situation where he is unable to tap into his full potential.

Children with ADHD also have the right to be protected

from teasing and other social traumas. They have the right to expect that the adults chairing their classrooms will help them negotiate peer relations when necessary. This can require a lot of intervention from teachers, both with regard to how others treat ADHD children, and how these children treat their fellow students. It's a two-way street.

Many more teachers know about ADHD now than five or ten years ago, but it still is not fully understood by a large enough spectrum of educators. As a result, many children with ADHD manage to avoid detection and go through high school or beyond before being diagnosed. They fail to get the kind of help and support in school that can prevent academic failure, poor social relations, and low self-esteem—and that's a right to which every young person is entitled.

In addition, many teachers are unaware of the broad, multimodal approach to treatment that has proved so effective with so many youngsters. They feel that Ritalin is the only answer to an ADHD child's problems and will recommend medication to his parents without explaining the many other treatment modalities that are available. This important information is a right to which every ADHD child is entitled.

Q: Our son's ADHD specialist has recommended that his teacher fill out something called the Conners teacher-rating scales. Could you explain what this is and how it can benefit our son?

A: The Conners teacher-rating scales (CTRS) is one of the most commonly used systems in the evaluation of children with ADHD. It contains thirty-nine questions requiring a rating of zero up to three, and it covers behavior, group participation, and attitude toward authority. Completed daily or weekly, it can shed invaluable light on an ADHD student's progress and indicate how well the child is responding to treatment and management. An abbreviated version of this scale is described earlier in this chapter.

Rating scales, such as the CTRS, also offer teachers a good followup report on an ADHD student. They provide informative details on the day-to-day experiences of the child, which in turn can help tailor a multimodal treatment approach, making it more effective.

Teachers spend a lot of time with ADHD children, so it's important to get their input. Rating scales can be completed in just a few minutes, which make them especially useful to teachers too busy for frequent phone chats with parents or a child's ADHD specialist.

Q: Our seventeen-year-old ADHD son will be going off to college next year, and we're fearful that this change in environment may cause serious problems. Are college instructors as adept at dealing with ADHD as high school teachers?

A: As ADHD becomes more widely known, an increasing number of colleges and universities are taking steps to make the educational experience easier and more productive for those with the condition. Some teachers still take a hard line when it comes to making special exceptions for students, but most realize that ADHD is a very real disorder that requires accommodation at the very least.

Some instructors, for example, are willing to give students with ADHD a little extra time on exams or let them take tests in a quiet location to avoid distractions. Others provide preferential seating to students with ADHD, allow them to tape record class lectures for later listening, and encourage them to type lecture notes into a laptop computer, instead of writing them by hand.

There are also steps your son can take to make college a little easier for him to manage. Living off campus rather than in a dorm, for example, may give him the privacy and lack of distraction he will need to concentrate on his studies. Dorm life isn't for everyone, but it can be especially difficult for people with ADHD.

Before your son goes away to college, you should help him become skillful and independent in handling his medication. It is going to be essential for him to be able to assess when and how much he needs. For example, he may need stimulants when he is doing his own work, but not in lectures; or it may be in lectures that without medication he cannot listen, focus, or understand. He will need to know how to vary the dose if necessary, but not to overuse it. His schedule and study habits are likely to change, and hence his needs for the medication will change. However, if the medication has been very helpful during high school, it is almost always certain that he should continue it at college.

Your son should be careful not to carry too heavy a class load each semester. If he has attention or distraction problems, too many classes may be an impossible burden.

It's also a good idea for your son to confer frequently with his instructors to review his progress in class and to discuss additional ways that he can study around his ADHD.

Finally, he should ask his guidance counselor if there is an ADHD support group on campus. Many colleges have them, and they can be an invaluable source of friendship and guidance if things get rough.

Q: My daughter's sixth-grade teacher is one of those people who doesn't believe that ADHD exists. In her mind, all of my daughter's problems are due to poor discipline and lack of motivation. This is completely untrue—my daughter wants desperately to learn, but her hyperactivity and impulsivity make it extremely difficult. We're at our wits' end. What do you advise?

A: Every school has one or more teachers like the one you've described. They're usually from the old school of education and believe that solid discipline is the answer to every problem child. Unfortunately, teachers like this can be a nightmare for children with ADHD because they fail to recognize the true cause of these youngsters' behavioral problems.

If this teacher refuses to talk with you about your daughter's problems, it's time to seek a higher authority. Schedule a meeting with the school principal or administrator to talk over the situation. Bring literature explaining what ADHD is and how it affects a child's personality and learning ability, and supplement it with pertinent information about your daughter from her doctor or ADHD specialist. Once you've convinced the principal that your daughter's problems are very real, ask for her help in converting your daughter's teacher. You might even want to bring in your daughter's ADHD specialist for a group discussion.

Go out of your way to make sure your daughter's teacher doesn't feel like you're ganging up on her. You want her as an ally, not an enemy. Be friendly and courteous, and present your case simply but completely. Explain that your daughter wants to learn, but that her condition requires certain allowances—then outline what these allowances should be. Ask for the teacher's help, and reassure her that all you want is what's best for your daughter.

If your daughter's teacher refuses to help even after all that, your choices are limited. You can ask that your daughter be transferred to a more progressive instructor or a different school. You may even consider placing her in a private school designed specifically for youngsters with ADHD.

Not all teachers are comfortable instructing children with ADHD. It's very possible that your daughter's instructor just doesn't have what it takes to handle these very special students. This doesn't mean that she's a bad teacher—she's probably very good. It just means that she's more effective with students who don't have learning disabilities, ADHD, or special needs.

Q: My twelve-year-old son enjoys school—except for recess. None of the other children want to play with him or have him on their team because of his inattention, hyperactivity, and other ADHD problems. This breaks my heart because it makes him so angry, frustrated, and sad. What can be done to make recess more enjoyable for a child with ADHD?

A: Most parents are so busy making sure their ADHD child is doing well in the classroom that they forget about the pitfalls of the playground.

Talk with your son's teacher to find out why the other children find your son so difficult to be around. Does he become aggressive and belligerent when he or someone on his team makes a mistake? Does he find it difficult to wait his turn during play? Does his inattention make him a poor team player? These and other problems are the main reasons children with ADHD do so poorly at team sports. They need a lot of teacher supervision, but it must be done carefully so that the child doesn't feel singled out or picked on.

You can help by doing a little role-playing and observation on your own. Play a variety of games with your son, and observe his behavior firsthand. Does he fly off the handle too easily? Is he a sore loser? Does he have a lot of difficulty paying attention? If you detect certain patterns, sit down with your son and talk about them. Point out these problems, and suggest alternative behaviors that will make him more fun to be around. Teach him how to curb his aggression and be a team player. Once he learns to recognize his problem behaviors and curb them, his playground angst should disappear.

A last resort is to let your son play with children a year or two younger than he is (if his teacher feels this is appropriate). Children with ADHD are typically less socially mature than their peers and have more in common with children who are slightly younger. If everyone feels comfortable with this situation, I see no reason why it shouldn't be allowed.

Again, this situation may be one in which you have to request more input and support from the school. Often playground activities are not closely supervised. Your ADHD specialist may be able to help in indicating to your child's teachers that their special guidance socially is just as important as their special input academically. Perhaps the presence of a teacher ready to intervene at the first sign of a problem on the playground will help. In addition, some suggested structured activities that can include the ADHD child may be less threatening and more successful than the usual totally unstructured and socially challenging recess period.

Often a teacher can guide an ADHD child towards possible friends by encouraging some joint activities. For example, a teacher could call upon the ADHD child and a buddy to do some task for her during playground time, thus helping the ADHD child to have a more successful social interaction. This can then be followed by parents helping their child to have a successful play date with someone the teacher has suggested as a likely friend.

Q: Is home schooling effective for children who have ADHD?

A: A growing number of parents, disenchanted with the state of public education today, are opting to teach their children at home. Whether this approach is effective for a child with ADHD depends on the child, the parents, and their home environment.

Youngsters with moderate ADHD may do better academically with a home education program because their parents can spend more one-on-one time with them than a busy teacher can. There are also fewer distractions in a home-school environment, so a child can study more effectively than in a hectic classroom.

However, home education isn't for everyone. Many children with ADHD have such severe behavior, attention, or impulsivity problems that their parents simply can't manage them well enough to teach them. They spend most of their time on discipline and very little on education. In extreme cases, a public special-education program is probably best. The teachers involved in such programs are specially trained to control children with ADHD and instruct them around their problem behaviors.

There are other advantages to public education. For example, being with children their age allows youngsters with ADHD to hone those all-important social skills, something that may be lacking in a home-school environment. And many youngsters, especially teenagers, find that public school provides the academic challenge they need to succeed later in life. It stimulates their intellect and provides personal successes that make them feel better about themselves. Praise from Mom and Dad is important, but praise from teachers and peers can work miracles when it comes to bolstering an ADHD child's self-esteem.

Before you decide to teach your child at home, you should discuss the situation at length with the child and his ADHD specialist. Is this something your child wants, or would he feel more comfortable with his friends in a public school? And how will home schooling affect his condition? These are very important questions. It's also a good idea to talk with other parents who have home-schooled their children to find out if you're up to the job. Parents with busy households or little ones running around often have trouble finding time to do the laundry, much less teach their ADHD child. Obviously, this isn't something that should be entered into lightly.

NINE

Your Choice

Throughout this book, we've maintained the assumption that you or your child has ADHD. Now it's time to ask yourself one last time whether this assumption is correct. Does your child really have ADHD? Or could his disruptive behavior and inattention—or your restlessness, labile temper, and poor focus—be caused by something that mimics some of the symptoms of ADHD?

Having analyzed the information in this book and examined all the facts in your particular case, perhaps you have concluded that your child does not meet the criteria for ADHD and that his strange demeanor must be the result of something else. A thorough differential diagnosis will help you and your doctor determine exactly what this might be.

But perhaps your answer is yes. Perhaps you've lived the behavioral nightmare of ADHD for years and, even without a professional diagnosis, have concluded with certainty that your child—or you, your spouse, or another family member—suffers with this very common syndrome.

Just to be certain, let's review the indications one more time.

ADHD is typically characterized by long-standing symptoms attributable to attention-focusing difficulties, distractibility, impulsivity, and/or hyperactivity. These symptoms interfere with a child's functioning at home and at school, the most common problem being poor academic progress despite a willingness to learn. In most cases, these symptoms have had an impact on a child's personality and emotional development since his earliest years.

Family life is repeatedly disrupted by the ADHD child's behavior. He is not able to develop or sustain strong friendships and suffers from poor self-esteem, frustration, anger, depression, and hopelessness. These emotions almost always compound his behavioral problems and interfere with his motivation.

Finally, despite the roller-coaster ride of love and hate you've experienced over the years, as parents you're deeply concerned about the possible long-term consequences of ADHD and want to do all you can to help your child so that he can have a normal and happy life.

If this summary sounds all too familiar, consider yourself part of the rapidly growing ADHD global family. As such, you probably still have many concerns regarding your role in the management of this often very disturbing and sometimes even bizarre and frightening disorder.

In this summary chapter, I'll answer your final questions on such topics as finding the right doctor, designing an individual treatment strategy for your child or yourself, and remaining an effective advocate.

Q: Now that my son's ADHD has been conclusively determined via a differential diagnosis, what do we do first? The whole situation has us completely overwhelmed.

A: Many parents assume that once their child's condition has been diagnosed, he'll simply take a pill and their troubles will be over. But in truth, diagnosis is just the first step in a very long and potentially frustrating journey.

The first thing you should do, as I've noted throughout this book, is thoroughly educate yourself and your son on his condition. Learn all you can about its many symptoms and management strategies. Then seek out a qualified physician or ADHD specialist for help in developing a multimodal approach to treatment. Ritalin is an effective first step, but as we know, it's not a panacea. Don't let anyone try to convince you that medication is all you'll need.

Q: What kind of ADHD specialist is best?

A: There are a variety of medical specialists whose training can help in the management of ADHD. However, a child psychiatrist is most specifically qualified to diagnose ADHD and institute a multimodal treatment plan. These specialists are fully trained doctors and hence are well grounded in the physical sciences and the biological aspects of human function. They also have several years of training in psychiatry with an emphasis on the problems of children and adolescents. As a result, a child psychiatrist is highly qualified to understand and examine the behavioral problems associated with ADHD, as well as the complex interplay between biology and environment that is commonly expressed in the disorder. The child psychiatrist is uniquely situated to assess all aspects of a person's functioning when he or she prescribes and manages medication.

It is also an integral part of a child psychiatrist's job to work with the different systems in a child's life. This includes school consultation, family therapy, and parental guidance, as well as collaboration with the educational specialists, pediatricians, pediatric neurologists, and social workers who are typically involved in a child's life and education. And of course, a child psychiatrist is trained in individual psychotherapy with children and adolescents.

Other professionals who may have expertise in one or more aspects of ADHD treatment include the child psychologist, pediatrician, pediatric neurologist, and special-education expert. However, none of these disciplines encompass the breadth of the medical, emotional, social, and educational aspects of ADHD in the way a child psychiatrist can.

Q: How can I find a child psychiatrist in my area who specializes in the treatment of ADHD?

A: Ask your pediatrician or primary care provider if he can refer you to a qualified child psychiatrist in your town. This often has to be the first step when looking for an ADHD specialist because many insurance companies and HMOs will not pay for specialized treatment unless you are referred by your primary care physician.

Even if you have a pediatrician, it may still be a good idea to discuss with your primary care provider some of your concerns regarding diagnosis and the planning of a multimodal treatment approach. Many pediatricians are not aware of the widespread effects of ADHD and still rely heavily on stimulant medication as the only component of treatment. Such an approach may be well intended, but it cheats the patient by ignoring the many other strategies that make up an effective management plan. Pediatricians may not be aware of the need for psychological services, nor of the need to work closely with the school and family, and hence may not suggest referral to an ADHD specialist.

If your pediatrician or family physician is unable to refer you to a child psychiatrist, you might want to call the American Academy of Child Psychiatry in Washington, D.C. at (202) 966-7300, or your local medical society for a list of child psychiatrists in your area. Another possible resource is a nearby medical school. The psychiatry department of a medical school can usually refer you to qualified psychiatrists. Many medical school psychiatry departments have a child psychiatry diagnostic center, like the Yale Child Study Center in New Haven, which can do a comprehensive assessment and differential diagnosis. If the center is too far away for an ongoing therapeutic relationship, they can often refer you to a specialist in your area for followup care. Your school or other families with ADHD children may also be helpful in suggesting a specialist in your area.

Q: We live in a very rural part of West Virginia, and there doesn't seem to be a child psychiatrist in our county. What should we do?
A: Unfortunately, many areas of the country are not served by a child psychiatrist versed in the treatment of ADHD. As a result, you may have to travel some distance to consult with one. This is necessary for the initial diagnosis and the formulation of a multimodal treatment plan, but could prove unrealistic for an ongoing professional relationship.

In cases like this, participation in an ADHD support group can be of tremendous help in determining and maintaining treatment goals. And even if you can't regularly visit your

ADHD specialist in person, do try to maintain regular contact over the phone, especially during the first few months of treatment.

If a child psychiatrist is out of the question due to distance or other factors, ask your primary care physician or officials at your child's school who they would recommend as an ADHD specialist in your area. But remember that this specialist may not be able to evaluate the whole situation. For example, if the person is a psychologist or educational specialist, he won't be able to evaluate or prescribe medication because he is not a physician. And if he's a pediatrician or pediatric neurologist, he won't be able to offer much by way of psychotherapy, nor will he be likely to get involved with your child's education.

Don't feel obligated to choose the first person you contact or even the second. Selecting an ADHD specialist is a very important and personal decision, and both you and your child should feel comfortable with the person you choose.

If you're lucky enough to receive the names of several area specialists, make a short list of three or four. Then make an appointment with each for an interview. Some doctors will talk to you on the phone, but others will prefer an in-office chat. Ask each specialist about his background and how he views the management of ADHD, as well as his feelings regarding a multimodal approach to treatment and the use of medication, psychotherapy, and family counseling; his willingness to work with your child's school, teachers, and tutors; and any other issues you feel are important. Then make your decision based on this information. Your goal is to find the most qualified individual for your child. Never settle for anything less.

Parents must often be the ones to coordinate their child's treatment and thus keep track of the many professionals involved in a multimodal program. It can be a time-consuming and occasionally frustrating job, but if you can't find a qualified child psychiatrist or other medically based ADHD specialist, you have little choice but to completely take over this coordinating role yourself.

This means making sure that all aspects of your child's functioning are assessed and that the treatment plan takes all of these aspects into account. The school may be able to do a careful educational assessment of associated learning difficulties and may then be able to refer you to a psychologist, whose further testing can look at educational, cognitive, attentional, and emotional issues. As a result of this testing, the psychologist can give you and your child's teachers a better perspective on issues affecting your child's emotional and academic success.

If significant learning problems are found, then you will have to arrange for tutoring, as well as work with the school to provide special support. Again, the child psychiatrist is very experienced in this role. However, if a psychiatrist is unavailable, you will have to work closely with the school and make sure they have all relevant information (for example, copies of any test reports) as they plan your child's program. If indicated by the testing or if either you or the school is concerned that your child has significant emotional and behavioral problems, you should find a psychotherapist experienced in working with children and ADHD sufferers. The psychotherapist must, of course, be in close communication with the doctor who is prescribing your child's medication.

So, you can begin to see the mammoth job involved in coordinating a multimodal treatment plan. But this coordinating effort is so extremely important. After all, your child is a whole person, though made up of many different aspects, and it is neither fair nor efficient to have multiple professionals working with him blindly, with no knowledge of what the others are doing. The child does not experience learning in school as vastly separate and unrelated to his social or family life and his physical well-being. And, of course, experiences in any one sphere are going to intimately affect his functioning in every other sphere. So it will make your life a lot easier, as a parent, if you can find an ADHD specialist to head your treatment team. But if you cannot, then you will have to be the energetic team leader yourself.

Q: What are the most important components when designing a multimodal treatment plan?
A: Once a definite diagnosis has been made, this will be a vital topic of discussion for you and your ADHD specialist. I

have examined several aspects of ADHD treatment in Chapters 4 through 8. Let's review them.

1. **Medication**. Stimulants, such as Dexedrine, Ritalin, and Cylert, as well as antidepressants, such as amitriptyline, Prozac, Zoloft, and Paxil are the medications most commonly used in the management of ADHD. They must be prescribed by a physician. This physician may be your primary care doctor, your pediatrician, a child psychiatrist, or a pediatric neurologist.

2. **Psychotherapy**. This is most effective in the hands of an experienced, well-trained therapist who is versed in several different approaches, such as insight-oriented therapy, supportive therapy, cognitive behavioral therapy, and group therapy. Most often, a child psychiatrist or child psychologist specifically trained in clinical work (as opposed to research) is best equipped to administer this component of the multimodal treatment plan.

3. **Behavioral modification**. Development of an appropriate regimen for home and school will require the assistance of the ADHD specialist and will probably involve rewards and perhaps punishments for targeted behaviors. Ideally, the ADHD child should take part in the planning so he sees it as a method designed to help him gain self-control and self-respect. His teachers, as well as other adults involved in his daily care, should also be part of the behavioral plan because consistency of approach is very important for success.

4. **Family counseling**. This may range from full-fledged weekly therapy involving all members of the family to occasional sessions with the parents and the ADHD specialist. Family counseling is encouraged to make individual therapy with the child easier, as well as help the parents develop strategies to work with the child at home. Family therapy may be conducted by a psychiatrist, psychologist, or social

worker, but it is most effective when the therapist is familiar with ADHD.

5. **Special education approaches**.
   a. *Classroom approaches*. These may include assigning an aide to give an ADHD child extra one-on-one attention, moving the child's desk to a less stimulating part of the room, or shaping the academic demands to more closely suit the ADHD child's needs, such as untimed tests.
   b. *Resource room help*. This means taking the child out of the classroom for special attention, both to work on weaker academic areas as well as on specific strategies for inattention, distractibility, and disorganization. This may be provided by a special-education teacher in the school or a trained study skills instructor.
   c. *Remedial tutoring outside school*. This may be recommended by the school or the ADHD specialist and usually involves a tutor working regularly with the ADHD child to strengthen weak academic areas. This includes help with regular schoolwork, as well as solidifying basic skills.
   d. *Special educational tutoring*. This is done by a tutor skilled both in understanding learning disabilities and in adapting a teaching approach to compensate for specific learning disabilities, such as deficits in memory or in visual-spatial processing. This specialist will also be able to help a child with ADHD develop specific learning strategies that will be useful throughout his life, such as enhancing note-taking skills and turning abstract visual concepts into verbal problems, when weakness lies in the visual sphere.
   e. *Changing schools*, either to one with a smaller student-teacher ratio or to a school specializing in children with ADHD and/or learning disabilities.

6. **Nonspecific approaches**, such as improving the ADHD child's general health with proper diet, regular exercise, a better-scheduled life, with adequate sleep and quiet time, and a more predictable family routine.

Q: Is it necessary for every aspect of the multimodal treatment plan to be applied in every case? If not, how should we decide which components are most important for our son?

A: Not everyone with ADHD needs all of the different treatment approaches. There are widely varying degrees of severity with ADHD, as well as varying symptom combinations.

Consider, for example, the differences between Peter and Stephanie, described in Chapter 6. Peter was highly symptomatic, so much so that even by age four the manifestations of his ADHD had intruded upon and affected every aspect of his life and that of other family members. In contrast, Stephanie's difficulties were much less visible or severe. They were initially seen as only academic and hence did not draw concern until she was eight, though it soon became clear that there were many emotional issues that also needed attention. These differences were reflected in the different multimodal approaches used in each case.

Peter needed nearly all of the components of the multimodal treatment approach, including individual psychotherapy, medication, behavioral modification at home and school, family counseling, and special classroom approaches. Approaches in the classroom included resource room activity to tutor Peter in weak areas and help him learn strategies to cope with some of his weaknesses. For example, this involved extra computer work for him, as his small-motor problems significantly hampered his writing skills.

Stephanie, on the other hand, clearly needed psychotherapy to deal with the emotional issues related to her ADHD. She also needed some individual tutoring in math and extra help in developing strategies for organization and for controlling the distractibility and impulsivity that sometimes caused her to be careless with her schoolwork.

In both cases, I needed to be available to consult with the

patients' schools and teachers, though, obviously, in Peter's case, this was a much more intensive interaction. At its height, it included the teachers sending me weekly rating scales of Peter's behavior and my preparing detailed recommendations for their approach to him in the classroom.

As I explained in Chapter 6, I believe psychotherapy can almost always be helpful to a child or adult suffering from ADHD. I do not believe, however, that medication is always necessary. It is certainly indicated when there are severe symptoms of hyperactivity, distractibility, or impulsivity, but it is rarely sufficient when used alone. The ADHD patient must learn other ways to control his symptoms, including psychotherapy, behavioral modification, and academic or work remediation.

When ADHD has severely distorted family relationships, it is important that family therapy be a component. This was the case with Philip, who was first described in Chapter 7. His marriage had suffered enormously due to his severe and previously undiagnosed inattention, impulsivity, and disorganization. Not only did these symptoms interfere with his professional work, but they made him a less consistent partner in the home. He was often insensitive to the needs of his wife and child, forgetful and emotionally unstable, with little forethought as to the consequences of his actions.

An important component of Philip's treatment was couples therapy, which helped with the damage to his marriage as well. He learned the importance of gaining the understanding and support of his wife as he struggled to improve his situation. He also needed a trial of medication, which, indeed, helped him to concentrate and organize himself. This led to improvement in his functioning both at home and at work.

Behavior modification is particularly helpful in cases where a pattern of disruptive behavior has been established. However, if this has progressed to the point of a serious conduct disorder or antisocial personality, it is unlikely that the ADHD patient will be sufficiently motivated to cooperate. Intensive psychotherapy may be necessary in conjunction with behavioral treatments. Medication can also help in such cases, though it is important to remember that there has already been damage to this person's ability to relate to others with trust and empathy that no amount of medication will alter. However, it may help with impulsivity and behavioral control and therefore make the individual more amenable to psychotherapy.

Thus, it can be seen that just as there is a wide spectrum of severity and type of symptoms in ADHD, so there is a wide spectrum of treatment plans. It is very important that your treatment plan be molded specifically to your family member's needs, a crucial job with which your ADHD specialist can help.

Q: Can you tell us the steps the ADHD specialist will take in setting up the multimodal plan? Which treatments should she try first?

A: There is no simple recipe, for example, "Start with Treatment Number 1. Add Number 2 if still symptomatic. Then add 3," and so on. It really depends on the symptoms of the individual and on how he works within his environment. It also depends on the history, the degree of distorted development and the secondary problems that have arisen as a result of the ADHD. This is why a careful assessment of all areas of functioning is an essential part of setting up the treatment plan.

However, I can give some general guidelines as to how I go about this in my practice.

1. A thorough assessment of functioning in all areas and of emotional coping skills, self-concept, and relationships.
2. First steps of treatment.
   a. *Medication.* If a person's ADHD is indeed detrimentally affecting his life in multiple areas, I am likely to recommend a trial of Ritalin or other stimulant, along with some initial problem-solving sessions. This is because stimulants are safe, economical, and very often quite helpful.
   b. *Problem-solving sessions.* If the patient is a child, the problem-solving sessions may focus on helping the child's parents to develop better coping

skills, to adapt household routines to better fit the needs of their child, and to assist in setting up strategies to help their child control his behavior. These sessions may also be used to design behavioral modification plans for home and school, if their child's behavior is particularly disruptive.

If the patient is an adult, the initial problem-solving sessions will focus on helping him better define the problem areas, whether they be problems at work, where his inattention and distractibility interfere, or whether his impulsivity is making interpersonal relations difficult. Once he has a clearer understanding of the problem areas, it may then be possible to devise strategies that can begin to make a difference immediately.

  c. *School consultation.* If the patient is a child, I will almost always consider school consultation to be an essential part of the management plan, even if it is only an initial contact to discuss medication needs and to recommend some classroom tactics to help the patient.

These initial problem-solving sessions allow me to evaluate the effect of the medication and to adjust the dose or type of medication as necessary while further evaluating the impact of ADHD on the patient's functioning in all spheres. If simple behavioral strategies and medication are not having the desired effect or if they are clearly not enough, due to the severity of the primary symptoms or the secondary effects on the patient's life, I will then recommend further steps.

3. Therapy, the next step. Therapy is necessary when the patient's ADHD has had long-standing effects on their functioning. The results may be poor self-esteem, poor social relations, anxiety and depression, as well as severe behavior and conduct disorders. Therapy is also necessary in ADHD patients who

have difficulty tolerating emotional states and in thinking about themselves or in using an internal narrative to process stimuli and to postpone action. And therapy is of course used in severe cases of inattention, impulsivity, and distractibility.

The focus of the therapy will depend on the nature of the difficulties. If they are largely secondary emotional difficulties, the therapy will focus on the need to develop insight. If the difficulties center on an inability to use language internally to process experience more fully—and hence have a tool with which to control impulsivity and focus attention—then the therapy will first focus on this skill. If the patient's difficulties center primarily on his relationships with his family, then family therapy may be indicated. Or if the patient's ADHD is severely interfering with his peer relations, group therapy can be helpful.

4. Branching out—treatment modalities in the school or work setting.

   a. *Special education or tutoring.* The primary concern for some children with ADHD may be their academic functioning. Some children have little if any hyperactivity or behavioral problems but may have significant inattention and distractibility. With these children, the first line of treatment may include energetic classroom help and special tutoring to develop strategies of dealing with their cognitive and attentional difficulties. If the inattention is severe, I sometimes also recommend a trial of stimulant medication, even in the absence of hyperactivity. Children with severe ADHD almost always need special educational or classroom approaches as part of their multimodal treatment plan, including behavioral modification strategies.

   b. *Work skills tutoring.* I will sometimes refer adults for special work skills tutoring if therapy or problem-solving sessions are not sufficient to help with a patient's severe disorganization, procrastination, and other work-related problems, such as time management, reading efficacy, ability to process information, writing difficulties, etc.

Q: Could you give us a few additional tips on designing an individual treatment strategy for our ten-year-old ADHD son? We want to make sure we're doing everything we can to guarantee a bright future for our child.

A: An effective individual treatment strategy must take many factors into consideration, including school, home, the child's social life, his relationship with parents and siblings, and his emotional state. Each of these must be addressed individually and also as parts of the big picture.

Parents must work closely together and spend time thinking about how family life can be structured so that it is most helpful to the ADHD child. This may involve setting up some behavioral contingency systems (as outlined in Chapter 5) and making sure that all of the children in the family are involved so as not to separate the ADHD child and make him feel as if he's the bad one.

At the same time, you should start having group family meetings on a regular basis. The meetings shouldn't focus exclusively on the behavior or treatment of the ADHD child, but should also include other family issues. Of particular importance are ongoing family problems and ways to deal with them that benefit all concerned.

During your first family meeting, it may be helpful to remind the ADHD child that the entire family is working together to help with his problems, not to control his life. Let him know, through words and actions, that you, as well as his brothers and sisters, are concerned about him and want to make things better.

This includes sharing with the ADHD child everything you've learned about the disorder. Emphasize repeatedly that the condition and its resulting behavior is not all his fault and that you'll be working closely together to find ways for him to deal with it.

At the same time, outline the kinds of professional help that will be provided at home, at school, and in therapy. Assure the child that you will be there to help him negotiate the world a little better and that he can talk to you any time he feels he has a problem.

In addition, involve the child in the planning of little details as well as big ones. For example, if the child needs a tutor, make sure he's comfortable with the person you've chosen. Let the child know you are taking his reactions and feelings seriously and are using all of this information to make the very best decisions regarding his treatment.

Explain to the child all you can about the different components of the multimodal approach to treatment. Tell him what his medication is, what it does, and how it will help him cope with his condition. Be equally up front about the need for psychotherapy, special classes, and other strategies. Make treatment a positive thing, not something to be afraid or ashamed of. This will give the child more control over his life and make him feel better about himself. Ignorance only breeds fear and anxiety.

While discussing treatment, remember that many ADHD children have difficulty with change at home and at school. If change occurs too quickly, it can cause anxiety, frustration, and anger. To avoid this, plan the child's treatment schedule in such a way that it easily becomes routine and doesn't overload the child with too much stimuli or activity. One child with whom I worked had a daily schedule that was so strenuous, she didn't receive her special educational tutoring until almost 8 p.m. Of course, by then she was exhausted and irritable because her stimulant medication was starting to wear off. Her parents meant well, but the program they had designed for her was too much, and it caused more harm than good. Remember that children need some free time during the day so they can relax and have a bit of fun.

School demands equal attention from the parents of an ADHD child. This was discussed at length in Chapter 8, but to reiterate, parents should work closely with school officials to ensure that their child's special needs are met. This means providing the school with as much data as you can regarding ADHD and your child's case in particular; bringing in an ADHD specialist, if necessary, to discuss treatment and management; and having the specialist give the school specific recommendations on how to help your child learn as effectively as possible. Stay involved with the school and your child's teachers to make sure your child's school experiences are the best they can be.

Q: What about self-help? Aren't there things I can do for myself now that I know I have ADHD?

A: Yes. First, educate yourself about ADHD by reading books and discussing the disorder with your specialist. The more you understand about how this underlying disorder has affected each area of your life, the better you will be at improving your situation.

Next, educate the significant others in your life. This may include family, friends, and work colleagues. The more they understand about your difficulties, the more they will be able to help you.

Then it is time to structure and organize your life. While an ADHD specialist can be a valuable advisor or coach in this task, there are steps that you can follow on your own.

1. Define the problem. You should start by defining your problem areas. Write them down. One at a time, break each problem down into its components. It may help to ask yourself just what aspect of the task or situation makes it difficult for you.

    For example, the problem of being perpetually late may have several typical causes. It may be that you don't plan activities ahead of time and have no real idea how long it takes you to do things. Or the problem may be with your distractibility. While you may plan to do something and have adequate time to get to it and do it, you may be repeatedly distracted from the task.

2. Brainstorm solutions to each component of your problem. Use paper and pen to write down *all* solutions and alternative ways of doing things that come to mind.

3. Mentally test your solutions. Here you begin to use

your critical faculty and, in your imagination, go through the solutions and assess the likely outcome.

4. Critically plan your solution. Here you can discard the ideas that clearly won't work and begin to plan your new strategies for coping with certain situations.

   For example, after defining the problem of lateness, you have come up with some solutions: "Run or drive faster. Just get more done in a day! Wear three wristwatches; set three alarms. Begin by estimating the time for each activity you plan to do in a day, write it down, and as you actually do the activity, record the length of time it took. Compare the estimate with the actual time." Well, you will soon see that some solutions, like the last, are better than others, like the first three. You can discard the ideas that clearly come from your impatience, impulsiveness, and self-punitive feelings, and begin to see that if you allow yourself to tackle problem-solving in this way, you can actually come up with some good solutions.

5. Add organization and structure to your life. This change could benefit all aspects of your life. You can start with external structure. This may include ordering your possessions; organizing your time with lists and schedules; using filing systems, notebooks, and lists as external memory banks and reminders; and minimizing distractions in your workplace. Such external structure can also help internally: the more information you structure and record externally, the less you have to be trying to remember and deal with in your mind. In other words, you can minimize the clutter and distractions in your mind by making some of your tasks, reminders, and organizing needs external and concrete. Then you can better focus on what is essential.

6. Define tasks more clearly. This may include breaking down tasks into smaller components, prioritizing them, and taking into account your own attention span and need for variation, breaks, and physical ac-

tivity. Perhaps you work best in forty-five-minute chunks, or perhaps you work best with a long expanse of uninterrupted time, in order to better focus your attention. Then plan your work accordingly.

7. Use time-out strategies to deal with intense emotions. If a major part of your difficulty stems from impulsive actions and heated emotional outbursts, then you can begin to train yourself to deliberately take time out when emotionally aroused. This may mean counting to ten, or it may mean actually going somewhere to cool out. During this cool-out period, follow several mental steps: Define the problem. What upset you and why? What is your impulsive solution, and is that really the best way to react? What would be an alternative way of handling the situation? What is the outcome of that reaction or action likely to be? Is there an even better way of handling the situation? This process allows you to delay impulsive action and to practice bringing your inner reflective skills to bear on the situation. This is often very difficult for ADHD sufferers. As I have explained in Chapter 6, psychotherapy is often necessary in order to strengthen these inner reflective skills. However, setting up a disciplined time-out strategy can be an enormous help in gradually making this reflectiveness become more automatic and in making intense emotional states more tolerable.

Q: I've decided to tutor my ADHD daughter in a few academic areas in which she's weak. Could you offer some tips on how to make this situation go smoothly for both of us?

A: You're to be commended for taking such an active role in your daughter's education. Few parents have the time or the inclination to tackle such a problem on their own.

The first thing you should do is consult with your daughter's instructors to make sure you're on the same wavelength as to your daughter's specific needs and goals. While you're talking, ask the teachers if they have any special texts, workbooks, or advice that will make your tutoring job a little easier for all concerned.

Make sure your tutoring sessions are conducted in a quiet room with few distractions and that your daughter's medication (if she's on any) is at full effectiveness. Strive for short, daily sessions that improve her understanding of the topics at hand and complement what's being taught in class. And take frequent breaks, especially if your daughter is hyperactive. Extended tutoring sessions should be avoided because they can overtax your daughter's mind, make her cranky or anxious, and result in conflict. When it's obvious that she is no longer willing or able to pay attention, stop and make a date for the next day. Begin each new session with a brief review of what was discussed previously.

Always maintain a positive approach. Compliments and encouragement go much farther than reprimands and scoldings. Always try to set your daughter up for success rather than failure. And try to reward her in some small way when she accomplishes something truly remarkable. But most importantly, don't become discouraged if your daughter's progress seems agonizingly slow. It's not uncommon for ADHD children to learn in spurts, with extended periods of little progress. Maintain a good attitude, and your sessions should go very well.

Two final suggestions: Try to end each tutoring session on a high note, preferably with an activity that your daughter enjoys. This will make tutoring a fun activity, rather than a chore, and hopefully something she will look forward to. And once you've closed the textbooks, take off your "teacher hat" and put it away. It's tempting to play the role of instructor all the time, but that will only put undue pressure on your mother-daughter relationship. Teach only during your daily tutoring sessions; then let it go. You're an instructor for an hour a day, but a mom for the other twenty-three.

In fact, for some families, there has been so much friction around homework and academic success that it is much better for the tutoring needs to be met totally outside the family. In such cases, it is important to mend the child-parent relationship, and for the parent to take the role of teacher would be counterproductive to that process. In addition, conflicts and emotional issues between the parent and child may hinder both the child's motivation and his ability to focus on his work. A tutor can remain objective and outside those emotional issues and does not already have a long history of conflict with the child.

Q: Our ADHD specialist has suggested that we write down the governing rules in our family and place them where everyone can see them. I've never really given this much thought. What kinds of rules should we consider that will most help our eight-year-old ADHD son?

A: Having rules in writing is a wonderful way for ADHD children to remember what's expected of them, without having to be constantly nagged by Mom and Dad. It reminds other family members too. The process of making rules can be a worthwhile family activity. At a family meeting, talk about why rules would be a good idea, and ask the children for their opinion on the value of rules. It may be helpful to broaden the discussion, at first, to rules at school, in society, and so on. And ask them to consider the pitfalls of having no rules at all.

Then ask every family member to think up some rules. Perhaps you could devise a plan whereby everyone comes up with five household rules, then schedule another meeting to discuss these rules and make a final list. While you, as parents, cannot guarantee that the final decision will be a totally democratic process, taking the input of the children seriously can give them a sense of self-respect, and confidence that your authority will not be used arbitrarily just to control them.

House rules are different for every family and are usually established based on a child's specific ADHD symptoms. For example, if a child is very hyperactive, rules might include: "We do not leave the table until we are finished with our meal," or "Running through the house is unacceptable." A few good rules for all to live by include the following.

- Everyone must pick up after themselves.
- Verbal or physical abuse is never acceptable.

- Do not interrupt when someone else is speaking.
- Everyone's opinion is valid. Listen before answering.
- Homework must be completed before the television can be turned on.
- Chores must be completed before allowance is awarded.
- There will be no screaming (or fighting) in the house.
- If you see a problem, offer a solution.
- ADHD is not an excuse for lazy behavior. Everyone must pull his weight.

Q: My husband's parents are aware that our seven-year-old son has ADHD and requires discipline and structure, yet they persist in undermining our efforts to keep our son on his treatment plan. I know they love their grandson, but their interference is causing serious problems. What can we do, short of banning them from our house?

A: Most grandparents love to spoil their grandchildren, and your husband's parents are no exception. Grandparents often express their love by doting on a child, buying him gifts, and letting him do what Mom and Dad seldom allow. This can cause minor problems with a healthy, normal child, but it can be counterproductive if a child has ADHD.

Separating your son from his grandparents is an unacceptable solution. It would almost certainly cause a terrible rift between you and your in-laws and would probably make your son miserable. Instead, try a little education. Take your in-laws aside, and explain to them that their loving efforts are undermining the important management strategies you have established for your son's condition. If you haven't done so already, explain what ADHD is, how it affects your son's behavior at home and at school, and exactly what you're doing to help keep his problems under control.

Then enlist their help. Explain what they can and cannot do with your son (such as let him run wild when he wants or avoid doing his chores or homework), and offer acceptable alternatives to their "anything goes" approach to grandparenting. Perhaps special activities or times with grandparents can be part of your son's rewards for fulfilling his obligations. If they still resist, ask your ADHD specialist to talk with them. Hearing the same words from a doctor or other expert often works wonders.

Most importantly, always tell your in-laws how much you appreciate and love them and how happy you are that they are involved in your son's life. Grandparents can be a tremendous source of love and inspiration for a child and extremely helpful when it comes to the management of ADHD. Do what you must to enlist them as allies. No doubt they'll be more than happy to help once they fully understand your situation.

Do remember though, that being with his grandparents may be the one place where your son feels unconditional acceptance and doesn't have the history of angry recrimination and disruption that has made the behavioral strategies necessary at home. Sometimes it may be helpful for him to let his hair down a little.

Q: Does ADHD have to be a lifelong condition?
A: This is a difficult question to answer. There are worrisome indications that many children with ADHD don't grow out of it and have the potential for serious problems in adulthood. But there are also indications that effective help early on can change that outcome.

It is important for parents to realize that they can indeed act to ensure a more positive outcome. And as their children grow older, they can and should become strong champions of their youngster's individual motivation, development, and success. It's similarly important that children learn to become their own vocal advocates, and parents can help their children develop this ability. This training will benefit them greatly when they grow up.

There is strong clinical evidence that the majority of youngsters diagnosed with ADHD will continue to manifest some symptoms well into adulthood, if not for the rest of their lives. But that doesn't mean they should let the condition rule their existence. Effective management techniques, psychotherapy, education, and the use of stimulant medication and antidepressants can go a long way toward helping anyone with ADHD live a normal, healthy, happy life. As I have described in the preceding chapters, adequate attention given to all aspects of the ADHD sufferer's life can make an enormous difference. In fact, as I describe in Chapter 6, I believe it is possible, with therapy, to change the underlying disabilities, not just temporarily ameliorate the symptoms, as with medication.

Q: My child has severe ADHD, and I'm afraid that her condition means she'll have to settle for less in everything she does from now on. Is this a valid concern, or am I worrying needlessly?
A: Studies have shown that adults with ADHD are usually less professionally advanced, don't do as well economically, and have more troubled relationships. But it doesn't have to be that way; quite a bit can be done to prevent these problems from developing. This includes not only medication and academic help, but also psychotherapy, which can delve into the more subtle effects that ADHD has on self-esteem and interpersonal relationships. It's an essential part of the multimodal treatment plan that can dramatically help the long-term outcome.

It's common for parents to feel bleak about the future of their ADHD children. Often they've suffered for years with their child's disruptive and unpredictable behavior, desperate for any information on what causes it and what can be done to bring it under control. And a diagnosis of ADHD doesn't mean their problems are over. It means that the real work is just beginning.

That's why the parents of youngsters with ADHD should view their ADHD specialists as a resource for themselves as well as their children. Don't hesitate to turn to the experts in your life for help, especially during the most difficult periods. In addition, seek the advice and emotional support of other parents who have dealt with this situation.

Most importantly, remember that you're not the only parents who have suffered through this. Thousands have been there before you, and you can learn through their experiences. The fact that your child has ADHD doesn't mean you're bad parents or that your child is a "bad seed." It's a chronic medical problem, just like diabetes, and must be thought of as such.

Q: I don't know if I'm up to the demands of my son's ADHD management program. It's so much work, and there's no light at the end of the tunnel. Please help me.

A: There's no denying the fact that the management of ADHD can be extremely difficult and time-consuming and that the parents of children with the syndrome are called upon to make a greater sacrifice of time and money than ordinary parents. But believe me, it's worth it. Through your hard work, your child will be able to deal with his condition and, hopefully, go on to meet all of life's challenges with enthusiasm, never settling for less than he's entitled to.

However, it is important that you have some support for your feelings of frustration and hopelessness. This support can come in the form of your spouse or other family members, other parents of ADHD children, and parent groups and associations, as well as your ADHD specialist. Talking about your frustrations to others familiar with the disorder can help you gain a better perspective and can often help you find solutions to problematic issues.

Remember, too, that at times your frustration mirrors that of your child. You can certainly use your own feelings as a barometer of how the ADHD sufferer in your family is feeling. This may be just the time to be giving him some extra support. In addition, your hopelessness may be a sign that something more is needed in the treatment plan, so again, it may be time to reassess the whole management plan.

It is important for you, as a parent or spouse of an ADHD sufferer, to practice the skills that the person with the disorder needs to learn. These include being able to talk about your feelings, as well as use problem-solving strategies and even time-out strategies to deal with intense feelings that seem intolerable. Using these skills, starting with something as simple as sharing your feelings of frustration and hopelessness with your spouse, can shed more light on your feelings, can allow the feelings themselves to become more tolerable, and can lead to more useful patterns of thinking and problem-solving. This process can then also lead to an inhibition of impulsive action, as well as to a decrease in wild mood fluctuations. Other general stress-reducing techniques that can benefit every member of the family, including the ADHD sufferer, include relaxation techniques, listening to music, exercise, and so on.

Of course, some frustration is inevitable due to the long-standing nature of the disorder and to the manner in which it affects all aspects of development and especially interpersonal relations. Obviously, you must never give up on your child. It's hard to remain motivated and optimistic in the face of overwhelming problems and slow change, especially if your child's ADHD is just one of many family difficulties. So take small steps and enjoy every success, no matter how minor.

It's easy for me to tell you this because I see people in your position almost every day. By the time most parents come to me, they've had it. They see nothing good coming from their work, and they feel frustrated, angry, and hopeless. I tell them that they may have to make serious sacrifices, just as with any serious medical condition, but that doing so will most definitely show results. They *can* make a difference.

Sometimes parents feel guilty about their child's suffering, and this makes it hard for them to set limits on just how much they are willing to sacrifice in the care of the ADHD sufferer. So do make sure the time you put in with your ADHD child is effective, and make sure that you use other resources as well. Your other children and spouse need you, and you have your own needs to fulfill, so sometimes it is essential that you use baby-sitters or other family members to help out. Older ADHD children can benefit enormously from sleep-away camps that specialize in their needs. Such a stay, even if just for a week, can give the family a needed break, while also teaching the ADHD child to handle himself in new situations and to enhance his social skills.

Q: I'm trying very hard to be a strong advocate for my thirteen-year-old son in the community and in school, and so far it's working pretty well. How can I maintain this difficult role in the years ahead?

A: Being an advocate for a child with ADHD can be a full-time job and a lifelong one as well. But it can also be tremendously fulfilling.

Advocacy covers many areas, as I'm sure you've found. In school, it means working with officials and teachers to ensure that your child is given every opportunity to learn. Sometimes this means being a bit pushy, especially if school officials refuse to take your child's special needs seriously.

On the home front, advocacy may mean going head to head with your insurance carrier or HMO to receive coverage for your child's multimodal treatment regimen. It also means educating friends, neighbors, co-workers, and family members on what ADHD is, how it affects a child's behavior, and how they can help.

Advocacy also means maintaining a continuing voice in the local community to ensure that special services are available for everyone with ADHD, children and adults alike. It means intervening on your child's behalf if he has difficulties with the Boy Scouts or some other social group by explaining to officials what ADHD is and how they can most effectively deal with it.

Foremost, your ongoing role as advocate involves being your child's "extra ego," meaning the part of the mind that helps negotiate the real world. Youngsters with ADHD have far more difficulties in this area than most normal children, and your continued support is essential.

Of course, as your child grows older, it may become more difficult for you to intervene in a direct way in every area of his life. In fact, it would not be appropriate for you to do so. But you can certainly help him now to develop the skills and the sense of confidence he will need to be his own advocate. If he understands that he has a neurological syndrome that is not his fault and that he has a right to expect certain needs to be met, he will become a more confident advocate for himself. Similarly, it is essential that he should know as much as possible about his disorder, particularly about his own cognitive and academic difficulties and possible strategies that help him. For example, when in college, he will have to let his professors know about special needs, such as untimed exams or particular aids for note-taking or writing papers, and so on.

Q: Do adults with ADHD need advocates too?

A: In a manner of speaking, yes. Most adults with ADHD are quite capable of taking care of themselves, that is, of being their own advocates. But sometimes the problems and issues associated with ADHD become so intense that the ADHD patient feels overwhelmed. In times like these, family members may need to act as advocates on their loved one's behalf.

As with child advocacy, this can cover a lot of territory. For example, it may involve explaining to friends, neighbors, and family members what ADHD is and how it affects the patient's behavior; or battling with your insurance company to ensure that medication and other forms of treatment are fully covered (many companies see ADHD only as a childhood disorder and are reluctant to reimburse treatment for adults); or working closely with the patient to help him avoid the day-to-day obstacles that can make life so miserable for people with ADHD.

In most cases, however, being an advocate for an adult with ADHD simply means offering ample amounts of love, compassion, and, most importantly, understanding. Dealing with ADHD can be extremely difficult when you're a child. But it's even more arduous when you're an adult.

TEN

Resources for the ADHD Family

Support and Networking Organizations

The daily management of an ADHD child is seldom something parents can handle entirely on their own; even the most ardent caregivers need help and support at one time or another. Your doctor or ADHD specialist is one valuable source, but there are also a lot of benefits to joining an ADHD support group. Being with people who share and understand your joy and heartache can make the task of living with an ADHD sufferer so much easier.

There are support and networking organizations in almost every region of the United States and Canada. Following are some of the largest and best known:

Children and Adults with
  Attention Deficit Disorders
  (CHADD)
National Headquarters
499 NW 70th Avenue,
  Suite 101
Plantation, FL 33317
1-800-233-4050 (voicemail
  only) or 954-587-3700

ADDult Information Exchange
  Network
c/o Jim Reisinger
P.O. Box 1701
Ann Arbor, MI 48106
313-426-1659

ADDult Support Network
c/o Mary Jane Johnson,
  Organizer
2620 Ivy Place
Toledo, OH 43613

Attention Deficit Disorder
  Association (ADDA)
P.O. Box 972
Mentor, OH 44061
1-800-487-2282 (recorded
  message) or 216-350-9595

The Attention Deficit
  Information Network, Inc.
  (AD-IN)
475 Hillside Avenue
Needham, MA 02194
617-455-9895

Learning Disabilities
  Association of America
  (LDA)
Jean Peterson, Executive
  Director

4156 Library Road
Pittsburgh, PA 15234
412-341-1515

National Center for Learning
  Disabilities (NCLD)
381 Park Avenue South,
  Suite 1401
New York, NY 10016
212-545-7510

National Information Center for
  Children and Youth With
  Disabilities
P.O. Box 1492
Washington DC 20013-1492
202-884-8200

Self-Help Clearing House
Northwest Covenant Medical
  Center
25 Pocono Road
Denville, NJ 07834
201-625-9565

Professional Organizations

The following organizations can provide valuable information regarding the diagnosis and management of ADHD, as well as refer you to ADHD specialists in your area:

American Academy of Child
  and Adolescent Psychiatry
3615 Wisconsin Avenue NW
Washington, DC 20016
202-966-7300

American Academy of
  Pediatrics
141 Northwest Point Blvd.
Elk Grove Village, IL 60007
847-228-5005

American Occupational Therapy
  Association
4720 Montgomery Lane
Bethesda, MD 20824-1220
301-652-2682

American Psychiatric
  Association
1400 K Street, NW
Washington, DC 20005
202-682-6000

American Psychological
  Association
750 1st Street NE
Washington DC 20002
202-336-5500

American Speech-Language-
  Hearing Association
10801 Rockville Pike
Rockville, MD 20852
301-897-5700

Council for Exceptional
  Children
1920 Association Drive
Reston, VA 20191-1589
703-620-3660
(This organization includes an Educational Resources Information Center on handicapped and gifted children that provides information and a clearinghouse)

The Orton Dyslexia Society
Chester Building, Suite 382
8600 LaSalle Road
Baltimore, MD 21286-2044
410-296-0232

Educational Resources

There is a tremendous amount of educational material available regarding the management of ADHD. The following organizations and companies can help you locate specific books, workbooks, videos, and catalogs:

ADD Warehouse
300 NW 70th Avenue,
  Suite 102
Plantation, FL 33317
954-792-8944

The Attention Deficit Resource
  Center
1344 Johnson Ferry Road,
  Suite 14
Marietta, GA 30068

The Rebus Institute
1499 Bayshore Blvd.
Burlingame, CA 94010
415-697-7424
(Provides up-to-date literature on the relevance of the Americans with Disabilities Act (ADA) to adults with ADHD and learning disabilities, especially in relation to employment situations)

ADHD Newsletters

Many national ADHD support organizations publish regular newsletters detailing the latest in ADHD management techniques, medical studies, and related legislation. Subscription prices and publication schedules vary from group to group. Write or call for information.

The ADHD Report
Guilford Publications
Russell Barkley, Editor
72 Spring Street
New York, NY 10012
800-365-7006

ADDendum (for adults with ADD)
Paul Jaffe, Editor
c/o CPS
5041-A Backlick Road
Annandale, VA 22003

Challenge, the Newsletter About Attention Deficit in Children and Adults
c/o Jean Harrison, President
P.O. Box 488,
West Newbury, MA 01985
888-239-4737

ADDult News
c/o Mary Jane Johnson
ADDult Support Network
2620 Ivy Place
Toledo, OH 43613

CH.A.D.D.ER and CH.A.D.D.ER BOX
CHADD National Headquarters
499 Northwest 70th Avenue, Suite 308
Plantation, FL 33317
954-587-3700

The Rebus Institute Report
1499 Bayshore Boulevard, Suite 146
Burlingame, CA 94010
415-697-7424

State and National Advocacy Groups

Advocacy is an integral part of being an ADHD caregiver, whether it's for a child or an adult. The following organizations provide the latest information on advocacy issues and can help cut through the red tape when you have problems with school officials or government bureaucrats:

ADD Advocacy Group
(Colorado residents only)
8091 South Ireland Way

Aurora, CO 80016
303-675-5337

Resources for the ADHD Family 243

CHADD National State
 Networking Committee
499 NW 70th Avenue
Suite 101
Plantation, FL 33317
954-587-3700

Equal Employment Opportunity
 Commission
1801 L Street NW
Washington, DC 20507
202-663-4900

Department of Justice
Civil Rights Division
Office of Americans with
 Disabilities Act
P.O. Box 66738
Washington, DC 20035-6738
202-514-0301

ADHD Books For Adults

It's impossible to know too much about the diagnosis and management of ADHD. The following books are extremely helpful to families who have just learned of the disorder, as well as those who have lived with it for years:

A Parent's Guide to Attention Deficit Disorders: The Children's Hospital of Philadelphia, Lisa J. Bain (Doubleday).

ADD and Creativity: Tapping Your Inner Muse, Lynn Weiss (Taylor Publishing).

ADD and the College Student: A Guide for High School and College Students with Attention Deficit Disorder, Patricia O. Quinn, M.D. (Magination Press).

The ADDed Dimension: Everyday Advice for Adults with ADD, Kate Kelly (Scribner).

The ADD Hyperactivity Workbook for Parents, Teachers and Kids, Harvey C. Parker (Impact Publications, Plantation, Florida).

ADD Kaleidoscope: The Many Facets of Adult Attention Deficit Disorder, Joan Andrews and Denise E. Davis (Hope Press).

ADD Success Stories: A Guide to Fulfillment for Families with Attention Deficit Disorder, Thom Hartmann and John J. Ratey (Underwood Books).

ADD: Helping Your Child—Untying the Knot of Attention Deficit Disorders, Warren Umansky, Ph.D. and Barbara Steinberg Smalley (Warner Books).

ADHD A Teenager's Guide, James J. Crist (Center for Applied Psychotherapy).

ADHD and Teens: A Parent's Guide to Making It Through the Tough Years, Colleen Alexander-Roberts (Taylor Publishing).
ADHD in the Schools: Assessment and Intervention Strategies, George J. DuPaul and Gary Stoner (Guilford Press).
ADHD/Hyperactivity: A Consumer's Guide for Parents and Teachers, Michael Gordon (GSI Publications).
Adult ADD: A Reader Friendly Guide to Identifying, Understanding, and Treating Adult Attention Deficit Disorder, Tom Whiteman et al. (Pinon Press).
Adventures in Fast Forward: Life, Love, and Work for the ADD Adult, Kathleen G. Nadeau (Brunner/Mazel).
All About A.D.D.: Understanding Attention Deficit Disorder, Mark Selikowitz (Oxford University Press).
All About Attention Deficit Disorder: A Comprehensive Guide, Thomas W. Phelan (Child Management Inc.).
Answers to Distraction, Edward M. Hallowell, M.D., and John J. Ratey, M.D. (Bantam Books).
Are You Listening?: Attention Deficit Disorders: A Guide for Understanding and Managing Overactive, Attention Deficit and Impulsive Behaviors in Children, Don H. Fontenelle (Front Row Experience).
Attention Deficit and the Law: A Guide For Advocates, Peter S. Latham, J.D., and Pamela H. Latham, J.D. (JKL Communications).
Attention Deficit Disorder and Learning Disabilities: Reality, Myths and Controversial Treatments, Barbara D. Ingersoll and Sam Goldstein (Doubleday).
Attention Deficit Disorder: ADHD and ADD Syndromes, Dale R. Jordon (Pro Ed).
Attention Deficit Disorder: Helpful, Practical Information: A Guide for Parents and Educators (Guide for Parents and Educators Series), Elaine K. McEwan Adkins (Harold Shaw Publishers).
Attention Deficit Disorders in Adults: Practical Help for Sufferers and Their Spouses, Lynn Weiss, Ph.D. (Taylor Publishing Company.).
Attention Deficit Hyperactivity Disorder: A Guidebook for Diagnosis and Treatment, Russell A. Barkley, Ph.D. (Guilford Press).

Attention Deficit Hyperactivity Disorder: Questions and Answers for Parents, Gregory S. Greenberg and Wade Horn (Research Press).

Attentional Deficit Disorder in Children and Adolescents, Jack L. Fadely and Virginia N. Hosler (Charles C. Thomas Publishers).

Attention Deficit Hyperactivity Disorder: A Clinical Guide to Diagnosis and Treatment, Larry B. Silver, M.D. (American Psychiatric Press).

Beyond Ritalin, Stephen W. Garber, Ph.D., Marianne Daniels Garber, Ph.D., and Robyn Freedman Spizman (Villard).

Do You Have Attention Deficit Disorder?, James Lawrence Thomas et al. (Dell Publishing Company).

Dr. Larry Silver's Advice to Parents on Attention Deficit Hyperactivity Disorder, Larry M. Silver (Psychiatric Press).

Driven to Distraction: Recognizing and Coping with Attention Deficit Disorder from Childhood through Adulthood, Edward M. Hallowell, M.D. and John J. Ratey, M.D. (Touchstone/Simon & Schuster).

Give Your ADD Teen a Chance: A Guide for Parents of Teenagers with Attention Deficit Disorder, Lynn Weiss, Ph.D. (Pinon Press).

Helping the Child Who Doesn't Fit In, Stephen Nowicki, Jr. and Marshall Duke (Peachtree Publishers).

Honey, Are You Listening?, Dr. Rick Fowler and Jerilyn Fowler (Thomas Nelson).

The Hyperactive Child, Adolescent and Adult, Paul Wender, M.D. (Oxford University Press).

The Hyperactive Child Book, P. Kennedy, L. Terdal, and L. Fusetti (St. Martin's Press).

Hyperactive Children Grown Up: ADHD in Children, Adolescents and Adults, Gabrielle Weiss, M.D., F.R.C.P. and Lily Trokenberg Hechtman, M.D., F.R.C.P. (Guilford Press).

Inside Attention Deficit Disorder: A Collection of Thoughts and Feelings on ADD by an Adult Who Lives It, Susan Alfultis (Available through ADDA).

Is Your Child Hyperactive? Inattentive? Impulsive? Distractible?: Helping the ADD/Hyperactive Child, Stephen W. Garber, Ph.D., Marianne Daniels Garber, Ph.D. and Robyn Freedman Spizman (Villard).

The Link Between ADD and Addiction: Getting the Help You Deserve, Wendy Richardson (Pinon Press).

Managing Attention Disorders in Children: A Guide for Practitioners, Sam Goldstein and Michael Goldstein (Wiley Interscience Press).

Maybe You Know My Kid: A Parent's Guide to Identifying, Understanding and Helping Your Child with Attention Deficit Hyperactivity Disorder, Mary Cahill Fowler (Birch Lane Press).

Moving Beyond ADD: An Effective, Holistic, Mind Body Approach, Rita Ellena Kirsch and Avery Hart (Contemporary Books).

Negotiating Parent-Adolescent Conflict, Arthur L. Robin and Sharon L. Foster (Guilford Press).

The Other Me: Poetic Thoughts on ADD for Adults and Parents, Wilma R. Fellman (Specialty Press).

Out of Chaos!: Understanding and Managing ADD: Its Relationship to Modern Stress, Sanjay Jasuja (Esteem House).

Out of the Fog: Treatment Options and Coping Strategies for Adult Attention Deficit Disorder, Kevin R. Murphy and Suzanne Le Vert (Hyperion).

Overload: Attention Deficit Disorder and the Addictive Brain, David K. Miller et al (Andrews & McMeel).

Rising to the Challenge: A Styles Approach to Understanding Adults with ADD and Other Learning Difficulties, Sally R. Snowman (Jones River Press).

Ritalin: Theory and Patient Management, edited by Lawrence L. Greenhill, M.D. and Betty Osman, Ph.D. (Mary Ann Liebert Press, New York City).

Smart Kids with School Problems: Things to Know and Ways to Help, Priscilla Vail (New American Library).

Teenagers with ADD: Parents Guide (The Special-Needs Collection), Chris A. Zeigler Dendy (Woodbine House).

Women with Attention Deficit Disorder: Embracing Disorganization at Home and in the Workplace, Sari Solden (Underwood Books).

You Mean I'm Not Lazy, Stupid or Crazy?, Kate Kelly and Peggy Ramundo (Tyrell and Jerem Press, Cincinnati, Ohio).

Young Hyperactive Child, Jan Loney (Haworth Press).

Resources for the ADHD Family

ADHD Books For Children

Coping with ADHD is a herculean task for many youngsters. The following books explain in easy-to-understand terminology how the syndrome works and what children can do to manage their symptoms:

I Would If I Could, Michael Gordon (GSI Publications).

Jumpin' Johnny: Get Back To Work, Michael Gordon (GSI Publications).

Keeping A Head in School, Melvin D. Levine, M.D. (Educators Publishing Service).

Learning to Slow Down and Pay Attention, E. Dixon and K. Nadeau (Chesapeake Psychological Services, Annandale, Virginia).

Making the Grade: An Adolescent's Struggle with Attention Deficit Disorder, Robert N. Parker and Harvey Parker (Impact Publications, Plantation, Florida).

My Brother's A World-Class Pain: A Sibling's Guide to ADHD/Hyperactivity, Michael Gordon (GSI Publications).

Putting on the Brakes: Young People's Guide to Understanding Attention Deficit Hyperactivity Disorder (ADHD), P.O. Quinn and J. Stern (Magination Press)

Instructional Videotapes

Many people find that they learn more about ADHD by hearing someone talk about it rather than by reading books. As a result, instructional videotapes have become a valuable supplement to the available literature. Many of the following videos can be obtained through the larger national support organizations:

ADHD: What Do We Know? and *ADHD: What Can We Do?*, Russell Barkley, Ph.D. *Both videos available through Guilford Press Videos, Guilford Publications Inc., New York.*

ADHD in the Classroom: Strategies for Teachers, Russell Barkley, Ph.D. *Available through Guilford Press Videos, Guilford Publications Inc., New York.*

Medication for ADD: Attention Deficit Disorder, Thomas W. Phelan and Jonathan Bloomberg, M.D. (Child Management Inc. [CMI] Products).

Adults with Attention Deficit Disorder, Thomas W. Phelan (Child Management Inc. [CMI] Products).
Attention Disorders: The School's Vital Role, Edna D. Copeland (3C's of Childhood, Inc., Atlanta, Georgia).
Answers to ADD: The School Success Kit, John F. Taylor (Sun Media, Salem, Oregon).
It's Just Attention Disorder, Sam Goldstein and Michael Goldstein (Neurology, Learning and Behavior Center, Salt Lake City, Utah). *Video specifically for children.*

ADHD Homepages and Websites on the Internet

As more and more people bring computers into their homes, the Internet has become an invaluable source of information and discussion on social and medical issues—including ADHD. Following are just a few of the ADHD-related Websites and homepages currently on-line. A search engine can easily help you find others.

CH.A.D.D. On-line (http://www.chadd.org/). Offers up-to-date news and information regarding ADHD studies, legal action and conferences.

ADD Warehouse (http://www.addwarehouse.com/). Specializes in products for ADHD and related problems. Offers on-line catalog.

ADD or ADHD Info Line (http://www.alcasoft.com/add/). Provides information regarding the diagnosis and treatment of ADHD, as well as family, school, and social issues.

ADD Coach (http://web.addcoach.com/partnercoach/addcoach/). Provides current information and resources for professionals who assist those with ADHD.

ADD Treatment and Research Center (http://www.cpgs.com/add/). Provides information and a wide range of services for adults and children with ADHD.

ADHD Interventions for Teachers (http://comp.uark.edu/~aussery/adhd/other.html). Provides information and resources for professionals who work with ADHD children and adults.

ADD/ADHD Online Newsletter (http://www.nlci.com/nutrition/). Monthly on-line newsletter for parents and other

caregivers in the treatment of ADHD; provides news and information, references, Q&A, and comments by readers.
Dr. Wright's website (http:/www.geocities.com/HotSprings/Spa/4218/)

Other Sources of Help and Information

Adult ADHD Clinic
University of Massachusetts
  Medical Center
361 Plantation Street
Worcester, MA 01605
508-856-2552
(Internationally renowned for treatment and research in child and adult ADHD)

Pharmaceutical Division
CIBA-GEIGY Corporation
Public Relations Department
556 Morris Avenue
Summit, NJ 07901
908-277-7082
(Offers a listing of ADHD support groups throughout the United States)

References

CHAPTER ONE

Still, G.F., "The Coulstonian Lectures on Some Abnormal Physical Conditions in Children," *Lancet*, 1: 1008–1012, 1077–1082, 1163–1168, 1902.

Hohman, L.C., "Post-Encephalitic Behavior Disorder in Children." *Johns Hopkins Hospital Bulletin*, 33: 372–375, 1922.

Ebaugh, F.G., "Neuropsychiatric Sequelae of Acute Epidemic Encephalitis in Children," *American Journal of Disease in Children*, 25: 89–97, 1923.

Bradley, C., "The Behavior of Children Receiving Benzedrine," *American Journal of Psychiatry*, 94: 577–585, 1937.

Rapoport, J.L., Buchsbaum, M.S., Zahn, T.P., Weingartner, H., Ludlow, C., and Mikkelsen, E.J., "Dextroamphetamine: Cognitive and Behavioral Effects in Normal Prepubertal Boys," *Science*, 199: 560–563, 1978.

Wender, P.H., "Some Speculations Concerning a Possible Biochemical Basis of Minimal Brain Dysfunction," *Annals of the New York Academy of Sciences*, 205: 18–28, 1973.

Knobloch, H. and Pasamanick, B., "Syndrome of Minimal Cerebral Damage in Infancy," *Journal of the American Medical Association*, 170: 1384–1387, 1959.

Clements, S.D., and Peters, J.E., "Minimal Brain Dysfunction in the School Age Child," *Archives of General Psychiatry*, 6: 185–197, 1962.

Neuwirth, S., et al., "Attention Deficit/Hyperactivity Disorder," National Institute of Mental Health, NIH Publication No. 94-3572, 1994.

Zametkin, A.J., Nordahl, T.E., Gross, M., et al., "Cerebral Glucose Metabolism in Adults with Hyperactivity of Childhood Onset," *New England Journal of Medicine*, 323: 1361–1366, 1990.

Lou, H.C., Henricksen, L., Bruhn, P., et al., "Focal Cerebral Hypoperfusion in Children with Dysphasia and/or Attention Deficit Disorder," *Archives of Neurology*, 41: 825–829, 1984.

Weiss, G., Hechtman, L., Milroy, T., and Perlman, T., "Psychiatric Status of Hyperactives as Adults: A Controlled 15-Year Follow-Up of 63 Hyperactive Children," *Journal of the American Academy of Child Psychiatry*, 24: 211–220, 1985.

CHAPTER TWO

Werry, J.S., Weiss, G., and Douglas, V., "Studies on the Hyperactive Child: I. Some Preliminary Findings," *Canadian Psychiatric Association Journal*, 9: 120–130, 1964.

Campbell, S.B., Szumowski, E.K., Ewing, L.J., Cluck, D.S., and Breaux, A.M., "A Multidimensional Assessment of Parent-Identified Behavior Problem Toddlers," *Journal of Abnormal Child Psychology*, 10: 569–592, 1982.

Wolf, P.H., "The Natural History of Crying and Other Vocalizations in Early Infancy," *Determinants of Infant Behavior* (Vol. 4), B.M. Foss, Editor.

Fiedler, M.F., Lenneberg, E.H., Rolfe, U.T., and Drorbaugh, J.E., "A Speech Screening Procedure with Three-Year-Old Children," *Pediatrics*, 48: 268–276, 1971.

Waldrop, M.F., Bell, R.Q., McLaughlin, B., and Halverson, C.F., "Newborn Minor Physical Anomalies Predict Short Attention Span, Peer Aggression, and Impulsivity at Age 3," *Science*, 199: 563–565, 1978.

Mendelson, W.B., Johnson, N.E., and Stewart, M.A., "Hyperactive Children as Teenagers: A Follow-Up Study,'' *Journal of Nervous and Mental Disease*, 153: 273–279, 1971.

Kramer, J. and Loney, J., ''Predicting Adolescent Antisocial Behavior Among Hyperactive Boys.'' Presented at the annual meeting of the American Psychological Association, 1979.

Winnicott, D.W., ''Transitional Objects and Transitional Phenomena,'' *International Journal of PsychoAnalysis*, 34: 89–97, 1953.

CHAPTER THREE

Borland, B.L. and Heckman, H.K., ''Hyperactive Boys and Their Brothers: A 25-Year Follow-Up Study,'' *Archives of General Psychiatry*, 33: 669–675, 1976.

Feldman, S.A., Denhoff, E., and Denhoff, J.I., ''The Attention Disorders and Related Syndromes: Outcome in Adolescence and Young Adult Life,'' *Minimal Brain Dysfunction: A Developmental Approach*, L. Stern and E. Denhoff, Editors, Masson Publishing.

Weiss, G., Hechtman, L., Perlman, T., Hopkins, J., and Werner, A., ''Hyperactive Children as Young Adults: A Controlled Prospective 10-Year Follow-Up of the Psychiatric Status of 75 Children,'' *Archives of General Psychiatry*, 36: 675–681, 1979.

Weiss, G., Hechtman, L., and Perlman, T., ''Hyperactives as Young Adults: Self-Esteem and Social Skills,'' *Canadian Journal of Psychiatry*, 25: 478–483, 1980.

Mendelson, W.B., Johnson, N.E., and Stewart, M.A., ''Hyperactive Children as Teenagers: A Follow-Up Study,'' *Journal of Nervous and Mental Disease*, 153: 273–279, 1971.

Weiss, G., Minde, K., Werry, J.S., Douglas, V.I. and Nemeth, E., ''Studies on the Hyperactive Child VIII: Five-Year Follow-Up,'' *Archives of General Psychiatry*, 24: 409–414, 1971.

Minde, K., Lewin, D., Weiss, G., Lavigueur, H., Douglas, V., and Sykes, E., ''The Hyperactive Child in Elementary

School: A Five-Year Controlled Follow-Up," *Exceptional Children*, 38: 215–221, 1971.

Minde, K. Weiss, G., and Mendelson, N., "A 5-Year Follow-Up of 91 Hyperactive School Children," *Journal of the American Academy of Child Psychiatry*, 11: 595–610, 1972.

Satterfield, J., Hoppe, C.M., and Schell, A.M., "A Prospective Study of Delinquency in 110 Adolescent Boys with Attention Deficit Disorder and 88 Normal Adolescent Boys," *American Journal of Psychiatry*, 139: 797–798, 1982.

Morrison, J.R., and Stewart, M.A., "A Family Study of the Hyperactive Child Syndrome," *Biological Psychology*, 3: 189–195, 1971.

Cantwell, D.P., "Psychiatric Illness in the Families of Hyperactive Children," *Archives of General Psychiatry*, 27: 414–417, 1972.

Morrison, J.R., "Diagnosis of Adult Psychiatric Patients with Childhood Hyperactivity," *American Journal of Psychiatry*, 136: 955–958, 1979.

Morrison, J.R., "Childhood Hyperactivity in an Adult Psychiatric Population: Social Factors," *Journal of Clinical Psychiatry*, 41: 40–43, 1980.

Mannuzza, S., Klein, R.G., Bessler, A., Malloy, P., and LaPadula, M., "Adult Outcome of Hyperactive Boys," *Archives of General Psychiatry*, 50: 565–576, 1993.

Spencer, T., Wilens, T., Biederman, J., Faraone, S.V., Ablon, J.S., and Lapey, K., "A Double-Blind, Cross-Over Comparison of Methylphenidate and Placebo in Adults With Childhood-Onset Attention Deficit Hyperactivity Disorder: An Open Clinical trial," *Journal of Clinical Psychiatry*, 57: 184–189, 1996.

CHAPTER FOUR

MacKay, M.C., Beck, L., and Taylor, R., "Methylphenidate for Adolescents with Minimal Brain Dysfunction," *New York State Journal of Medicine*, 73: 550–554, 1973.

Varley, C., "Effects of Methylphenidate in Adolescents with Attention Deficit Disorder," *Journal of the American Academy of Child Psychiatry*, 22: 351–354, 1983.

Wood, D.R., Reimherr, F.W., Wender, P.H., and Johnson, G.E., "Diagnosis and Treatment of Minimal Brain Dysfunction in Adults," *Archives of General Psychiatry*, 33: 1453–1460, 1976.

Wender, P.H., Reimherr, F.W., and Wood, D.R., "Attention Deficit Disorder (Minimal Brain Dysfunction) in Adults: A Replication Study of Diagnosis and Drug Treatment," *Archives of General Psychiatry*, 38: 449-456, 1980.

Walen, C.K., "Does Stimulant Medication Improve the Peer Status of Hyperactive Children?" *Journal of Consulting and Clinical Psychology*, 57: 545–549, 1989.

Barrickman, L., Noyes, R., Kuperman, S., et al., "Treatment of ADHD with Fluoxetine: A Preliminary Trial," *Journal of the American Academy of Child and Adolescent Psychiatry*, 30: 762–767, 1991.

Riddle, M.A., King, R.A., Hardin, M.T., et al., "Behavioral Side Effects of Fluoxetine in Children and Adolescents," *Journal of Child and Adolescent Psychopharmacology*, 1: 193–198, 1990–1991.

Gammon, G.D. and Brown, T.E., "Fluoxetine Augmentation of Methylphenidate for Attention Deficit and Comorbid Disorders," *Journal of Child and Adolescent Psychopharmacology*, in press.

CHAPTER FIVE

Carlson, C.L., Pelham, W.E., Milich, R., et al., "Single and Combined Effects of Methylphenidate and Behavior Therapy on the Classroom Performance of Children with Attention Deficit-Hyperactivity Disorder," *Journal of Abnormal Child Psychology*, 20: 213–232, 1992.

Gittelman-Klein, R., Abikoff, H., Pollack, E., et al., "A Controlled Trial of Behavior Modification and Methylphenidate in Hyperactive Children," *Hyperactive Children: The Social Ecology of Identification and Treatment*, C.K. Whalen & B. Henker, Editors, Academic Press.

Index

Addictive personality, 64, 67, 71–72
ADHD
  causation theories, 21–23
  diagnosis of, 4, 13–14, 22–29
  gender differences, 3, 12, 16
  history of knowledge about, 16–18
  incidence of, 3, 18
  and life-span. *See* specific developmental stages
  and marketplace, 19
  positive characteristics of, 18–19, 72
  secondary characteristics, 13, 15–16
  secondary effects, 5
  signs/symptoms of, 13–16, 19–20, 63–64
  subtypes of, 14
  as syndrome, 2–3, 12
  terms used for, 3
Adjustment disorder, in differential diagnosis, 27
Adolescents, 49–56
  anti-social behavior, 53
  case examples, 52–55, 149–153
  diagnosis, 20
  normal developmental issues, 49–50
  psychotherapy for, 148–152
  signs of ADHD, 19, 25, 49–51
  social development of ADHD, 50–51
  and trust, 176–177
Adult ADHD, 57–75
  careers and ADHD, 72–73
  case example, 64–66
  continuation from childhood, 23, 57–61, 232–233
  diagnosis of, 20–21, 62–64
  diagnostic problems, 61–62
  and emotional problems, 67–68
  positive characteristics of ADHD, 72
  problems in adulthood, 57–58, 60–61, 71–72

INDEX

Adult ADHD *(continued)*
  psychotherapy for, 152–157
  relationship problems, 71–72, 73–74, 159, 164–165
  research studies related to, 59–60
  and residual ADHD, 58
  signs/symptoms of, 19
  treatment of, 74–75, 81–82
  women, 66–67, 70–71
Aggression, and Ritalin, 96
Allergies, and ADHD, 122–123
Alopecia, Ritalin side-effect, 92
Alternative treatments, 123–126
  amino acid therapy, 123
  anti-candida treatment, 125
  biofeedback, 124
  integrative sensory training, 124–125
  vitamin megadoses, 124
Americans with Disabilities Act (ADA), coverage of ADHD, 76
Amino acid therapy, 123
Anafranil, 101
Anger, parental, 177–178
Antidepressants, 98–100
  benefits of, 99
  mechanisms of action, 98–99
  side effects, 99
  tricyclic type, 98–99
  types of, 98–100
Antisocial personality disorder, 68–70
  in differential diagnosis, 27–28
  incidence and ADHD, 5, 38, 61, 67, 68–70
  research studies on, 69
  signs of, 68
Anxiety, 16, 67
Appetite, and Ritalin, 91
Arousal
  infancy, 33–34
  meaning of, 33

Artificial sweeteners, 122
Attention, components of normal attention, 21–22
Attention deficit hyperactivity disorder. *See* ADHD
Auditory perception disabilities, 191

Bed-wetting, 53
Behavioral problems
  adolescents, 53
  adults, 60–61
  antisocial personality disorder, 5, 38
  oppositional defiant disorder (ODD), 15, 27
  school-age children, 43–44
Behavior modification, 104–115
  in classroom, 199–200
  cognitive-behavioral treatment, 107–108
  contingency-management programs, 106–107
  and doing chores, 116–117
  effectiveness of, 105
  in home, 108–112
  ignoring disruptive behavior, 112–113
  outside the home, 114–115
  and parental participation, 108–111
  rewarding positive behavior, 110–112
  with stimulant medication, 108
  time-out, 113–114
  traditional modalities, 104
Benzedrine, 80
Beta-blockers, 101
Biofeedback, 124
Birth trauma, 21
Boredom, 53, 63
Brain damage, and ADHD, 21
Bupropion hydrochloride, 99

Index

Cancer issue, Ritalin, 97
Candida infection, 125
Carbmazepine, 101
Careers and ADHD, 72–73
  best jobs, 72–73
  job discrimination, 76
  positive aspects of ADHD, 72
Change, difficulties related to, 44
Chores at home, parental techniques for child, 116–117
Class clown, 44
Classroom. *See* School
Clonidine, 100
Cognitive-behavioral treatment, 107–108
Colic, 20, 25, 31, 35, 40
College attendance, and ADHD student, 204–205
Computers, for note-taking, 198
Connors' Teacher-Rating Scales (CTRS), 194, 203–204
Contingency-management programs, 106–107
Creativity, 18
Crisis points, 178
Crying, ADHD infant, 35–36
Cylert, 74, 80
  beneficial aspects of, 80–81, 88–89
  benefits over Ritalin, 82, 83
  dosage, 84
  mechanisms of action, 87–88
  research studies on, 82

Depression, 16
  in differential diagnosis, 27
  and women, 66–67, 153
Desipramine, 98
Developmental stages. *See* Lifespan; specific developmental stages

Dexedrine, 74, 80
  beneficial aspects of, 80–81, 88–89
  dosage, 83–84
  mechanism of action, 22, 87–88
  short/long acting forms, 84
Dextroamphetamine. *See* Dexedrine
Diagnosis, 4, 13–14, 22–29
  and adults, 62–64
  differential diagnosis, 26–29, 31–32
  DSM-IV criteria, 13
  initial detection, 20–21, 23–24
  of learning disabilities, 191–193
  scope of testing, 24
  signs/symptoms of ADHD, 13–16, 19–20
Diagnostic and Statistical Manual IV (*DSM IV*), diagnostic criteria, 13
Diet and ADHD
  artificial sweeteners, 122
  food additives, 122
  food allergies, 123
  sugar, 120–122
Differential diagnosis, 26–29, 31–32
  importance of, 31–32
  problems/disorders mimicking ADHD, 26–29
Discrimination, and Americans with Disabilities Act (ADA), 76
Distractibility, 43
  classroom interventions for, 195–197
Dopamine, and stimulant drugs, 22, 84, 87
Douglas, Virginia, 17–18
Drug abuse, 53, 72
  in differential diagnosis, 28
Drug interactions, and Ritalin, 93
Dyslexia, 191

INDEX

Eating behavior, ADHD infants, 36
Eating disorders, 70–71
Emotional problems, and adult ADHD, 67–68
Emotions
  ADHD and toleration of, 47, 48, 65, 115, 155
  helping child talk about, 170
  and use of stimulant drugs, 89, 91
Encephalitis, 17, 28
Encopresis, 40–41, 48
Environmental factors, in ADHD, 22
Exercise, and ADHD, 126–127, 179

Fabrication, 45, 47, 53, 54
Facial tics, and Ritalin, 92
Family, 159–185
  advocacy and ADHD family member, 160, 168–169, 236–237
  anger and ADHD child, 177–178
  child/adolescent lack of response to parents, 176–177, 179–180
  coaching of social skills by, 168–169
  communication with school, 171
  crisis points, 178
  education about ADHD, 161–162, 167
  family problems, in differential diagnosis, 27
  family therapy, 75, 163–166
  grandparents, dealing with, 231–232
  and homework assistance, 180–181
  household rules, suggestions for, 230–231
  marital conflicts and ADHD child, 185
  mistakes related to ADHD, 172–174
  parent/child relationship and ADHD infant, 34–35, 38, 70, 139
  pets in, 184–185
  relationship patterns and ADHD, 166–167
  sibling conflicts, 166, 182
  telling members about ADHD, 176
  therapist agenda with, 161–162
  and treatment, 129–157
  and treatment plan, 162
  tutoring by parents, 228–230
  and violent behavior, 183–184
Fearfulness, 16
Feingold Diet, 122
Fire setting, 53
Fluoxetine hydrochloride, 99
Food additives, 122
Food allergies, 123
  in differential diagnosis, 28
Food hoarding, 53
Forgetfulness, 13

Gambling, 72
Gender differences
  ADHD, 3, 12, 16
  girls with ADHD, 45–47
Genetic factors, 21
Girls with ADHD
  case example, 45–47, 146–148
  and promiscuity, 53
Growth suppression, and Ritalin, 94
Guilt of parents, 172, 235

Headaches, and Ritalin, 91
Heart function, and antidepressants, 99
Home
  acting out at, 115–116

behavior modification in, 108–112
doing chores, 116–117
lateness, prevention of, 117–120
See also Family
Home schooling, 208–209
Homework, difficulties with, 180–181
Hunger, in differential diagnosis, 29
Hyperactivity, 13
characteristics of, 15
historical view, 17
and sugar intake, 120–122
in young children, 25
Hypersensitivity reaction, Ritalin side-effect, 92

Imipramine, 98
Impulsivity, 13, 155
adults, 63–64
characteristics of, 15, 43
Inattention, 13, 37, 43
characteristics of, 14
Infancy, 32–39
baby–caretaker relationship, 34–35, 38, 70, 139
calming infant, 33–34
and causes of ADHD, 21, 22
and disrupted arousal states, 33–34
language development, 137–138
later development and ADHD, 37–38
research difficulties, 33
signs of ADHD, 20, 25, 31, 35–37, 138–139
Insurance coverage, for medication, 175
Integration disabilities, 191
Integrative sensory training, 124–125
Intelligence, high, and ADHD, 18, 20, 25

Intelligence tests, 189
Intuition, 18
Irritability, 19

Jobs. *See* Careers and ADHD

Language development
faulty development and ADHD, 37, 47, 139–140, 144
importance of, 137–138
Lateness, helping child with, 117–120
Learning, stimulant medication effects, 88
Learning disabilities, 15
diagnosis of, 191–193
in differential diagnosis, 26
types and ADHD, 191
Legal problems, 15, 53, 68, 69
Lethargy, and Ritalin, 91
Life-span
and ADHD, 23
adolescents, 49–56
adult ADHD, 57–75
infancy, 32–39
preschoolers, 39–42
school-age children, 42–49
Lithium, 101
Lock box method, 117
Lying, 45, 47, 53, 54

Maid service, 116–117
Mania, in differential diagnosis, 27
Marriage
conflicts and ADHD child, 185
marital problems and ADHD spouse, 71, 164–165
Medication
antidepressants, 98–100
clonidine, 100
and insurance coverage, 175
for obsessive-compulsive disorder, 101

Medication *(continued)*
  for secondary symptoms, 101
  venlafaxine, 100
  See also Stimulant drugs
Memory problems, 13, 63, 66, 191
Methylphenidate. *See* Ritalin
Minimal brain damage, use of term, 3, 12, 17
Motivation, lack of, 51–52
Multimodal treatment approach, 6, 74, 103–104, 129–130, 162
  components of, 217–219
  guidelines in setting up plan, 221–224
  implementation of, 219–221
Music, and concentration, 55

Nadolol, 101
Negative attention, 112
Neurological factors, in ADHD, 21–22
Neurotransmitters
  and antidepressants, 98–100
  and stimulant drugs, 22, 80, 87
Norepinephrine, and stimulant drugs, 22, 84, 87
Nortriptyline, 98

Obsessive-compulsive disorder, medications for, 101
Open classroom, 190
Oppositional defiant disorder (ODD), 15
  signs of, 27
  without ADHD, 27
Organization, and ADHD infant, 34
Output disabilities, 191

Parents
  parent-child relationship, and ADHD infants, 34–35, 38, 70, 139
  See also Family

Paxil, 70, 99
Pediatrician
  and diagnosis, 24, 39
  and finding therapist, 167–168, 213–214
Pemoline. *See* Cylert
Perseveration, 44
Pervasive developmental disorder, in differential diagnosis, 26
Pets, and ADHD child, 184–185
Phobia, 67–68
Physical examination, and diagnosis, 24
Playground activities, 206–207
Positron emission tomography (PET), 22
Premenstrual syndrome, 70
  medication for control of, 70
Preschoolers, 39–42
  case examples, 39–42, 141–146
  and psychotherapy, 140–146
Private school, 202
Procrastination, 63
Promiscuity, 53
Propranolol, 101
Prospective study, 60
Prozac, 99, 101–102
  and ADHD, 100
Psychiatrist, locating ADHD specialist, 213–216
Psychological tests, and diagnosis, 24
Psychotherapy, 129–157
  and ADHD patient, 136–140
  for adolescents, 148–152
  and adult ADHD, 152–157
  benefits of, 6–7, 134–135, 140
  curative mechanisms, 135
  elements of, 130–131
  patient/therapist relationship, 133–134

Index

for preschoolers, 140–146
process of, 132–133
and school-age children, 146–148
use of language, power of, 134–135, 144–146
Psychosis, Ritalin side-effect, 92

Rebound effects, Ritalin, 95, 96
Relationships, 19
adult ADHD, 71–72, 73–74, 159, 164–165
baby–caretaker relationship, 34–35, 38, 70
benefits of stimulant drugs, 89
marriage, 71, 164–165
patient/therapist, 133–134
school-age children, 47–49
therapeutic interventions for, 56
See also Family; Social development
Research studies
prospective studies, 60
retrospective studies, 59–60
Retrospective studies, of adult ADHD, 59–60
Ritalin, 74, 79–98
abuse of, 97–98
age and use of, 55
and aggression, 96
beginning use, 82–83
beneficial aspects of, 80–81, 88–89
black market sale, 85
cancer issue, 97
child/adolescent opposition to, 90–91
as controlled substance, 85
drug interactions with, 93
and growth suppression in children, 94
mechanism of action, 22, 84, 87–88

monitoring of use, 85
overprescription issue, 86
prevalence of use, 86
rebound effects, 95, 96
research studies, 82, 84–85
short/long acting forms, 84
side-effects, 91–92
stopping, Ritalin vacations, 95
uses other than ADHD, 84
Routines, to avoid lateness, 118–120

School, 187–209
accommodating ADHD child, 190, 200–201
adjustment difficulties and ADHD, 42–44
and advocacy parental role, 200–202
college students, 204–205
Connors teacher-rating scales, use of, 194, 203–204
family communication with, 171
home schooling, 208–209
interventions for distractibility, 195–197
learning strategies with ADHD students, 197–198
and medication schedule, 193–194
misbehavior and ADHD, 199–200
play activities, 206–207
private/special schools, 202
regular conferences with teacher, 194–195
role in ADHD management, 188–189
structured versus open environment, 190
and student rights, 202–203
teachers and diagnosis, 189–190

School *(continued)*
  teacher skepticism about ADHD, 205–206
  and tutors, 200
School-age children, 42–49
  effects of ADHD, 42–43
  girls with ADHD, 45–47, 146–147
  psychotherapy for, 146–148
  signs/symptoms of ADHD, 25, 43–44
  and social development, 47–49
Secondary effects, 5
Seizures
  antidepressant side-effect, 99
  Ritalin side-effect, 92
Self-employment, 72–73
Self-esteem, low and ADHD, 44, 50, 61, 64, 68
Self-help, 226–228
  guidelines for, 227–228
Sensory impairment, in differential diagnosis, 26
Serotonin, 100
Sexual problems, 67
Siblings, conflict of, 166, 182
Sleep problems, infant ADHD, 20, 36
Social development
  and adolescents, 50–51
  parental assistance in, 168–169
  and school-age children, 47–49
  See also Relationships
Spanking, 112
Specialists in ADHD
  finding specialist, 167–168, 213–216
  types of, 213
Special schools, 202
Sports, problems with ADHD child, 179
Still, George, 16

Stimulant drugs
  adult use, 81–82
  beneficial aspects of, 80–81, 88–89
  choosing right drug, 82–83
  Cylert, 74
  Dexedrine, 22, 74
  dosage, 74, 83–84
  mechanism of action, 22, 80, 87–88
  paradoxical effect, 80
  prevalence of use, 79–80
  research studies on, 81, 82
  Ritalin, 22, 74, 79–98
  See also specific medications
Stomachaches, and Ritalin, 91
Sugar, 120–122
Suicide, 67, 68, 71
Support groups, benefits of, 174–175

Teachers. *See* School
Temperament, in differential diagnosis, 28
Tics, and Ritalin, 92
Time-out, 113–114, 228
Toddlers, signs of ADHD, 25
Toilet training, 40–41
Tourette's syndrome, 16
Traffic accidents, 60
Treatment
  adult ADHD, 74–75
  alternative treatments, 123–126
  behavior modification, 104–115
  and family, 161–167
  finding ADHD specialist, 167–168, 213–216
  multimodal approach, 6, 74, 103–104, 129–130, 162, 216–223
  psychotherapy, 129–157
  of secondary problems, 75

Index

self-help, 226–228
support groups, 174–175
treatment plan, importance of, 6–8
See also Medication; specific drugs; specific treatment modalities
Tricyclic antidepressants, 98–100
benefits of, 99
side-effects, 99
Tutors, 192, 200, 223–224
by parents, 228–230
work skills tutoring, 223–224

Venlafaxine, 76, 100
Violent behavior, 21, 25, 48, 64, 68, 72
family interventions in, 183–184
Viral disease, in differential diagnosis, 17, 28
Visual perception disabilities, 191

Vitamin megadoses, 124
"Vitamin R," 98
Vocalization, infancy, 37

Wechsler Intelligence Scale for Children (WISC), 189
Wellbutrin, 99
Women
case example, 64–65, 153–157
and depression, 66–67, 153
eating disorders, 70–71
premenstrual syndrome, 70
symptoms of ADHD, 66–67
See also Gender differences; Girls with ADHD
Work skills tutoring, 223–224

Yeast infection, 125

Zoloft, 70, 99, 101
Zoning out, 13, 15, 19, 25, 112

DR. JOSEPHINE WRIGHT is both an adult and child psychiatrist, with a busy private practice in New York City and Sharon, Connecticut. Her professional interests are varied. She has long been interested in the ways in which developmental disorders such as attention deficit hyperactivity disorder and learning disabilities interact with social and emotional development, and has worked with people of all ages who suffer from these disorders.

Dr. Wright was born in England and lived much of her childhood in Australia, where she received her medical degree. She has been living and working in the United States for almost twenty-five years. Dr. Wright is married and has two sons.